THEODOSIUS

THEODOSIUS
THE EMPIRE AT BAY

Stephen Williams

and

Gerard Friell

Yale University Press
New Haven and London

First published 1994 in the United Kingdom
by B. T. Batsford Limited.

Published 1995 in the United States by
Yale University Press.

Printed in Great Britain

Library of Congress catalog card number: 94-60725

International standard book number: 0-300-06173-0

A catalogue record for this book is available
from the British Library.

10 9 8 7 6 5 4 3 2 1

CONTENTS

PLATES

MAPS

ACKNOWLEDGEMENTS

Our thanks are due to the following: Ramsey MacMullen, as always, who has been helpful with suggestions; and thanks are also due for his generous permission to use his list of barbarian officers, included as our Appendix V. Geoffrey Wainwright and Stephen Johnson have both been very supportive. Among non-specialists who read drafts of chapters, whose comments were essential and whose encouragement was always warmly received, Alan Peachey, Herbert Jarmany and Liam Browne have our thanks.

S.W.

The support and assistance of friends and colleagues must be acknowledged, and of these I would especially like to mention Sally Pegg and Mike Embree. Also, and most importantly, I could not have done this without the support and patience of my wife, Teresa, whose help has been invaluable.

G.F.

For the illustrations, we acknowledge: Weidenfeld and Nicolson for plates 1, 8, 12–15; the British Museum for the four coin reproductions, plates 4–7; Deutsches Archaeologischen Institut Abteilung, Istanbul, for plates 2, 3, 9; Kunsthistorisches Museum, Vienna, for plate 17; English Heritage Academic and Specialist Publications and the Mucking Excavation Committee for plate 16; plates 10, 11, 19a are from the Studio Vista World Architecture Series, originally published by George Brazillier Inc., New York, in 1963 (we have been unable to trace the original copyright holders for these); plate 19b was provided by Tony Wilmott from his personal collection at just the right time; and for the magnificent picture of the Hoxne coin hoard (plate 18) we have to thank the generosity of the *Independent* picture desk, and their photographer, Brian Harris.

The facilities and helpful staff of the Joint Library of the Hellenic and Roman Societies were invaluable in our research.

To Patricia, Cordelia and Gabriel

S.W.

For Teresa; and for my family

G.F.

PART I
THE CRUCIBLE

'As for the Romans, after this defeat they gave up all hope of maintaining their supremacy over the Italians and began to fear for their own native soil and indeed, for their very existence, since they expected Hannibal to appear at any moment . . . Yet although without any doubt the Romans had been worsted in battle and their military reputation destroyed, because of the special virtues of their constitution and their ability to keep their heads, they eventually not only won back supremacy in Italy and later defeated the Carthaginians, but within a few years of this made themselves masters of the whole world.'

Polybius, *Histories* Bk III

I

ADRIANOPLE AND AFTER

The embassy which came to the Sacred Court of Valens Augustus, emperor of the East, at Antioch in Syria in the spring of 376 was certainly important, but on the surface at least its substance was not unusual. The Tervingian Goths (later known as Visigoths),[1] under their chieftains Alavivus[2] and Fritigern,[3] were encamped *en masse* on the northern bank of the Danube, opposite the Roman diocese of Thrace (Bulgaria and European Turkey, map II), and respectfully begged the emperor to grant them lands to settle within the empire, on the customary conditions of submission to Roman rule and the supply of fighting men for the imperial armies.[4] They explained that they had been driven from their homelands, after very fierce fighting, by new and savage invaders, the Huns. A fearsome, demonic picture was painted of these ugly nomad warriors who were so primitive they dressed in skins, had no houses nor land but seemed to live on horseback, and whose cavalry was irresistible.[5] They had defeated the Alans,[6] and in alliance with the survivors had overwhelmed the Greuthungian Goths,[7] driving them from their fertile lands westwards to the river Dneister.[8] The Huns and their Alan allies then attacked the Tervingi, who were unable to withstand this combined assault and were compelled to migrate.[9]

Valens and his ministers already knew something of these troubles, for they had been in continual contact, hostile and friendly, with Gothic tribes and their leaders for many years. Ten years earlier Valens had led his army against the Tervingi in a long, largely successful but inconclusive war, ending at last in a treaty with their leader Athanaric[10] which was concluded on a boat in the middle of the Danube, representing neutral territory.[11] The situation had now altered. The impact of the Huns had disrupted all of the societies beyond the Danube, including that of the Tervingi.[12] Athanaric had advocated continued resistance, but had been deserted by most of his people, who instead followed Alavivus and Fritigern in seeking asylum in Roman territory.[13] Athanaric, with the rump of his followers, had retreated into Transylvania,[14] having earlier (sometime before AD 367) sworn a solemn oath by his gods that he would never set foot on Roman territory.[15] He may also have feared a refusal by Valens to allow him to enter the empire following their long conflict in the 360s.[16]

Fritigern, by contrast, was more pro-Roman and prepared to compromise.[17] He was a leader of his people but not a king in the monarchical sense.[18] In common with nearly all other Germanic leaders he had no means of organised coercion and no state apparatus. His authority rested partly on his noble lineage, but more important was his prowess and success in war and peace.[19] He could exhort, threaten, persuade, but he could not compel. If he failed to deliver they would abandon him as they had abandoned Athanaric.[20] He therefore had to anticipate and guide their wishes with some skill, particularly through the lesser nobles who had the loyalties of the clans and subgroups.[21] The momentous decision to emigrate might have been suggested by him, but it required collective tribal agreement. Once taken, he could steer it but no longer prevent it.

The imperial policy of controlled barbarian immigration, *receptio*,[22] was long established. Provided it was on Roman terms — as part of the treaty following a victory, for example — it offered a simple means of recultivating deserted lands, securing a source of recruits for the army, and creating a safety-valve for the pressures of the tribes beyond the frontiers.[23] In consequence, a growing number of the subjects of Gaul, Italy and the Danube provinces were of barbarian origin (mainly Germanic) and semi-Romanised, as were most of the regular soldiers and officers in the army.[24]

Valens was uncertain what course to take. From his distant base at Antioch it was difficult to assess the scale of the problem. Tribal wars were always taking place in the remote steppe lands far beyond the Danube, of which the Romans had only a hazy knowledge. Sometimes, news of them only reached the civilised world long after they were over and the whole picture altered.[25]

Still, there were enough separate reports and petitions to indicate that this time something on a larger scale than usual was going on. The plight of the Goths seemed genuine, but what were their real numbers, and what scale of military threat would they present if refused?[26]

Although he had been emperor of the East for some twelve years Valens was neither a very astute nor a decisive ruler.[27] He owned his throne entirely to his elder brother, the great and warlike Valentinian, who had been elected emperor by the army and, against sincere advice,[28] had chosen his brother to rule jointly with him in the collegial custom which the beleaguered empire had followed for nearly a century.[29] Valentinian had ruled the West vigorously, throwing the invading Alamanni back across the Rhine, rescuing Britain from barbarian invasions, and crushing a separatist revolt in Africa.[30] Valens in the East had been overshadowed and implicitly protected by the ferocious military prowess of his brother,[31] but a year earlier Valentinian had died suddenly, of a stroke, while angrily haranguing some barbarian envoys.[32] The Western throne had passed to his teenage son Gratian, who also lived in the shadow of the heroic dead emperor.

Valens had to depend more than ever on his ministers in the Consistory,[33] men such as the Praetorian Prefect Modestus,[34] and the two finance ministers Fortunatianus[35] and Tatianus.[36] They mostly favoured acceptance, arguing that this addition of Gothic manpower would greatly strengthen both Valens' army and his treasury. The new supply of soldiers would relieve landowners of the duty to supply recruits, so that they could pay their taxes in gold instead.[37] This advice might be sound, but it may not have been disinterested. The new levies of gold would, of course, pass through the sticky fingers of these ministers and their clients all down the line. Barbarian tribal groups had been settled before, but rarely in such numbers.[38] The Tervingi promised 'submission' of course, but that was a diplomatic formula being used in the absence of any demonstration of Roman military superiority. How could they be controlled in practice? More reports were arriving of yet another Gothic people, the Greuthungi (later Ostrogoths),[39] having likewise migrated to the northern bank of the Danube. Would they too want admission?

Valens had little room to manoeuvre. The worst result would be a general Gothic invasion across the Danube, on a greater scale than anything for a century.[40] His armies along the Danubian frontier were hardly strong enough to repel such a threat, and he could not afford to transfer many troops from the East since a new war with Persia was looming.[41] He therefore accepted his ministers' advice and agreed to the immigration of the Tervingi across into Thrace. The Persian problem kept Valens at Antioch, so that he could not oversee this highly sensitive and important operation in person. Instead he sent instructions on conducting the immigration to his local officials.

Alavivus and Fritigern were informed of the decision. The great crossing was to be assisted with boats and rafts. Their people were to be given immediate provisions from state supplies, and later allotted suitable land to cultivate. In return, they promised peace with the empire and readiness to supply troops on request. As an earnest of the treaty[42] the two chieftains agreed to give a large number of hostages to the empire, and they were questioned on their adherence to the religion of the emperor, which was Arian Christianity.[43] Valens and his officials expressed great satisfaction at the bargain. And so, 'With such great eagerness on the part of these insistent men was the ruin of the Roman world brought in', wrote a contemporary historian some ten years later, with bitter hindsight.[44]

The Danube was swollen with rains. As the great host was ferried across in boats, on rafts or even hollowed tree-trunks, it quickly became clear that, with their families, wagons and livestock, their numbers were far greater than anticipated. Regulation proved virtually impossible. Some drowned in the crossing. Exactly how the warriors were to be disarmed is not clear, but the orders were either disregarded or impractical. The potential for exploitation of such a desperate mass was obviously recognised by many on the Roman side, and this was compounded by the huge logistical problem of feeding and supplying such vast numbers: a task which would have strained the most efficient and honest of administrators. Soon hunger and desperation were widespread amongst the immigrants.

The administrators in question, Count Lupicinus[45] and his colleague Maximus,[46] had their own priorities. Instead of organising rapid and judicious dispersal from the original great encampments, Lupicinus let hunger do its work until even dogmeat was being sold to the Visigoths[47] at extortionate prices, which sometimes included the enslavement of their children. Soon their indignation was close to exploding, and Lupicinus hastily mustered his troops and began the long overdue transfer to permanent and dispersed settlements further from the frontier. Revolt might have broken out then had not Fritigern, a shrewd strategist, disguised his anger at the treatment of his people and, presenting a reasonable face to the Romans, persuaded the Visigoths to bide their time.[48]

By this time the Greuthungi, likewise fleeing from Hunnic pressure, had also petitioned Valens for land south of the Danube.[49] However, now realising the extent of the Visigothic immigration and its problems, Valens refused to admit the Greuthungi. While Lupicinus and his forces were escorting the Visigoths away from the frontier zone the usual defensive river patrols seem to have been neglected, and the leaders of the Greuthungi — Alatheus[50] and Saphrax[51] — seized the opportunity to cross the river in makeshift boats with as many warriors as possible, hoping to follow and link up with Fritigern.[52]

Fritigern's main body, still under arms, moved obediently towards the city of Marcianople, near modern Varna, where there were ample markets to supply them. Here Lupicinus seems to have tried a very clumsy stratagem to separate the warriors from their leaders. In a show of friendship Alavivus and Fritigern were invited, with their bodyguard, to a banquet in the city while their followers were kept outside the city walls by a strong body of troops. The Visigoths protested loudly, both to the troops and to the local inhabitants, at being denied access to the markets and cheated once again. This quickly turned into a riot, then a battle, in which Lupicinus' troops were defeated. The news reached Lupicinus, who was apparently no longer sober, and he gave secret orders to cut down the Visigothic bodyguard and to hold Alavivus and Fritigern captive. However Fritigern had also heard the news, and with great presence of mind he calmed his host and explained that it was all a local commotion of no consequence; but, he pointed out, it might become dangerous if his people could not see their chieftain unharmed and be reassured by his presence. Lupicinus grasped the offer and Fritigern returned to his people, where he promptly signalled them to prepare for battle.[53]

Lupicinus and his forces were routed with great loss; characteristically he fled the field and disappeared into political oblivion. The result was probably the worst possible outcome: Valens, through the venality and incompetence of his officials, now had to face a war with the Visigoths well inside Roman territory, which proved to be inconclusive and destructive to the frontier provinces. Fritigern's horde moved through Thrace and Moesia, pillaging at will and drawing additional strength from Gothic and other barbarian slaves, earlier settlers from beyond the frontiers, miners fleeing harsh labour and peasants who revolted and joined the Visigoths. The Greuthungi[54] were now also established south of the Danube and added to the threat. Valens ordered more troops to the Danube area from the Armenian frontier, and appealed to Gratian in the West for assistance.[55] There were Roman successes in the following two years, but they did not achieve a decisive victory and the war could not be brought to a conclusion.[56] When Valens moved briefly to Constantinople the mob taunted him for his spinelessness and he quickly left the city again.[57]

Gratian was preoccupied with the Rhine frontier, but eventually achieved a major victory over the Alamanni[58] and in 378 he marched eastwards with a large field army to assist his uncle. Valens seems to have been in two minds. He welcomed his nephew's aid, but envied him his recent victory. Valens' own general Sebastianus[59] had recently won a battle against the Goths in the region of Adrianople (Edirne in modern Turkey). Since the Goths had already been weakened by years of fighting and recent defeats, surely he could deliver the final crushing blow himself without waiting for Gratian to share in the victory?[60]

By now Valens had assembled a considerable field army from all over the eastern empire, the largest concentration of force that had been seen for many years, commanded by men of a very different calibre from Lupicinus. The detailed preparations, false assumptions, blunders, opportunities and strokes of fortune that attend a defeat often seem indistinguishable from those of a victory. Perhaps all one can say is that Fritigern made mistakes, but Valens made more. The Roman army moved westwards, shadowing the Visigoths, and scouts reported — wrongly — that the enemy force was much smaller than their own. Fritigern, having been defeated by Sebastianus as a result of over-dispersal, concentrated his forces and sent urgent appeals to his Greuthungian allies to join him.[61] In the meantime he did all he could to delay the onset of battle.

Outside the great walled city of Adrianople Valens built a fortified camp and held a council of war[62]. Gratian's advance guard had already arrived and their commander, Richomer,[63] urged Valens to stay on the defensive and to await the arrival of the main western army. Victor,[64] Valens' Master of Cavalry (*Magister Equitum*), seconded this view. However, Sebastianus was all for launching an immediate attack, which was what Valens wanted to hear.[65] Ironically, if an attack had been made at once, the Gothic forces might have been caught unprepared and without reinforcements.

Messages of truce came from Fritigern, and Valens delayed. Fritigern declared that he had never wanted this war, that there was still time to avoid a battle and to reach a solemn, lasting peace treaty which would confine his people to Thrace. He added that the periodic display of the strength of Roman arms would be very welcome in helping to keep his ungovernable people in order.[66] Whether he suspected him or believed him, or detected signs of weakness in these overtures, Valens gave no reply but moved the whole army towards the enemy and halted about eight miles from Adrianople, his supply base. The Visigoths were in sight, drawn up in front of their own camp, a great laager of wagons.

Once again, an apparently desperate Fritigern sent envoys to parley. Possibly hoping to secure a victory without having to fight, Valens was now favourably disposed to a treaty and demanded high-ranking envoys to negotiate with. It was a blazing hot day on 9 August 378, and the frustrated men and horses were suffering from heat and fatigue. Fires had been deliberately started on the plain to add to their discomfort. By now Fritigern's allies were close by and he only needed time for them to deploy. He asked Valens to show his sincerity by sending, in his turn, high-ranking men as hostages. Richomer volunteered for the mission in an attempt to bring some order to the situation, but before he reached the Gothic lines fighting had already broken out and he was recalled. A body of Roman light cavalry had been skirmishing too close to the enemy and had been repulsed in disorder. The main body of the army now advanced, but without real coordination. The Roman cavalry on the left wing broke through the opposing forces and swept far ahead of the centre of the army, reaching almost to the Gothic wagon-citadel. Unsupported and disorganised, they were cut off and scattered, as the furious charge of the newly arrived Greuthungian and Alan forces under Alatheus and Saphrax drove off the Roman cavalry and outflanked and enveloped the exposed wings of the Roman infantry.[67]

> The infantry thus stood unprotected, their ranks so closely pressed that hardly anyone had room to draw his sword or free his arm . . . When the barbarians poured down in great hordes, trampling horses and men, and when in the tight press of ranks there was no room for retreat and no opening for flight, our soldiers, in supreme contempt of death, struck down their enemies ferociously while receiving their own fatal wounds. On both sides the strokes of axes split helmets and breastplates . . . In the great tumult the infantry, exhausted by the efforts and the perils of the fighting, no longer able to think or plan, their spears broken, rushed recklessly with drawn swords into the dense masses of the enemy, careless of their lives now that all escape was impossible. The ground, slippery with blood, gave them hardly any foothold, so they could only strain every nerve to sell their lives dearly, and so fierce was their resistance to the enemy assaults that some of them were killed on the weapons of their own comrades.

The narrator is the contemporary soldier and historian, Ammianus Marcellinus.[68] Though entirely surrounded by Gothic and Alan infantry and cavalry, locked in close ranks and presenting a point-blank target for missiles, the mass of the army fought on for many hours until, exhausted and decimated, the resistance finally became a rout. Valens' bodyguard fled with the collapse of the surviving units, and Victor attempted to rescue the Emperor with the last reserves of Batavian cavalry, but he was lost in the mêlée. It is indicative of the scale of the defeat that no-one knew for certain where and how Valens was slain. Victor, Richomer and a section of the army managed to escape with nightfall, but the great majority of troops and their commanders — perhaps 20,000 of the East's best fighting men —

lay on the battlefield.[69]

Ignoring Fritigern's orders, the Goths then besieged Adrianople itself where the Court, civil officials and treasury remained under a small garrison. Being quite unskilled in siegecraft, and vulnerable to the defenders' artillery, they had no success. Attempted treachery by some pro-Gothic troops inside the city was discovered and the perpetrators promptly executed. Frustrated in their attempts, the Gothic forces drifted off eastwards down the highway towards Perinthus and Constantinople.[70]

The staggering scale of the disaster sent a shock of disbelief through the East. The field army had been destroyed, but for a third who had escaped (and some elements not summoned for the campaign from their bases). In a turbulent time of wars and invasions nothing like it had been experienced in living memory. Ammianus justly compared it to Cannae, six centuries earlier, when the last Roman army in Italy had been annihilated by Hannibal and nothing stood between him and Rome. Gratian, learning the appalling news, withdrew with his army westwards to Sirmium (Mitrovica).[71] The East was leaderless and unable to put a major force into the field to resist the invaders. The impossible, the unthinkable, had happened. The shock and fear arising from the disaster are reflected in contemporary sources, especially since the loss of the emperor himself in battle indicated the true scale of events (it had happened twice in the tumult of the third century: Decius and his army being destroyed by the Goths in 251, and Valerian being captured by the Sassanid Persians in 260; but not before or since.[72]

The battle of Adrianople has repeatedly been seen since Ammianus as a turning point, both in the history of the Roman empire and in the history of warfare. Whilst it was certainly a great disaster for Rome, and completely changed the terms on which Romans and barbarians would deal in the future, it was not necessarily the 'beginning of the end' for the empire, and we will return to this thesis later.

In terms of military history, it has been commonly assumed that the outcome of the battle demonstrated the superiority of cavalry over infantry, which lasted until the late middle ages and the development of more effective projectile weapons. In our view this is a flawed approach, arising from a misunderstanding of the battle itself and the nature of the opposing forces, which ignores the vast bulk of evidence to the contrary, both in the later fourth century and in other periods. Adrianople was an infantry battle, decided by a series of tactical moves and accidents, and was no different in its troop composition and manoeuvring from most of the set-piece warfare of the day (see Appendix 1 for a detailed discussion of the military aspects of the battle).

Not everything went Fritigern's way. His warriors, living off the countryside at will, had little cohesion and, time and again, were unable to capture fortified cities or strongpoints. They were repulsed at Perinthus, and then suffered a minor defeat by some Saracen troops outside Constantinople itself. For over a century the empire, faced with a continuous belt of enemies, had invested in stronger fortifications for its cities and frontier posts. Strongly defended gateways, high, thick walls and projecting artillery bastions were now the pattern and in this crisis proved their worth. A sophisticated enemy like the Persians could capture such fortifications with engineering techniques and siegecraft — they had done so at Amida in 359 — but the Germanic peoples had neither the skills nor the organisation to do this.[73]

Repulsed at Constantinople, the Goths drifted west again, meeting no real armed resistance. Established colonies of Goths, already settled throughout the East in previous, peaceful settlements, now showed signs of disaffection. What Roman troops there were remained in the fortified strongpoints, isolated and lacking any strategic command. Richomer and Victor had joined Gratian at Sirmium, having escaped the wreck of Adrianople. Julius,[74] Master of the Army in the East (*Magister Militum per Oriens*), arriving from the eastern frontier, forestalled the possible desertion of existing Gothic settlers, on his own initiative, by a bloody stratagem. He invited them all to assemblies in the cities, where by a pre-arranged signal they were massacred.[75]

The most pressing decisions lay with Gratian at Sirmium, towards which the vestiges of power now gravitated in the form of generals with or without troops, officials with or without money, administrators with little or no control over their territories. At Sirmium there was at least an Emperor, an administrative centre, the core of a state apparatus and an intact army. Gratian was only twenty-two years old and now the sole ruler of the empire. Although the Rhine frontier was temporarily pacified it would not remain so for long without the military presence and attention of an emperor. Ever since Diocletian and Maximian, political wisdom had dictated that the empire's distances were too great, its frontiers too extensive, its enemies too many and strong for it to be ruled by one man for very long. The sons of Constantine[76] had painfully rediscovered this. Constantius,[77] having disposed of his brothers, had been compelled to share the imperial power with his cousins Gallus,[78] and then Julian,[79] even though he had murdered their father. By the end of Constantine's dynasty it was quite natural to expect Valentinian to appoint an imperial colleague to rule the other half of the empire.[80]

Gratian, who had already shown himself to be a more able general and ruler than Valens, recognised that in the current emergency there was little time for hesitation or delay. The East desperately needed a supreme military commander to rescue it from the wreck of Adrianople; and such a man would naturally expect to assume the purple, with or without the consent of the Western emperor. Who, then, was the best candidate?

The seemingly straightforward question, raised so frequently in the Roman empire, was fraught with dangers; it was almost a forbidden thought. So many emperors had been murdered, so many usurpers had made bids for the throne by military revolt, palace coup or provincial breakaway. It was not surprising that the imperial succession was the one question which it was strictly forbidden, on pain of death for high treason, to put to diviners, oracles, seers or mediums, whom so many people consulted on every other conceivable subject. Valens himself, in a bout of savage paranoia, had uncovered real or imaginary plots centring on secret occult consultations about who would succeed him, and many greater and lesser men had been tortured and executed.[81]

Even for a high official of the Sacred Consistory, to whom Gratian now put this question in all sincerity, a false step could spell ruin. Few of these ministers trusted one another. In addition to the prefects, field marshals, finance ministers, masters of offices, chamberlains and masters of the bedchamber and all the other posts in the increasingly oriental Court there were omnipresent official spies — the *agentes in rebus*[82] — whose duties included reporting any loose or potentially treasonable talk among the complex bureaucracy. Every high official lived with the knowledge that careless talk, even ambivalent political signals or innocent remarks, could suddenly cost him his position, perhaps even his life. Everyone wanted to back the right horse, since if the name put forward turned out to be the wrong one it was likely to be remembered by the *agentes*, and by the newcomer who was to wear the diadem. Such was the hazardous business of decision-making within the closed, glittering and stifling world of palace politics to which Gratian was now looking for honest advice.

In its long history the Roman empire had never articulated a clear and unambiguous method of imperial succession, partly because of the deep-rooted embarrassment about outright monarchy which dated back to Augustus, and partly because of the military emergencies of the third century. Dynasty and kinship ties certainly counted, in the manner of the old Roman family system, but they were not overriding. The senate and, above all, the army could legally elect an emperor, as they had elected Valentinian;[83] and it went without saying that the emperor had to be a competent military leader, or else he would soon be supplanted by one who was. This tradition had the advantage that immature or incompetent heirs could be dethroned or passed over quite legally, but its weakness was that any powerful and ambitious general was a potential emperor.[84]

When, long before, Valentinian had been debating whom to choose as an imperial colleague his trusted general and supporter, Dagalaif,[85] had given him very outspoken advice: if you are thinking of your family then appoint your brother, but if you are thinking of the empire then appoint someone else. As a German, who could therefore not aspire to the purple himself, Dagalaif could be disinterested; nor did his subsequent career suffer as a consequence. Later events had indeed indicated that the appointment of Valens had been a mistake.

Gratian was not tempted to a similar mistake. He too had a brother, named Valentinian after their father, who enjoyed the nominal title of Augustus,[86] but who was only seven years of age. Instead, the favoured candidate was a young man of great military promise who had fought an impressive and successful campaign in Moesia several years earlier;[87] but he had no reason to love Valentinian's dynasty. Flavius Theodosius the younger had been apprenticed in war and statecraft to his illustrious father, Count Theodosius,[88] who had been Master of Cavalry (*Magister Equitum*) in the West and a staunch support to Valentinian's throne. Within a short time of that emperor's death he had fallen victim to a court intrigue, and had been executed for treason.[89]

Protectorless, and with his career blighted, his son prudently retired to the family estates at Ceuta, near Valladolid in Spain,[90] where he was now, at thirty-two, quietly rebuilding his life. His immediate response to Gratian's urgent summons is not recorded, but rarely can anyone have been offered a more daunting commission.

2

THE BURDENS OF EMPIRE

Theodosius' family were provincial aristocrats, with a concentration of estates in Gallaecia (see map I) and the usual network of connections and influence through the upper classes of the Spanish and Gallic provinces.[1] Spain was a region where Christianity had taken hold early and, unlike the older Italian senatorial families, they were firmly Christians of the Nicene creed and numbered bishops among their friends and connections.[2] They first came to prominence with the elder Flavius Theodosius,[3] whose outstanding talents as a general brought him to the topmost military circles of Valentinian, playing an important part in the emperor's campaigns on the Rhine and upper Danube.[4]

In 367–8 he had carried out the major task of retrieving the disastrous military situation in Britain where, after years of mounting pressures and unheeded warnings, the armies had been overwhelmed by simultaneous invasions of Picts, Scots, Attacotti, Franks and Saxons.[5] From Count of the Army (*Comes Rei Militaris*)[6] he had been promoted to Master of Cavalry (*Magister Equitum*)[7] in the West.

On most of these campaigns he had taken with him his promising younger son, Theodosius,[8] beginning a rigorous apprenticeship in war and statecraft almost as soon as he was of military age. The youth had been quick to learn the skills of a commander, and to observe also the combination of force and diplomacy with which his masterful father divided and pacified the enemy in Britain. In 374, at the age of twenty-seven, he was given his own independent command as *Dux* in Moesia against the Sarmatians, and succeeded in defeating them and imposing favourable conditions of peace.[9]

The stage thus seemed set for a distinguished military career which, in the normal way, could in time lead him also to the highest commands. In the meantime his father had again been despatched on a difficult campaign, in Mauretania, to suppress a widespread revolt led by the Moorish usurper, Firmus.[10] The situation had been provoked by the extortions and gross maladministration of the governor Romanus,[11] whom Theodosius exposed and succeeded in having prosecuted. The campaign was one of attrition, conducted with skill and ruthlessness against considerably greater numbers, and was finally brought to a conclusion in 375 with the capture and suicide of Firmus. Then, in the immediate aftermath of victory, his patron, the emperor Valentinian, died suddenly, and in a very short time the blow fell. On imperial orders Theodosius was quickly arrested and executed at Carthage. Before his execution, which he faced calmly, he was baptised.[12]

The reasons for his sudden execution (let alone the formal charge) are unknown, and have promoted much modern conjecture. Although trusted by Valentinian he had certainly made enemies at court, including the friends of Romanus. Even more dangerous was the powerful Prefect of Gaul, Maximinus,[13] whose brother-in-law Theodosius had executed in Britain for plotting rebellion. Due to his background Theodosius naturally inclined to the Gallo-Hispanic senatorial faction at court, and had been friendly with the celebrated literary figure Symmachus.[14]

The unexpected death of Valentinian in November 375[15] created a political crisis in which the Pannonian faction at court moved quickly to secure their safety, proclaiming the boy Valentinian II Augustus at Aquincum[16] and posting the potentially dangerous general, Sebastianus,[17] safely out of the way. This move did not, however, prevent real power from descending on Valentinian's elder son, Gratian, at Trier.[18] It seems plausible that in this situation they would have seized any chance to eliminate Theodosius, perhaps their most formidable opponent and the natural focus of a rival faction.

There is another element in the story, which might also have added fuel to such a plot. Five years earlier the near-paranoid Valens had launched a series of savage trials for sorcery at Antioch. The accused had admitted under torture to seeking by divination the name of the man to succeed Valens as emperor. In this sad game a ring, suspended by a fine linen thread, moved randomly to various letters of the Greek alphabet and yielded the sequence φεοΔ (THEOD . . .). As a result one Theodorus,[19] a notary, was executed together with many others at Antioch. (The prophecy of course was ultimately fulfilled, as prophecies in Roman histories usually are.)

With Valentinian dead and Valens the senior emperor, Theodosius' enemies could have revived in the Augustus these superstitious fears, and added this weight to their design. If so, they must have had the weapon ready to hand, for they acted very rapidly while Theodosius was still in Africa and without easy access to the court. Whether they used the authority of Valentinian II or Gratian is not known. If the nightmares of Valens were a factor it would have been logical for him to destroy the son as well as the father, and indeed Ambrose[20] relates that for a time the younger Theodosius was in danger. He quickly withdrew into retirement on the family estates, which surprisingly had not suffered confiscation, and where the strings of influence were at least in the hands of his friends.[21] If he was a marked man the web of accusations was never completed before a sudden and decisive coup at Gratian's court removed the danger, with the execution of Maximinus and the violent purge of the whole Pannonian faction.[22]

The pattern of political opportunism in all these prosecutions, the speciousness of so many of the charges (treason? corruption?) illustrate the perpetually dangerous atmosphere in which top officials lived. For Theodosius the wheel had clearly turned, and a party friendly to his family was now uppermost at Gratian's court in the West. His uncle, Eucherius, and

Antonius, a relative by marriage, were amongst Gratian's high officials.[23] In time he might even be received back into favour, although it would be most unwise to anticipate this. But at least he was safe.

For three years he adapted easily to the life of a provincial aristocrat, overseeing his newly-acquired patrimony and attending to all the social duties it involved. In a dangerous world he had learnt prudence and diplomacy, but it would be wrong to think of him as simply biding his time. Like any other nobleman who has temporarily held office he would have kept in touch with changes at court through correspondence with his elevated family, friends and their clients. The upper classes of the empire constituted a reservoir of civil and military leadership on whom the government could always call, but many of them spent only short periods in office and, unless they were ambitious or greedy, lived a comfortable and pleasant life, especially in the Western provinces of Gaul, Spain and Italy.[24]

There is no reason to suppose that Theodosius was markedly different, nor that his diplomatic skill was merely the product of careful calculation. By temperament he was both emotional and felicitous. His talent for cultivating friends, relations and social equals, or dealing with clients and dependants, was the result of a genuinely warm, affable, outgoing nature, fond of society and naturally attractive to all who met him. *Civilitas, hilaritas, comitas* (the ease of dealing with every class of person in the expected manner)[25] were highly valued qualities in an elite which, far more than modern aristocracies, lived almost entirely in public. A prominent man who was unlucky enough to lack these personal graces, like Tiberius, was seriously handicapped.[26]

It was in this not unhappy period of retirement that Theodosius married Aelia Flaccilla, who soon gave birth to a daughter, Pulcheria, and a son, Arcadius.[27] Flaccilla was the precursor of a line of powerful imperial women who played an important role in the court politics and management of the empire.

In the autumn of 378 the full news of the disaster of Adrianople can scarcely have reached the western provinces before Theodosius received the emperor Gratian's urgent message from Sirmium, with the well-publicised offer of supreme military command in the East, and with it the truly formidable commission of somehow rescuing the central heartland of the empire from ruin.

The later panegyric stresses Theodosius' disinterested motives and his reluctance to accept, but this is largely rhetorical convention. An imperial offer of this significance and in these circumstances was tantamount to a command. In the absence of an imperial candidate to succeed Valens (he had no heir, and the crushing defeat of Adrianople must have ruled out any Eastern military commander) nobody could fail to see what the supreme military command implied, and was intended to imply. Though protocol may normally have allowed one to go through the motions of consideration, in this case events moved very quickly.[28]

Before the end of the autumn Theodosius travelled east, was appointed *Magister Militum* (Master of the Army) at Sirmium, and scored a rapid victory over the Sarmatians who, in the confused state of communications and defences, were threatening the western Danube frontier opposite Pannonia (see map I). This was no more than a preliminary to the far greater labour of clearing the Goths from the eastern Danube area, but it impressed Gratian and led quickly to the next, near-inevitable step. On 19 January 379, before the armies at Sirmium, Theodosius was acclaimed Augustus with direct rule over all the Eastern provinces, to which were added the Macedonian provinces, which had formerly belonged to Gratian's domain.[29]

The Roman empire of the late fourth century, whose rule Theodosius now shared with Gratian, was a very different entity from that of the Julio-Claudians and Flavians in the first century, or Hadrian and the Antonines in the second. The constant invocation of a changeless, eternal Rome by the orators and historians, their effortless comparisons with the fabulous Catos and Scipios of the distant past, was more than just a natural reverence for tradition and continuity. It verged on a classical hypnotic fixation, which continued even up to the Enlightenment when Gibbon was writing. It presented Rome as a kind of inviolate essence, transcending all upheaval and change, and in doing so soothed and blunted the critical faculties of many contemporaries who had to grapple with a radically different world.

The two centuries since Hadrian and the Antonines had seen convulsive changes on such a scale that the empire as a territorial and political unit had occasionally broken apart. The greater pressures of Germanic and other peoples in increasingly coherent groupings along the whole length of the Rhine and Danube, and the rise of a powerful expansionist Persia, had stretched the empire's military resources beyond their capacity. The frontiers had been repeatedly breached and the Gallic and Danubian provinces progressively devastated. As troops were urgently needed on every threatened front the armies had operated independently of a single controlling centre, and their loyalties to a general who could pay them had superseded their loyalty to a distant emperor. While the empire was being assaulted by external enemies it was simultaneously racked by military anarchy as rival generals fought for the throne. In the half-century between 235 and 285 there were 15 'legitimate' emperors and many more brief usurpers. Nearly all had died violently, in civil war or simple assassination by their own soldiers and lieutenants.

Slowly and with great difficulty these empire-wide disorders had been mastered by a series of Danubian military emperors, of whom the greatest were Aurelian, Diocletian and Constantine. By 330 the empire had been rebuilt, but in a new form. It was now more centralised, absolutist and organised on semi-military lines for an indefinite siege. The more open, civic character of the second century had become narrow, autocratic and hierarchical. A greatly expanded army and an elaborate, uniformed bureaucracy supported the imperial throne, and exacted in their turn a far higher, more oppressive and pervasive level of taxes in cash and kind, in goods and services. Emperors themselves used every device to elevate themselves above their soldiers and subjects by adopting a public image of semi-divine beings in glittering palaces, surrounded by an oriental, hieratic ceremonial, and by becoming correspondingly insulated from society outside of their courts.

Rome itself had ceased to be the effective centre of the government of the empire. These functions were now concentrated on the newly-established imperial capitals strategically located near to the threatened frontiers and the main communication routes: Trier, Milan, Aquileia, Sirmium, Salonica, Antioch and, above all, the new and splendid city of Constantinople. The traditional gods that had guided a small city on the Tiber to world empire had been largely displaced by the radically new religion of Christianity, whose bishops now cooperated with the state and increasingly resembled government officials.

The reconstruction had been heavy-handed, painful and — in many ways — insensitive to the values and spirit of the urbane civilisation that had once existed. It was a product of sheer necessity, created by practical, semi-cultured soldier-emperors, and it was far from stupid. The frontiers, partly contracted, had been stabilised and heavily fortified, and had generally held. Deserted land had been settled with Germanic colonists under Roman control and authority. The crippling civil wars for the throne had been largely surmounted by the new devices of dual emperors of East and West, the deliberate separation of civil and military chains of command in the elaborately graded bureaucracy, the subdivision of the provinces into smaller administrative units and the almost magical ceremonials of the elevated imperial cult.

It had only been achieved at enormous and permanent social costs, some obvious, some hidden, whose effects were working through in the later fourth century. The margin of effective resources on which emperors could draw had grown smaller. Wealth and power had polarised drastically, and the process was self-perpetuating. The traditional senatorial aristocracy had, through intermarriage and the absorption of smaller landowners, increased their *per capita* landed wealth many times over since the early empire. Added to these was the new, parvenu aristocracy of the imperial mandarins, Constantine's *clarissimi*,[30] who operated the upper levels of government. These two classes had a direct interest, as both landowners and imperial officials, in passing the financial burdens — as much as possible — on to the poorer and less powerful below them, and in this they succeeded.

Despite the recovery of the empire in the later third century, and also through much of the fourth, the problem immediately facing Theodosius as Augustus of the East was nothing less than the simple survival of the state. Since Adrianople the empire had lost, crucially, the military initiative. Long sections of the eastern Danube were no longer functioning frontiers. Main communication lines were insecure, and the great Visigothic nation in arms was moving unhindered over hundreds of miles of the Balkans, causing great destruction and attracting Gothic slaves and *coloni* to its ranks.[31]

Gratian and Theodosius still possessed organised forces, and there were other scattered garrisons and units throughout Thrace, as well as intact, but remote, forces in Egypt, Syria and the rest of the Orient. The Western army was, of course, still in being but it could not be thrown completely into the conflict on the middle and lower Danube without exposing the Western provinces. Both emperors knew that in strength, fighting quality and morale the Eastern forces were nowhere near ready to match Fritigern and his allies in set battle. The losses suffered in first-class trained troops, the temporary loss of nerve in the survivors and its inevitable effects on other parts of the army could not be repaired overnight.

The emperors had some assets, if these could be husbanded and deployed skilfully. The fortified cities, though isolated, were well provisioned and garrisoned and held out securely. As Fritigern knew very well, the Goths had no skill in siegecraft, and he consistently urged his followers to avoid the cities, declaring that he had no quarrel with walls.[32] They were very formidable as a concentrated force, but it was immensely difficult for Fritigern to keep them concentrated, or even impose on them a general direction and purpose. They had great problems feeding themselves and their families, and readily dispersed over large areas plundering and foraging, but neither storing nor planting, and making no adequate preparations for the next year. For the present Theodosius' best prospects were with a prudent policy of attrition, starvation, local engagements on favourable terms and exploiting whatever splits might appear among the Goths. The sweeping follies of Valens' grand decisions were now having to be paid for, and it was not surprising that Theodosius' strategy of recovery was one of marked pragmatism, opportunism and caution.

Among the many acclamations and salutations to the new ruler was an address to him by Libanius, the celebrated rhetorician of Antioch,[33] now in his sixties, which struck a strong patriotic note over the disaster of Adrianople. Some, he says, have accused our armies of cowardice, incompetence and lack of training. But on the contrary they were heroes, worthy of the greatest Roman traditions. They fought and died where they stood, and their valiant emperor died with them, refusing the disgrace of flight and true to the finest examples of our ancestors. The heaps of bones of those who fell around their emperor are the monument to their valour. Theodosius could only have welcomed such sentiments, badly needed as they were to steady public morale.

Proclamations and exhortations issued from Sirmium. In the true traditions of imperial doublespeak the fine gold coins announcing joint rule bore the legend *Victoria Augg*, with the winged victory figure, for all the world as if there was something to celebrate.[34] (In much the same way, coin legends such as *Securitas, Prosperitas* or *Concordia Militum* were usually signs of invasions, economic hardship or army revolts.) An imperial decision of February 379 endorsed and encouraged the ad-hoc regional administration of court officials and generals (*palatini*) in the separated areas of the East, giving them a free hand.[35]

The two Augusti struggled through the winter of 378–9 to assemble a government and army for the East. These had to be in existence by the spring, when the main fighting season began and the Goths would again be on the move. Several of Theodosius' high-ranking supporters in Gratian's court now either took office under him or recommended others who did. Olybrius, Praetorian Prefect of Illyricum, became Prefect of the East and acted as the controlling link in the transfers, which included the finance minister Tatianus and the *Magister Militum*, Sapores. Syagrius, Gratian's *Magister Officiorum*, recruited a number of high officials, as did Eutropius, the historian, recalled like Theodosius from political retirement shortly after Adrianople.[36] After a successful early campaigning season in Pannonia, Gratian had secured the position to the extent where he could leave matters in the hands of his generals and his imperial colleague. Leaving a portion of the army with Theodosius, Gratian and his court then left Sirmium for the West where trouble was again threatening from the Alemanni and Vandals on the Rhine frontier.

Theodosius' immediate need was to secure an Eastern capital and base of operations. It is striking evidence of the confused state of the Balkans that Constantinople itself was impractical, as were all the other strongpoint cities along the great strategic highway: Perinthus–Adrianople–Phillipopolis–Serdica–Naissus. In effect, the vital east–west communications artery for troops and supplies was for the present unusable, and its regular supply depots vulnerable to the Goths. Theodosius and his forces instead moved south-east to Salonica, the well-protected imperial capital with a great harbour on to the Aegean, to which supplies of all kinds could be imported from Egypt and Asia. From here roads radiated east to Constantinople, north to Naissus and Illyricum, and west and south into Thessaly. His action followed that of his father ten years earlier: sent to rescue Britain from a combined barbarian invasion, Theodosius the Elder had first secured a strong base in London, and then systematically set about dividing and defeating his enemy.[37] But the crisis Theodosius had to deal with now was incomparably graver.

With a core of a professional army and its officers to build around, Theodosius and his agents used every possible device to fill up the ranks, as a stream of laws indicate, beginning in July 379 and continuing throughout the next few years.[38] Conscription and the hereditary obligation to serve were both established in law, and were now applied with the greatest vigour in the territories which Theodosius controlled. The sons of soldiers were combed out of the ranks of the bureaucracy. Landowners were pressurised anew for recruits, with heavy penalties for those offering slaves or menials, and capital punishment for those harbouring deserters. Even the wretched malingerers who had mutilated their thumbs to avoid conscription were ordered in at the rate of two per recruit demanded. In addition, Germanic recruits were eagerly sought from whatever source — even Gothic prisoners or deserters. Other barbarian mercenaries were engaged on easy contracts which permitted them to return home provided they supplied a substitute. Trained units were also recalled from Egypt.[39]

Even when distributed among more seasoned formations, conscripts of whatever quality would take some time before they could be useful soldiers. This was, of course, rendered even more difficult when they were utterly reluctant, and when the morale of the professional army absorbing them was itself shaky. Many ran away when they could, and landowners, always short of labour, connived at this, as the furious laws testify: landowners or their overseers harbouring deserters will be burnt alive; tax collectors discovering deserters will gain generous immunities from their civic obligations; slaves informing on deserters will immediately gain their freedom; and deserters themselves will die by the sword — although there are strong indications that the army was often willing to overlook technical desertion by raw recruits, provided they returned to the standard. Like his father in Britain Theodosius was making a deliberate choice here. To have imposed vigorous military law on these waverers would have resulted in a small, highly disciplined force, but not the large army that Theodosius needed to assemble if he was to wrest the initiative from Fritigern.

Tantalisingly, we have almost no detailed accounts of the campaigns of 379–82. The confused narratives of Zosimus, the hints of Themistius, the attested movements of the two emperors and other fragmentary sources still do not add up to a complete and coherent picture; but some features are clear. Firstly, if Fritigern had any strategic objective beyond simple plunder and supply he failed to impose it on his followers; secondly, it was a war of manoeuvre, modest engagements and attrition against the Goths, especially by holding the strongpoints, denying them food supplies and exploiting splits amongst them; thirdly, Theodosius continued to depend heavily on Gratian's military support for whatever successes were achieved.[40]

Finally, and most importantly, by 381 neither Theodosius nor Gratian any longer aimed at destroying the Goths, even had they been able to. Conventional civilian opinion doubtless expected a crushing victory to avenge Adrianople, but Theodosius had no wish to risk everything on another great set-piece battle. All the strategy of his reign indicates how acutely aware he was of the military manpower shortage. If he lost this last Roman army in the East there would be nothing left. Even if he won the losses could leave him gravely weakened against the next inevitable threat. Far better to conserve both Roman and Gothic manpower, achieve military dominance over the barbarians, and then wean their warlike energies into his own service.

One further factor to take into account in this change of approach is that in 381 there was a further incursion across the Danube, this time by predominantly Hunnic groups. Although it was repulsed it was a sure sign of the continuing level of threat beyond the immediate problem of dealing with the Goths, and no doubt inclined Theodosius in the direction of reaching an accommodation with them.[41]

The main military action of 379 had been a minor victory over the Visigoths in Thrace by Theodosius' general Modares. His role is particularly significant since he was a convert to the Roman cause of considerable standing among the Goths, possibly even related to Athanaric. His support for Theodosius suggests that it was still an attractive prospect for barbarians of high standing to enlist and serve as Roman officers, rather than seek to lead federate groups; it may also indicate that Rome was again gaining the upper hand.[42] Whether as a result of this defeat, or due to the exhaustion of supplies in Thrace, or both, the Visigoths then moved west into Illyricum. Theodosius had spent almost all that year rebuilding an army, raising recruits and transferring forces from the eastern frontiers. By late 379 he was reportedly enrolling Goths themselves into the Roman army in large numbers, which again suggests that there had been a shift in the perceived balance of power.[43]

That winter, at Salonica, Theodosius fell gravely ill, to the point where in February 380 he seemed to be dying. Like his father he received the solemn sacrament of baptism, from bishop Acholius, which would purge him of all sin. His generals did not suspend their operations and preparations — they could not, but the imminent prospect of another imperial succession crisis could not have raised their confidence. Events showed just how flimsy was the advantage recently gained, and how dependent everything was on the life and will of one man. The enemy was not slow to seize the opportunity. Once again the Visigothic hordes washed southwest, this time into Thessaly, while their Greuthungian cousins pushed into Pannonia. Once again they plundered and caused great destruction but were unable to take the walled cities, and once more an appeal for help went out to Trier; Gratian realised that he and his armies would again be needed to assist the desperate position in the East.[44]

However, Theodosius made a full recovery by the spring, which he quite naturally attributed to the divine grace of baptism and the countless prayers and masses said on his behalf. Soon afterwards he was to throw his full imperial authority behind the Nicene bishops, and unify the doctrine and worship of the church by the force of law.

In March-April 380, with a heterogeneous, unpromising force, whose numbers can only be conjectured but which probably did not exceed 10,000, Theodosius now prepared to move against the Visigoths. The sufferings of the affected provinces were so great that it is hardly surprising that some of them cooperated with the Goths. In the north-east (near modern Pleven in Bulgaria) the city of Nicopolis had fallen, probably handed over by its population despairing of any assistance. Fritigern's main forces were now based on Moesia Superior (eastern Serbia), and now moved south into

Macedonia. Theodosius risked a confrontation and, in one or more engagements, was worsted but not disastrously. His new, raw army was still no match for Fritigern's warriors, and he was forced to withdraw while they besieged the cities of Macedonia and Thessaly and plundered their hinterland.[45]

The cities, although poorly garrisoned, held out, and the Goths were content to settle for a sizeable tribute in goods and supplies and then to move on. By now they had learned not only the futility of trying to take fortified cities, but also the advantage of regular 'taxation', which left the inhabitants with enough to recover, as opposed to the total pillage of an area, which leaves them with nothing and cannot be repeated. As soon as they had moved on Theodosius provided the cities and forts with proper garrisons, and then moved by rapid marches to Constantinople from where he sent urgent requests to Gratian for military aid, and at the same time imposed new, emergency taxes on all the cities within his reach.

Gratian had his own crisis, in the shape of an invasion of Pannonia by Fritigern's allies under Alatheus and Saphrax. He was apparently successful in controlling the assault, and soon after came to a treaty agreement with them which allowed them to settle in Pannonia. This may have been the expedient result of a less than decisive victory or, even if it was conclusive, it may have been a necessary device to free troops to assist Theodosius while neutralising the threat that they would again return east to aid Fritigern.[46]

At all events Theodosius was assured of military aid, and much of the summer and autumn of 380 was spent in planning this joint enterprise. Both emperors travelled to Sirmium to concert future operations, either directly or through their generals, and Theodosius' propaganda stressed always — as well it might — the harmony and cooperation between them. In November Theodosius entered Constantinople in triumph. This was a propaganda demonstration, for he had personally achieved almost nothing. The populations of Thrace, Macedonia, Thessaly and Moesia had suffered atrociously, and there is no doubt that some of them, especially the poorest peasantry, actually cooperated with the Goths by directing them to the richest pickings, or even joining them when there was nothing left to lose.[47]

Nonetheless, Theodosius' ceremonial entry was devised to restore public confidence and morale, and signal to the nobility, church and people of the metropolis that Rome now had the upper hand and the dire emergency which had begun with Adrianople was now overcome. This propaganda received a welcome boost in January 381: the former Tervingian leader, Athanaric, who had originally split with Fritigern and led his followers into Transylvania rather than plead for entry into the Roman Empire, was old and sick.[48] He had been ousted by Fritigern who had been maintaining his contacts north of the Danube and seeking to consolidate his dominant position among the Goths. Athanaric had no choice but to apply as a humble supplicant to Theodosius, asking permission to settle inside the empire with the rump of his followers.[49]

Theodosius seized the opportunity and exploited it to the full. Athanaric and his small band of followers were in no bargaining position: they were throwing themselves on Roman clemency. With great ostentation Theodosius and his imperial retinue met Athanaric several miles outside the city, and greeted him as an honoured royal guest. Here was a chance to demonstrate to the whole Gothic world the advantages of alliance and cooperation with Rome. Display, pomp and illusion were going to accomplish what could no longer be done by main military force. Nowhere was better equipped to do this than the fabulous capital of Constantinople.

The city which was to dazzle the crusaders eight centuries later certainly had the desired effect on Athanaric, with its impression of quite limitless wealth which Rome had always presented to the Germanic imagination: 'I have now seen what I often had heard of, though I did not believe it', declared Athanaric at the sight of the palaces, the great public squares, the hippodrome, the shimmering churches, the immaculately drilled guards, the harbour choked with shipping and the throng of peoples of all nations. 'Truly the emperor of Rome is a god on earth, and whoever lifts a hand against him is asking for death.' This was just what Theodosius wanted all Goths to hear, and he took pains to ensure that they did.

A fortnight later Athanaric died in the city. He was already sick, and there was no suggestion of anything untoward. Theodosius, sensing a further opportunity, laid on the most magnificent state funeral with full royal honours, and himself led the procession. Large numbers of Visigoths had been assembled at Constantinople for the occasion, and they were deeply impressed. Athanaric's retinue of warriors readily agreed to serve in Theodosius' army, and to accept the duty of frontier defence. In purely military terms this made little difference to the balance of forces, but it had a significant psychological effect on both Goths and Romans.[50]

The campaigning season of 381 opened with an offensive by a fully professional Western army, commanded by Gratian's Frankish generals Bauto and Arbogast, assisted by whatever effective forces Theodosius could add. It succeeded in driving Fritigern out of Macedonia, out of Illyricum altogether, and back to his devastated starting point in Thrace. In three years of ostensibly victorious plundering since Adrianople the Visigoths had achieved almost nothing. At last there were real Roman victories to show, although it still took most of another year of attrition, starvation and divisive diplomacy before Roman ascendancy could translate itself into the concrete shape of a peace treaty.[51]

At some time about this point Fritigern disappeared from the scene, either because he died, or because he had lost the support of the mass of his followers as so many Germanic war leaders did.[52] Much of 382 was taken up with pressing the advantage home against the Visigoths, who were penned into ever narrower areas of a devastated Thrace, and it was not until October that this strategy finally bore fruit.

The final treaty with the Visigoths, signed on Theodosius' behalf by his generals Saturninus, Richomer and others, was concluded on 3 October 382.[53] It accepted the Visigoths as settlers in Thrace, and — in outward appearance and official pronouncements — it seemed to have reversed the disaster of Adrianople six years earlier, returning to the *status quo ante* of 376 when Valens accepted them as new settlers. Theodosius' propagandists, especially Themistius, stress the picture of Gothic defeat and submission. Once again, it seemed, even the most catastrophic of Roman defeats could eventually be reversed due to the resourcefulness and ultimate invincibility of eternal Rome.[54]

> We have seen their leaders and chieftains, not making token submission of a tattered banner, but giving up their weapons and swords with which up to that day they had held sway, and clinging to the knees of the emperor. . . .

Such was the picture. In this case the reality was not just subtly different, but radically so. It was not based on Roman ascendancy but on Roman weakness. The treaty ratified a whole shift in the strategic balance: it was not one of Roman accommodation of a defeated or subdued enemy, as had hitherto been (or perceived as) the rule. This was more like a treaty between equals. The Visigoths were not distributed as *coloni*, nor were they subject to Roman administration; they were acknowledged as an allied people with their own territory. Their military obligations to the empire were not to supply recruits who would be integrated into the Roman army structure, but to fight *en masse* when required as a national contingent under their own leaders. Unlike previous immigrants their tribal structure and identity remained intact. Though nominally subject to the empire they were, in effect, a foreign nation in arms established on Roman territory.

Theodosius and Gratian clearly knew what they were doing. The change in policy between 378 and 382 is reflected in the altered tone of Themistius' orations, stressing the clemency and goodwill of the emperor rather than his warlike prowess; and even more clearly by the reception of Athanaric in 381. To defeat the Goths militarily was either impossible, or simply too costly in the present state of the empire, especially since the Huns and Alans were wrecking the earlier political balances to the north of the Danube and were also carrying out raids into Roman territory, as in 381. The policy of accommodation was the best that could be had in the circumstances. It was not without risk, but any other policy involved an even greater risk.

There is some evidence that the senatorial classes, too, sensed that the treaty was not quite business as usual. Their dislike of it sprang less from political anxieties than from resentment that these barbarians were being treated as virtual equals. In the senatorial universe it was axiomatic that barbarians were inferior to Romans, just as slaves were inferior to the freeborn and plebeians to the nobility. Yet here was an emperor of good breeding showering honours on these savages. There is a strain of special pleading in Themistius:

Which then is better: to fill Thrace with corpses or with farmers? To fill it with graves or with people? To travel through wildernesses or cultivated lands? To count those who have perished, or those who are ploughing? . . . I hear from those returning from there, that they are remaking the iron from their swords and breastplates into hoes and sickles, and that those who formerly loved Ares now worship Demeter and Dionysius.[55]

By the end of the year it seems Theodosius had definitely regained the initiative, although the Visigoths were neither destroyed nor expelled from imperial territory, as conventional public opinion doubtless expected. Theodosius had not the strength to do this, and he therefore had to divide and weaken the enemy. But, more significantly, he may not even have wished to destroy them, had it been within his grasp. The overall strategy of his reign strongly implies that he was always conscious of the scarcity of manpower at a time of unabated external threats. His margin for error was very thin. With very great effort he had put together a new army after Adrianople; if he lost that, there would be nothing left. He was not at all attracted by an 'annihilating' victory, if that meant very high losses in Roman (and Gothic) troops, which would only leave him gravely weakened against the next inevitable challenge. Far better to aim for ascendancy over the volatile barbarians, and draw on their manpower for his army.

3

IMPERIAL DIVISIONS

The military breathing space, the fragile stability on the Danube and Rhine frontiers and the concerted policies of the two imperial colleagues were abruptly shattered in the spring of 383. In an unexpected but obviously popular revolt, Magnus Maximus,[1] the military commander in Britain (*Comes Britanniarum*),[2] was declared Augustus by the acclamation of the army, and quickly crossed with powerful forces to Gaul, where the local army units soon joined him.[3]

Gratian was with the court and army in northern Italy, preparing for a campaign in Raetia against the Alemanni.[4] On hearing the news he broke off the campaign and moved as quickly as possible northwards with his most mobile forces. From Verona in mid-June he reached the region of Paris in about a month.[5] There the two armies manoeuvred uneasily around each other for some five days, with scouts, skirmishers, deserters and messengers passing to and fro. It was one of those fluid, crucial scenes, enacted so often before, when the disputed and very marketable loyalties of the troops came to the fore. They would all rather be paid than fight, and they knew their services would still be in high demand whoever won. The professionalism and military prestige of Maximus, and his careful cultivation of the army, won the day. A section of Gratian's Moorish cavalry[6] went over to Maximus, and after that the emperor's support quickly crumbled. Finally his own honoured general Merobaudes,[7] twice consul, one of Valentinian's great and most successful commanders, deserted to Maximus. At this devastating blow, Gratian broke off and fled south with only 500 cavalry.[8]

With these drastic defections in his army Gratian must have realised the hopelessness of his position in Gaul, and that his only chance of safety lay in reaching Italy again.[9] Unwisely he seems to have halted at Lyon, perhaps with the dubious promises of refuge and support from the city governor. The halt was enough to allow Maximus' general Andragathius[10] to reach Lyon, where Gratian was delivered up and executed on 25 August 383. He was twenty-four years old. There is still no clear reason why Gratian's support crumbled so quickly. He was the son of the great Valentinian, and although still young he had been emperor for eight years, during which time he had campaigned extensively and successfully against the major enemies of the empire; indeed he had been sole emperor in the brief period after Adrianople before he appointed Theodosius as his colleague, and had been the principal agent in holding the empire together in the face of the

Visigothic victory. He was certainly no untried boy emperor. However we do have the testimony of Ammianus,[11] who suggests that despite considerable energy and promise as a young emperor Gratian may have been falling prey to the seductions of absolute power and neglecting his political standing.

Maximus established his capital at Trier,[12] the great imperial capital of Valentinian close to the Rhine frontier. Generally, the coup was bloodless. The court officials and supporters of Gratian were allowed to go into retirement,[13] and were quickly replaced by Maximus' own picked men (although two of Gratian's supporters, Leucadius and Narses, were saved only by the intercession of bishop Martin of Tours).[14] Maximus lost no time in sending embassies to the two legitimate emperors. To the twelve-year-old Valentinian II at Milan the offer was of peace, but on condition the boy henceforth submit himself to Maximus' tutelage at the palace of Trier.[15] Simultaneously his Grand Chamberlain (*Praepositus Sacri Cubiculi*) was despatched to Theodosius at Constantinople. The message was simple. Apart from the merest diplomatic excuses, such as that his officer had exceeded his orders, no apology or regret was expressed for the murder of Gratian. Instead, Theodosius was offered the straight choice: peace and alliance, or all the hazards of civil war?[16]

Although the immediate causes of the revolt are not clear the pattern was only too familiar. Several times in the past hundred years major military revolts had occurred in the Gallic provinces, the most successful being that of Constantine himself in 307. The lands beyond the Alps, essentially the dioceses of the two Gauls, Spain and Britain, formed a relatively self-contained and defensible region, and once a powerful military ruler had full control of them it was very costly and difficult to dislodge him. Some usurpers, such as Postumus[17] and Carausius,[18] had been content to rule a separate regional *imperium*; others, like Constantine and Magnentius,[19] used a Gallic empire as the stepping stone to Italy and control of the West.

Two things are clear from the circumstances of the revolt. First, it succeeded so rapidly that Maximus must have made thorough preparations, with secret agreements and the suborning of Gratian's armies. Second, he obviously calculated, wrongly, that there was a good chance of being accepted by Theodosius as imperial colleague, provided he secured his victory quickly.

This was almost certainly more than just a reckoning of the balance of forces and distances, for Maximus and Theodosius were well known to one another. They may even have been distant kinsmen. Certainly they were compatriots, social equals and, before Theodosius' elevation, military peers. Maximus was a Spaniard[20], probably from Gallaecia, and the two had fought together in Britain and Africa in the campaigns of the elder Theodosius. Maximus may even have played some part in helping Theodosius to the throne. When he sent the very frank embassy to Constantinople, it was to a man who already knew his loyalties, character and abilities well: no persuasive protestations were necessary.

Classical sources give as the principal cause of the revolt Gratian's loss of army support due to the immoderate favours he showed to his chosen bodyguard of Alan cavalry, even to the point of adopting their nomadic hunting dress. More generally, he is reproved by Ammianus[21] for his neglect of state business and unbecoming indulgence in hunting and wild beast fights. These latter faults are stock reproaches from a senatorial viewpoint, but would hardly matter much to the armies provided Gratian proved himself as a commander and looked after their interests. Again, there were Alans and all kinds of other tribal units serving in the largely 'barbarian' army,[22] and it is difficult to believe such resentments alone could have been a major cause of disaffection.

More plausibly, the spirited but still politically inexperienced Gratian may simply have been lacking in vigilance. In his marches, campaigns and courtly progresses he had neglected the northern, Gallic provinces in favour of Italy.[23] The specific motives of Maximus can only be conjectured; certainly he had every reason to feel poorly rewarded. As a strong and experienced commander, the peer of Theodosius, he might even have been a possible candidate for the purple himself after Adrianople (other great generals such as Merobaudes or Bauto were excluded by their barbarian origins). When so many other of Theodosius' Spanish colleagues were filling the great prefectures and ministries of the East,[24] he could at least have expected a post of *Magister Militum* or Count of the Household Troops (*Comes Domesticorum*) instead of simply the commander of Britain.[25]

But revolutions, even in Britain, had to be based on more than one man's discontents. The youth Gratian had campaigned respectably and generally successfully against the enemies on the Rhine,[26] but in military prowess and leadership he still bore no comparison to his great father Valentinian, hammer of the Germans; he had ruled from Trier, and his aggressive campaigns and great fortification programmes[27] contrasted sharply with the son's heavy reliance on his generals, and his acceptance of huge settlements of Greuthungian and Alan armed 'allies' in Pannonia.[28] It is possible that many veteran officers yearned for a return to this strong, thoroughgoing military regime in Gaul, and that Maximus' agents and promises fostered this feeling against the distant and careless Gratian.

Whatever Theodosius' immediate reaction to the *fait accompli*, he was in no position to fight a major civil war at present. Maximus was in secure control beyond the Alps, the Danube frontier barely stabilised and the Visigothic treaty still fresh and untested. The last occasion of a comparable civil war had been Constantius' suppression of the Gallic usurper Magnentius thirty years earlier, which had involved the enormous costs of an empire-wide expedition, and such crippling losses at the eventual victorious battle of Mursa that the field armies and frontier troops had been weakened for many years afterwards. The imputations of some historians, ancient and modern, that Theodosius was well disposed towards Maximus because he did not march immediately west to avenge Gratian, betray a poor grasp of the sheer magnitude of such a military undertaking at this time.

Knowing this, Maximus had hoped Theodosius would agree to a simple carve-up of the empire between them, with Valentinian in Italy overshadowed and reduced to symbolic status only. In this he miscalculated the residual loyalty to the dynasty of Valentinian, both in Theodosius himself and in the government at Milan, who quickly and fearfully closed ranks around the boy emperor, dreading a further *blitzkrieg* on Italy by Maximus. Determined to deter or avert it if they could, they appealed to Theodosius for help.

Theodosius gave no answer to Maximus' peremptory question: alliance or war? He no doubt calculated that Maximus, for all his threats, was no more capable than himself of mounting a full empire-wide civil war at this juncture. Though Theodosius could subordinate personal feelings to political considerations, he was an emotional man who had every reason to feel gratitude towards Gratian. The manner of Maximus' embassy, the assumed kinship, cynically arrogant *realpolitik* and sheer insolence were an affront to his visible dignity, at a time when this mattered more than ever. For him to accord immediate recognition to an outright rebel would be most damaging, and he had no need to do it while Maximus did not control Italy — which was, indeed, the key to the situation.

At Milan the court of Valentinian II was dominated by his mother Justina, widow of the great Valentinian, the old loyalist Praetorian Prefect, Petronius Probus, hastily called out of retirement, and the redoubtable bishop Ambrose.[29] By the time Maximus' envoy, Victor, had travelled to Milan, Ambrose had already been despatched north to Trier to negotiate an accommodation. Ambrose was instructed by Maximus that the boy Valentinian should come to Trier with his mother 'as a son to his father' — in short, that the separate government in Italy be extinguished. Ambrose temporised, as too did his colleagues at Milan. First he replied that a young boy and his mother could hardly make the journey in the depths of winter; then, that his mandate did not empower him to negotiate such a step as this.

Maximus detained him at Trier until his own envoy Victor returned empty-handed. While Ambrose himself was returning to Milan, yet another, separate embassy from Valentinian passed him on its way to Trier. The details and outcome of these worried negotiations are unknown, but the delays served their purpose: by the winter the troops of Milan had occupied the Alpine passes into Italy, and Maximus' option of a rapid invasion had been lost.[30]

Next summer Theodosius himself apparently set out with a military force to the West, with the declared aim of chastising Maximus, but this seems not to have been a serious expedition, which would have been extremely difficult to mount in such a short time. It was most likely a public relations gesture, intended to tell opinion in the East that Maximus was being treated as a usurper, and to stiffen the resolve of the Milan government, which it succeeded in doing. There is no evidence that Theodosius' force travelled any further west than Beroea in Thrace, although Valentinian was at Aquileia in September 384 and there may have been a conference of the two.[31]

There was thus extreme tension and suspicion between Maximus and the other two emperors, but it stopped short of war. In the same year (384) Valentinian's general Bauto led a campaign into Raetia (Switzerland) to expel a minor invasion of Iuthungi. His force was composed of mobile Alan and Hun mercenaries,[32] and Maximus saw it as a transparent threat to himself. He protested loudly that barbarians were being employed against him, a Roman. From Milan, Ambrose replied diplomatically that the Iuthungi threatened not just Italy, but Maximus' own frontiers as well; the campaign was in fact on behalf of both of them,[33] and it was brought to a conclusion without leading Gaul and Italy into conflict. Such disputes as this presupposed, however grudgingly, some mutual acknowledgement of the *status quo* and a common interest.[34] By the end of 384 there was an effective truce between the three imperial capitals, which Maximus had every incentive to develop into a more established legitimacy.

During his four years as ruler of the Western provinces he made no overtly threatening moves, and maintained some form of communication with both Theodosius and the court of Valentinian at Milan. In 386 Maximus' brother, Marcellinus,[35] had travelled to Milan on his behalf and returned safely. This coincided with a further embassy by Ambrose to Trier, and at least partial recognition by Theodosius in the East (below, pp. 43). Maximus made much of his Catholic orthodoxy, perhaps hoping to open and exploit divisions between the Arian court of Justina, the mother of Valentinian, and the fiercely Catholic Ambrose. (There had indeed been conflict between the parties, leading to a virtual siege of Ambrose in the *Basilica Portiana* by the largely Gothic garrison of Milan, which tried — in vain — to enforce a perfectly legal and constitutional move to allow freedom of worship to the Arian congregation of the city.)[36] Valentinian was reproved in patronising fashion by Maximus for tolerating Arianism within his territories, in contrast with the zeal with which Maximus himself had adopted and enforced Catholic Christianity.[37]

Maximus had been baptised soon after assuming the purple — possibly immediately following the murder of Gratian in late 383[38] — and thenceforth pursued a rigorously orthodox religious policy, marked by the notorious execution of the bishop Priscillian,[39] the first execution for the radically new offence of heresy (although the case was finally held before civil officials, and the death penalty may have been due more to the identification of the Priscillianist heresy as Manichean, and therefore treasonable). It is conceivable that Maximus was also demonstrating his orthodoxy, in contrast to the toleration of Arianism at the court in Milan, to his equally devout and rigorous compatriot, Theodosius.

However, if this much of Maximus' propaganda was aimed at reconciliation with Theodosius, other elements must have been designed to bolster his standing within army and political circles within his own territory: he scorned the Frankish origins of Valentinian's generals, and also the high favour shown to barbarians by Theodosius himself. This would seem to be a posture, rather than any real anti-barbarian conviction on the part of Maximus — according to Ambrose Maximus had boasted of his barbarian support,[40] and his own general Andragathius, responsible for the capture of Gratian, was of barbarian origin;[41] the whole issue is reminiscent of the justification used for his initial move against Gratian. Anti-barbarian rhetoric was a standard feature of public statements, but not a genuinely held belief among those who understood the military realities of the day.

Theodosius had not stopped Maximus, but he had at least limited the damage: he had refused recognition, forestalled an expansion into Italy, and bolstered the authority of the court of Valentinian at Milan, which still controlled Italy, Africa and the western Danube provinces. After this experience Theodosius clearly recognised that he had to prepare for an eventual civil war with Maximus. He now opened negotiations with the new Great King of Persia, Shapur III, with the aim of stabilising the Eastern frontier by treaty so that it would not need the presence of large forces in the near future.

Persia was the only neighbouring state of comparable power and sophistication, and although the two empires had gone to war periodically over the centuries the zones of dispute were well recognised and the intervening peace treaties more stable and durable. The two empires had been formally at peace since the failure of Julian's invasion in 363 and the subsequent treaty of Nisibis.[42] Diplomatic exchanges usually centred on the control of the shifting buffer zones, client kingdoms and fortified towns between them.

A renewal of peaceful coexistence was essential now that a new monarch was on the Persian throne. Already certain allied Saracen tribes on the frontier had revolted against Rome, requiring a punitive expedition. A Persian embassy to Constantinople in 384 was followed by a reciprocal embassy to Ctesiphon, led by one of Theodosius' most trusted associates, the general Flavius Stilicho.[43] Of Vandal origin but, like his Germanic military colleagues, thoroughly Romanised, he had risen rapidly through the cavalry commands. He later displayed considerable political as well as military skills, to a degree still rare among Germanic commanders. The negotiations with Persia were protracted (384–7), and after Stilicho's initial embassy were continued through subordinates. They concerned the two empires' respective influence in the interposed kingdom of Armenia, and eventually culminated in an agreement, ratified in 387, to partition the country directly under two client kings. Territorially it was a retreat on the Roman side: one-fifth of the country acknowledged Roman overlordship as against four-fifths Persian. However it gave the security Theodosius badly needed, which might not have been obtained with a more independent, unified Armenia which could play one side off against the other.

41

Throughout this period Stilicho was steadily advanced. He was promoted to Count of the Stable (*Comes Sacri Stabuli*, in charge of the supply of horses for the armies, then *Comes Domesticorum*, and, most importantly, was awarded the singular distinction of marriage to Theodosius' niece Serena on his return from the Persian embassy in 384. She was the emperor's adoptive daughter and so Stilicho became his son-in-law. Such a marriage was the clearest signal that henceforth Stilicho was elevated above other court and military officers, to the very right hand of Theodosius' throne, in the dangerous years ahead.

After the brief military demonstration of 384 Theodosius took other steps to shore up the Milan government and its young and inexperienced boy emperor, and to establish a protective umbrella over Italy that would deter and exclude Maximus. In 385 he appointed as Praetorian Prefect of Italy Flavius Neoterius,[44] an experienced and highly regarded man who had been his Prefect of the Orient during the Gothic emergencies. In Africa, the granary of Italy, he gave the supreme military command to the Moorish noble Gildo,[45] who had served with distinction under the elder Theodosius in the war against Firmus,[46] and was bound by close ties of clientship to the family.

These moves still fell short of filling the semi-vacuum that was the real political position in Italy. It was ruled by a child, and however honest and competent his supporters there was no established, respected machinery of regency.[47] The late third century under Diocletian had officialised the principle that emperors must be capable military commanders and must lead their armies in person. The fourth century under Constantine and his sons had reaffirmed the practice of collegiate rule and reasserted the principle of dynastic succession. Sooner or later these requirements must clash, and a fatal flaw in the hereditary method come to the fore: boy emperors had been unheard of for the last century — they would simply have been murdered and replaced by the nearest capable general.

The fate of Gratian might have been warning enough. If he had intended to displace Valentinian Theodosius could have established a strong regime in Italy, combining supreme civil and military authority and commanding the loyalty of the armies: in effect, a legitimate counterweight to Maximus. That he did not do this suggests that Theodosius was too much of a legitimist, too loyal to the dynasty of Valentinian to take such a step. The situation common in the fifth century — of a supreme military commander wielding power in the name of an imperial figurehead — had not yet emerged. Theodosius was also intent on the eventual succession of his own sons to the throne, and their future inheritance may have played its part in his decision to support the young Valentinian. He therefore followed the middle path: support for Valentinian, alongside partial recognition of Maximus while he secured the East and his own position.

The government of Italy therefore devolved on Justina, bishop Ambrose, Neoterius and — to a lesser extent — the generals Bauto and Arbogast. Of these the outstanding figure is Ambrose, whose political talents and powerful personality now had room to expand, in competition with Justina for the mind and soul of Valentinian. He came to be perhaps the most influential churchman in an age of great bishops. Son of a Praetorian Prefect of Gaul, he was raised in the senatorial ruling classes and wielded political power with confidence, holding an Italian governorship before his sudden election as bishop of Milan in 374, following his attempts to impose law and order on the violent quarrels of the Arian and Nicene factions.[48] In his new role he combined high culture, political experience and an unflagging zeal for Nicene orthodoxy and the claims of the church. As bishop of the principal and legitimate Western imperial capital[49] he seemed to combine nearly all the qualities most needed by his time and situation — except military leadership.

Theodosius was content to avoid open war for the present, especially while the Persian frontier was being secured and the Danube still very vulnerable. In parallel with his prudent preparations for war[50] was a certain apparent relaxation of tensions, a move towards normalising relations short of full political ties and acknowledgement of co-imperium. Maximus' Prefect, Flavius Euodius, had his consulship for 386 legally recognised in the East,[51] and imperial portraits of Maximus were even displayed at Alexandria by Theodosius' Prefect, Maternus Cynegius.[52] Diplomatic exchanges were renewed between Trier and Milan with Ambrose undertaking another mission, ostensibly to secure the return of the body of Gratian, which Maximus had kept unburied as a bargaining counter, but the mission was a failure.[53]

The main Danube frontier had been at least manageable since 382. A small revolt near the city of Tomi in eastern Thrace was quickly suppressed by the general Gerontius, but overall the new barbarian settlements were being integrated peacefully into Theodosius' polyethnic territories and army. This fragile accommodation was again threatened in 386, in what seemed a repetition of the events leading to Adrianople. A large population of Greuthungi had occupied the northern bank of Danube in arms, and petitioned Theodosius' officials for permission to settle within the empire, with the clear threat of invasion if this was refused.[54] After all the difficulties of war and diplomacy with the Visigoths which only now seemed to be bearing fruit, such a new immigration so soon could have wrecked the whole framework of cooperation.

Theodosius treated it as a simple invasion threat and concentrated his main military effort against it. His general Petronius Probus[55] was able to engineer a great deception which lured the invaders into their boats for a massed crossing, and then ambushed them with a far stronger naval force:

When the signal was given, the Romans sailed out in large ships with very strong oars, and sank every boat they encountered. Because of the great weight of their armour, none of the warriors who jumped overboard were saved. The boats that escaped ran into other ships along the shore . . . none could penetrate this barrier of Roman ships. The slaughter was greater than in any previous naval battle, and the river was choked with bodies and weapons. . . .[56]

A serious invasion was thus thwarted, but the threat may well have contributed to Theodosius' curious quasi-recognition of Maximus in 386.

The army Theodosius and his generals had rebuilt since Adrianople was adequate to manage the central Danube and garrison the Orient, but it was a different matter to mount a great offensive in the West in addition. Such a campaign army needed an extra tier of first-class cavalry and infantry forces, conscripts, mercenaries, siege engineers and other specialist units, with all the enormous volume of supplies and equipment that went with them, established in depots along the great military highways and in strategic cities. Not surprisingly such preparations involved increased taxes on the cities and estates of the East, on top of what was already a very heavy burden. At Alexandria there had already been popular demonstrations against Theodosius, but the resentment boiled over into a far more serious explosion at Antioch in the early spring of 387.

Riots, demonstrations and commotions of all kinds were commonplace among the plebs of the great cities of the East. They were often an extension of the mass excitements of the theatre or hippodrome, and would sometimes be incited and orchestrated by the same professional cheer-leaders (*euphemiai*) who stimulated the applause at these entertainments. They could be triggered by many things, but sometimes would take on a clear political tone when the anonymity of a crowd of many thousands allowed them to shout back at their city magistrates, governor or even the emperor — as when Valens had been jeered for his feebleness by the mob at Constantinople.[57]

At Antioch, as elsewhere, the *lustralis collatio*, the tax in gold on artisans and merchants, had already borne very heavily on the city, affecting most of its inhabitants. In the new year a further tax, the *aurum coronarium*, was levied on the landowning curial class who formed the city's governing council. This was traditionally a 'free donation' to the emperors, on the occasions of anniversaries when a special donative was expected by the armies. When the imperial announcement of the tax was read out the city council and other leading men went in a legally correct deputation to the governor to request a reduction in the amounts.

However, they were immediately supported by an apparently well-rehearsed and vociferous mob, protesting and calling on God, which rampaged about the city damaging buildings, and then returned to the governor's residence where his besieged staff feared he would be lynched. The next step was irrevocable. Unable to break into the governor's palace, the mob tore down the panel portraits of the emperor, and then the bronze statues of Theodosius, his father and members of the imperial family, breaking them up and dragging them with abuse through the streets. These images were the most sacred political icons of the empire, the holy objects in the universal cult of the godlike Augustus, whose sanctity Christianity had never succeeded in diminishing. They stood in every law court and public place as the witness to oaths, they preceded the armies on parade and in battle, and were the palpable focus of every expression of loyalty. Everyone knew that to desecrate them was the clearest gesture, not of grievance but of treason and revolt, after which there could be no going back.[58]

After the mob had burned the house of one leading citizen and looked set to fire other parts of the city the militia finally intervened and quickly dispersed them. Shortly afterwards the Count of the East arrived with a small military force, arrested several of those involved in the arson, and proceeded to investigate the treasonable destruction of the imperial images. A report of the incident went to Constantinople, the assumption being that the leading citizens were clearly implicated in the riots — which seemed to be confirmed when many of them sought to leave for their country estates at short notice. Meanwhile, the actual or presumed leaders of the mob were tried and executed, some by burning alive, despite the custom of an amnesty on executions during Lent.

Theodosius would not have been unaware of the financial burdens being imposed, but they were just as onerous to other cities. Antioch had a reputation for its fickleness, addiction to vice, luxury and theatres, its proneness to riot and blithe indifference to government which had now culminated in the ultimate challenge. When the imperial commissioners Caesarius and Hellebich finally arrived they announced that this great metropolis of millions, jewel of the East, capital of emperors and of the great Seleucid kings before them, was to lose all civic status, land and revenues, and become a tributary to the small nearby city of Laodicea.

It was not a realistic penalty: the great and populous capital city could never be governed from a small suburban town. It was a spontaneous outburst of Theodosius' anger, a thunderbolt reasserting imperial power and warning just what he could do if he wished. The long process of delay and communications between Antioch and Constantinople gave time for reflection. Heads continued to roll, men were imprisoned, estates confiscated. In the meantime the city had sent bishop Flavius and the senator Hilarius to plead humbly for mercy from Theodosius. His own commissioners, uncertain how to proceed, referred back for further instructions, and by this time his hot temper had not merely cooled, but was swinging in reaction towards clemency. The status of Antioch was restored and a general pardon issued. Theodosius even commended the magistrates of Antioch for their public spiritedness in taking up their city's cause. Hilarius was rewarded with a governorship. On this and other occasions Theodosius enlarged warmly on the quality of mercy in a sovereign, in terms almost reminiscent of Marcus Aurelius.

For an emperor under considerable strain, on the verge of a civil war for survival and faced with simmering disaffection over the tax burdens, this gesture shows Theodosius at his most human: quick to anger, but then capable of recognising his own impulsiveness and being dissuaded. The war with Maximus could not long be delayed, once Ambrose had returned from his last embassy to Trier empty-handed and fearing for the peace. Among other sentiments Maximus had allegedly exclaimed how much he regretted not having taken Italy immediately after Gratian's death when he had the chance. There could be no doubt of his designs on Italy and the West, nor that he was well aware of Theodosius' war preparations.

4

CATHOLIC ASCENDANCY

When Constantine made his historic alliance between the Roman state and the Christian church he had hoped, among other things, that this new, energetic and disciplined religion would buttress his unified empire with a unified faith.[1] He was frustrated and disappointed. With the lifting of the persecutions and the gracious entry of the church into an earthly establishment, deep disagreements of doctrine and organisation all came into their own. The very tenacity that, a few years earlier, had resisted all attempts by Diocletian, Galerius and Maximinus to break the church by force was now active in its internal disputes.[2] The leaders of any successful revolution soon split into factions, each convinced that they alone embodied the true spirit of all that has been fought for, against the others who have diluted or betrayed that spirit. Bishops who had faced prison, torture and death rather than make the near-conventional gesture of offering a pinch of incense to the *genius* of the emperor were not now going to compromise their principles in a fudged unity simply because the emperor demanded it. Constantine had encountered as an ally what Diocletian before him had encountered as an enemy: the extraordinary stubbornness of this religion which set doctrinal purity above all considerations of state policy or civic harmony. He too only half-appreciated how radically different this religion was.[3]

Traditional paganism shared many elements with emerging Christianity, but the concept of heresy was something quite new. Precise formulation of doctrine had been unimportant to paganism: it was felt to be beside the point, in the manner of Hinduism then and now. What mattered was tradition, myth and ritual, the symbolic expression of deep social verities. The many divinities answered these enduring needs, and people might speculate about their natures without disturbing their roles. Even the newer mystery cults which tended towards a syncretist monotheism, such as the cult of *Sol Invictus*,[4] were quite relaxed about the manifest variety of gods and heroes, seeing them merely as palpable aspects of the Divine One, whose reality lay behind them all.

Christianity could have absolutely none of this. Its roots were not Hellenic but Judaic. It had inherited the jealous, militant monotheism of Exodus, as well as the pre-eminent Judaic concern with the Law. All other gods were evil demons, if they existed at all. Once and only once had the Divine assumed human form, in the supreme mystery of Christ's incarnation. If the nature and message of Christ was allowed to be vague or disputable then the whole promise and authority of faith, church and priesthood rested on sand. No sacerdotal authority, no finality; no finality, no Gospels; no Gospels, no Christ.

Truth and error in doctrine were therefore of cardinal importance, but for the most part they were treated not as intellectual error in the manner of philosophy or law, to be resolved by logical argument or the appeal to authoritative texts. From very early on, especially in the African churches, doctrinal disputes assumed a surprising bitterness, the disputants seeing in each other not sincere mistake but wilful blindness, inspired either by treacherous motives or the malign influences of diabolic agents, ever ready to ensnare souls. The Donatist, Cyprianic, Arian, Sabellian, Macedonian and countless other controversies were full of such vituperation, which sometimes went beyond anathemata to physical violence and the employ-ment of fanatical mobs. Except in rare moments false opinion in religion was not sharply distinguished from demonic infection, malicious intent, or crime. With the concept of heresy gradually emerged its corollary: the dangerous idea that belief itself (as distinct from ritual conformity) is a kind of voluntary behaviour which can be changed by coercion. This attitude was to be prevalent in Christianity for over a thousand years.

The principal doctrinal questions naturally concerned the nature of Christ. Almost all sides were agreed on two cardinal points. First, that Christ is literally Divine, not just divinely inspired or chosen, which of course was true of the prophets. Since there is only one God, Christ is therefore of a piece with the Father in some important sense. Second, however, Christ is not identical with the Father in the strict sense of individual, numerical and qualitative identity (in the way that, for example, Octavian is identical with Augustus).

Beyond these apparently conflicting propositions very little was agreed, and it is perhaps not surprising that the most scholastic and wonderful metaphysical controversies arose from them. It was, of course, important to define the nature of Christ (insofar as this was permitted to finite minds), and to settle the faithful in a clear and distinct doctrine, but it is unlikely that these hydra-like arguments did much to comfort the simple Christian. What they did was offer a field-day to the inveterate Greek love of philosophical dispute, which had its revenge on the shackles of Christian dogmatism by opening a Pandora's box of chimerical and unedifying Christological disputes that racked the Church for centuries. As the famous visitor to Constantinople observed, this is a city where every slave and artisan is a profound theologian. Ask one of them to change some silver and he explains instead how the Son differs from the Father. Ask another the price of a loaf of bread and he replies that the Son is inferior to the Father. Ask a third if your bath is ready and he tells you that the Son was created out of nothingness.[5]

The relation between Son and Father could not be strict identity: that was the Sabellian or 'Patripassionist' heresy, whose opponents ridiculed it as entailing that the Father literally suffered and died on the cross. But if it was not strict identity, what was it? The most far-reaching of all the fourth-century disputes concerned the heresy of Arius, a presbyter of Alexandria. He held that Christ, though sharing uniquely in the Divine nature, was created by the Father and is therefore of distinctly subordinate status, belonging to the created order. This was vigorously opposed by Alexander, Arius' bishop, as tending towards two divinities (Ditheism).[6]

Arianism also seemed to invite doubts about the status of the clergy and Christ's redemptive mission. If Christ was part of the created order, how far could the Divine quality he had exercised on earth be bequeathed undiminished into the future? Could his consecrated priests really claim to exercise an unbroken, unaltered charismatic power transmitted from the apostles? Or were they merely the elected ministers of the faithful, without special spiritual powers beyond their godly lives and fitness for their office?

A synod at Alexandria condemned Arius as a heretic, but he moved to the East where his influence grew. The Alexandrians advanced the opposing doctrine of *Homoousios*, that Father and Son are identical in essence (*ousia*) but distinct in person (*hypostasis*), but this merely compounded the problem. (At this point we might echo the great philosophical novelist Robert Musil, and suggest that readers who are impatient with metaphysics simply skip the next five paragraphs.)

In Aristotelian philosophy the essence of a thing is that necessary principle which makes it the thing it is and not another thing, as opposed to its contingent properties or components which might not have belonged to it. Thus, sphericity is essential to a ball, while its colour is contingent. If God is one, then identity of essence must mean numerical identity, and the distinctness of persons merely different subordinate aspects of this oneness — which came close to the Sabellian heresy.

But, if Father and Son merely *share* the essence of Divinity, as two horses share the essence of horsiness, then how can they be other than numerically two Divine beings — two gods — whether or not one is subordinate?

The Arian counter-formula was *Homoiousios*, namely that Father and Son are of 'like' essence, as a perfect copy is like its original. This is clearly qualitative, not numerical, identity: two peas can be indistinguishable, but they are still two peas, not one. But this position was almost impossible to reconcile with the Oneness of God, which Arianism still professed. For, if Oneness is an essential and not an accidental property (and surely it must be), then how can such an essence logically be shared by more than one subject? The two indistinguishable peas both share the property of 'uniqueness', but only in the logically trivial sense that *every* numerically distinct particular is unique in some respect. Whatever the Oneness of God means, it must be more than that.

It is no part of our intention here to enter into these issues, but rather to register their importance in the development of the new religion of the Roman state. However, recent analytical philosophy since Leibniz and Frege has made some progress since Aristotle on the notoriously difficult problems of identity, including personal identity; it does not seem that the central Christological disputes were genuinely insoluble.[7] They appear to have contained contradictions which only became sharper as the terms of the arguments were more carefully defined, and which could only be avoided by abandoning one or other cardinal principle of the faith.

As a last resort, of course, it might be claimed that the nature of the transcendent God does not come under the logical rules of identity that apply to everything else, abstract or concrete, universal or particular. But this was to admit that it is all an incomprehensible mystery, which many war-weary spirits were willing to concede as the century went on. The theologians had simply taken on a new metaphysical ballast that was too heavy for them, as they lurched anew into the Appollinarian, Nestorian and Monophysite controversies. We can perhaps understand how easy it was for Mohammed to blow the whistle on the whole confusing game, with the simple, uncompromising assertion that God Is One.

But these things mattered supremely at the time, among laymen and clergy. The condescending Gibbonian attitude of enlightened amusement rings very hollow today. The universe in Gibbon's day seemed to rest in the safe and intelligible certainties of Newtonian mechanics, Euclidian geometry and Aristotelian logic. All three have now been overturned and we are gloriously at sea again. Many humanistically educated people today believe, by proxy, in fantastic metaphysical doctrines they do not begin to understand (and which moreover offer not a shred of help to our values and our lives). The teachings of particle physics and cosmology, of the antimatter universe, of quarks, superstrings, and the primordial soup in which quantum fluctuations *ex nihilo* somehow led to the Big Bang: all our culture assures us, in a way very uncomfortably like an act of blind faith, that the physicist priesthood that propounds these mysteries must know what it is talking about.

Constantine had no understanding of these subtleties and no patience with them. Indeed, he was little concerned with Christ at all.[8] He had opted for the God of the Christians against *Sol Invictus* because it had seemed to offer the best promise of divine favour for the Roman state, which it was the emperor's duty to secure by the proper forms of worship. The church had been granted many special privileges by him, and in return he wanted unity in it, not continual quarrelling over hair-splitting matters.[9]

As *Pontifex Maximus* the emperor had always regulated the state cults and religion in general, and Constantine quite naturally intervened in the Christian disputes. In 325 he called, for the first time, a general or oecumenical council of some 300 bishops from all over the empire, at Nicaea in Bithynia.[10] By a large majority it condemned Arius, whom Constantine then banished. It also confirmed the superior ecclesiastical jurisdiction of the sees of Alexandria, Antioch and Rome over other cities, and endorsed a church organisation following the boundaries of the existing provinces. Constantine played a major role in the debates, and although he did not take complete control of the Council it became obvious that imperial authority could be brought to bear, decisively, in church disputes.[11]

The appearance of doctrinal unity, the one subject of the whole operation, was illusory. The Alexandrian formula of 'identical essence' was still interpreted by Arian sympathisers merely in the sense of similarity, and before long Arius himself was quite ready to accept it and seek reinstatement. The new Alexandrian bishop, Athanasius, was violently opposed to this, and conducted such an intemperate campaign against crypto-Arianism that he became a pestilential nuisance, even by the standards of the day, and convinced Constantine that he was the main obstacle to unity. Another council was therefore called at Jerusalem, which condemned Athanasius, and readmitted Arius and his followers on the basis of the Janus-like Nicene faith.

By Constantine's death two camps were solidifying, the divisions very roughly following the Latin and Greek halves of the empire (except for Egypt). In the West, especially at Rome, there was a fervent attachment to the identity of essence of Father and Son, and limited patience for fine philosophical distinctions; in the East, a subtler leaning to Arianism which spawned several variants, and a disdain for the Western bishops as intellectually naive. The difference of languages certainly contributed to the disputes over definitions and meanings. The split turned into open schism at the council of Serdica.[12] The new emperor, Constantius, was pro-Arian and did much to undermine the Nicene party. Supported by the Arian bishop Eusebius of Nicomedia, he manipulated special councils at Arles, Mursa, and Constantinople, and finally had the Arian formula of 'like essence' declared orthodox.[13] Next year he died, and the apostate emperor Julian, intent on restoring paganism, cynically encouraged the Christian rivalries in the hope that the factions would destroy one another. But Julian ruled only three years. He tried to purge the officer class of Christians, including one of his best generals — Valentinian — who was unanimously elected emperor soon afterwards.

Among all the excommunications and exiling of bishops the state's involvement was steadily growing. Many bishops positively welcomed the use of imperial authority against rivals and heretics, and only wished the emperors would go further. They seemed blind to the accompaniment, that the state was slowly turning the church into something like an arm of the imperial bureaucracy. One who saw and feared this was bishop Hosius, who warned Constantius: 'Do not meddle in church affairs, give no orders in these matters, but be instructed by us. God has placed imperial power in your hands, but the church He has entrusted to us.'[14]

So far heresy had not been actually criminalised, and the clergy ran only the risks of ejection and exile. Nor had there been very vigorous measures against paganism. Constantine had enjoined toleration, and did not object to the dedication of temples in his honour, provided only that 'superstitious' rites — mainly sacrifice — were avoided.[15] His sons had ended the public subsidies to temples, demolished a few of them and forbade sacrifice, without much effect. Although official sacrifice to the genius of the 'divine' emperor ceased, almost all other forms of the state cults, as well as the exalted cult of the emperor himself, continued as before. By the time of the battle of Adrianople the East was predominantly Arian under the patronage of Valens, but with a strong Nicene minority grouped around bishop Basil of Caesarea. The West was staunchly Nicene, under the patronage of Gratian and the leadership of Alexandria and Rome.

The early Christian emperors were doubtless sincere in their faith, but they never forgot that they were Roman emperors first and foremost. They listened to bishops as they listened to other advisers, built them churches and gave them more generous subsidies than the traditional pagan cults had received, and were baptised by them, usually on their deathbeds, but they were not dominated by them. They used the church to further their own ends, and constantly played one faction off against another or resorted to crude imperial authority to get their way. The Arianism of Constantius and Valens owed something to the fact that Arian clergy were considered to be easier to manage, with their weaker apostolic claims. The spiritual guidance of emperors, including the safe steerage of their immortal souls, was not allowed to deflect their secular policies, nor interfere with the crimes that go under the heading, Reasons of State.

Theodosius was in a very different mould, as the literature of the Catholic Church has fulsomely acknowledged. He was a devout Nicean, in keeping with his whole Spanish background and the society that filled his court at Salonica and Constantinople. He took the teachings of the church and the condition of his own soul very seriously indeed. Unlike Constantine he was a Nicean before he became emperor, and he had never followed any other doctrine, never weighed the pros and cons of rival gods. After assuming the purple he remained a faithful Son of the Holy Church, and in matters of religion he saw entirely through its eyes. He allowed the church a political influence that no previous emperor had done, and the church, principally in the person of bishop Ambrose of Milan, was duly appreciative:

> . . . a pious emperor, a merciful emperor, a faithful emperor, concerning whom the Scripture has spoken. . . . What is more illustrious than the faith of an emperor whom sovereignty does not exalt, pride does not elevate, but piety bows down?[16]

So long as Valens reigned the Arian clergy of the East were secure, but with the elevation of Theodosius at Sirmium came the very clear message that their days were now numbered. For all of 379 Theodosius was absorbed by the Gothic war. In August Gratian, under the influence of Ambrose, took an important step towards legal persecution of heresies in the West, reversing his father's more tolerant policies: all heresies were prohibited by law. Those still holding heretical opinions risked punishment if they preached them.

Then, at Salonica in February 380, Theodosius issued a comprehensive edict defining and enforcing Nicene orthodoxy, one of the most significant documents in European history:

> It is Our will that all peoples ruled by the administration of Our Clemency shall practise that religion which the divine (sic) Peter the Apostle transmitted to the Romans . . . this is the religion followed by Bishop Damasus (of Rome) and by Peter, bishop of Alexandria, a man of apostolic sanctity: that is, according to the apostolic discipline of the evangelical doctrine, we shall believe in the single Deity of the Father, the Son and the Holy Ghost under the concept of equal majesty, and of the Holy Trinity.
>
> We command that persons who follow this rule shall embrace the name of Catholic Christians. The rest, however, whom We judge demented and insane (*dementes vesanosque*), shall carry the infamy of heretical dogmas. Their meeting places shall not receive the name of churches, and they shall be smitten first by Divine vengeance, and secondly by the retribution of Our hostility, which We shall assume in accordance with the Divine judgement.[17]

Thus the unity among Christians, which Constantine had vainly sought, was to be imposed directly by law.

The edict was issued even before Theodosius was suddenly prostrated by illness in the spring, and military direction temporarily frustrated.[18] Contrary to a common tradition the edict was not a consequence of his baptism by bishop Acholius at the crisis of this disease, but baptism clearly confirmed his devotion and orthodoxy. At that time it was the most solemn of sacraments, involving the remission of sins and the binding of the person to the community of the faithful. It was commonly received not at birth, but at some significant point in the soul's pilgrimage — especially the nearness of death (as Theodosius' father had been baptised before his execution). It was natural for Theodosius to attribute his recovery in the late spring to this potent instrument of grace, and the fervent prayers of clergy and people. When he finally entered Constantinople in state in November 380 it was as a zealous son of the Catholic church, as well as a successful Roman emperor. Immediately a systematic purge of Arian clergy was launched, and measures prepared against other damnable heresies.[19]

To unite the formerly beleaguered Nicene clergy of the East Theodosius needed an adroit and tough bishop of Antioch (the principal see of the East), and found one in Meletius, rather than the rival candidate, Paulinus, supported by the bishops of Rome and Alexandria.[20] The purge against Arianism was not an edifying affair, as even its supporters admitted. Demophilus, the principled Arian bishop of Constantinople, refused to subscribe to the Nicene creed and was deposed immediately. The Arian clergy were supported by popular demonstrations, and at Constantinople the new Nicene priests were installed in the churches only by armed force, though a number of Arian clergy converted and kept their posts. Theodosius received Gregory of Nazianzus graciously, and with a typical theatrical flair mounted an imposing ceremony for his enthronement as bishop, accompanying him in solemn procession to the Church of the Apostles. Even so, it required a stiff guard against the jeering crowds, and Gregory himself, a gentle man, related sadly that it was more like the entry of a hostile conqueror into a defeated city. Removal of the other Arian bishops from the Eastern cities triggered an undignified scramble for the vacant sees, and a heightened atmosphere of intrigue.

A new law of Theodosius decreed banishment not just for the Arian heresy, but also 'the contamination of the Photinian pestilence' and 'the crime of the Eunomian perfidy', which should be banished from the hearing of men.[21] The Photinians were very close to the Sabellians in stressing the oneness of God; while the Eunomians, who seem to have aroused Theodosius' special animosity, were a kind of ultra-Arians who dwelt on the fundamental differences between Father and Son. The ferocity of the laws against them was exceeded only by those against the unfortunate Manicheans. They were outside the Christian fold altogether but, unlike other pagan religions, had both doctrines and an organisation that resembled the Christian church, and were thus a special threat.[22]

In May 381, despite the needs of war, Theodosius summoned a new oecumenical council at Constantinople to heal the long-standing doctrinal schism between East and West on the basis of Nicean orthodoxy. The fair way of doing this would have been a truly empire-wide council in the manner of Nicaea, and at one stage Gratian seems to have expected one, meeting at Aquileia, but it was not achieved. The council was naturally dominated by the Greek bishops; Rome and Milan were not represented, and even Timothy of Alexandria arrived later and participated reluctantly, but it was to claim full oecumenical authority.[23]

The council was presided over by Miletius of Antioch, who was emphatically repudiated by the absent Damasus of Rome and Ambrose of Milan, who still supported Paulinus. All was managed fairly skilfully until suddenly Miletius died, and the council was in danger of foundering in confusion. Gregory, innocently, proposed Paulinus as the new bishop of Antioch in a gesture of conciliation to the West, and brought down an unexpected storm on his head. His allies abandoned him to the cynical manoeuvres of the Macedonians and Egyptians, who challenged his right to the see of Constantinople on a technicality despite his sponsorship by the emperor.[24] Theodosius' support for Gregory had already become lukewarm. Unable to bear the intrigues and recrimination Gregory offered his resignation, which Theodosius, to his dismay, accepted. The council then nominated the Miletian bishop Flavius for Antioch, and for Constantinople the unusual candidate Nectarius[25] — the distinguished Praetor of Constantinople, who had not yet even been baptised. But he was a respected figure, free of faction, a capable administrator with no special axe to grind. Gregory retired sadly to Cappadocia to write his autobiography.

The council went on to define orthodoxy, including the mysterious Third Person of the Trinity, the Holy Ghost who, though equal to the Father, 'proceeded' from Him, whereas the Son was 'begotten' of Him. The principal role of the Holy Ghost seems to have been the spiritual vehicle whereby the divinity could be conceived by a mortal virgin woman. They also condemned the Apollonian and Macedonian heresies, clarified church jurisdictions according to the civil boundaries of dioceses, and ruled that Constantinople was second in precedence only to Rome, because Constantinople was the New Rome — a view stoutly rejected by Rome and Alexandria.[26]

In July 381 a new law of Theodosius formally expelled Arian clergy from their churches (the Arian clergy of Constantinople had already been ejected by Theodosius in 380), and stipulated, diocese by diocese, those Catholic bishops who were to be recognised, communion with whom would qualify lesser clergy to hold their churches: Nectarius of Constantinople, Amphilocius of Iconium, Helladius of Caesarea, and so on.[27] Antioch was tactfully omitted from the list: Theodosius wisely refrained from using public law in the bitterly disputed claims of Flavius and Paulinus.

Although the Western bishops still fought against several of these appointments they welcomed the council's doctrinal rulings and sent thanks to Theodosius for his restoration of Catholics.[28] This attitude was confirmed the following year at a council in Rome under bishop Damasus, but it continued to condemn the ruling which ranked the see of Constantinople second to Rome, since this was based purely on the historic and political status of the two capitals. In response to this, Damasus promulgated for the first time a very different argument. The ecclesiastical primacy of the bishop of Rome, he declared, rested not on the City's standing, nor the decisions of any synods or councils, but on the Roman martyrdoms of Peter and Paul, and the text of Matthew 16, 18: 'Thou art Peter, and upon this rock I will build my church . . .'. Thus began a theory of Roman papacy, potent with future consequences.[29]

These differences did not prevent general communion of East and West being re-established after a schism of thirty years. The thorny questions, no longer doctrinal, were left to one side. The councils of 381 and 382, backed firmly by imperial law, succeeded at last in ratifying the unity of the organised Christian church, which had eluded Constantine.

The last act of Arian resistance occurred in Milan, where Valentinian's forceful mother Justina, herself an Arian, had not given up the struggle against Ambrose and his Catholic following. She persisted in her efforts at the imperial court to secure toleration for the remaining Arian minority, and actually succeeded in persuading her young son to issue a law in January 386 permitting Arian congregations to assemble and worship freely; this was despite Theodosius' earlier law, and her need for his support against Maximus.[30]

Ambrose and the Catholic party were outraged and castigated her as Jezebel. The decisive clash came when she demanded one of the Milan churches, the *Basilica Portiana*, for Arian worship. Ambrose and his flock barricaded themselves in the church, law or no law, and challenged her to do her worst. To evict them forcibly in a mainly Catholic city would involve rioting and bloodshed. The Gothic garrison of Milan was Arian, but to set the army against the people was a move Justina was not prepared to make. Reluctantly, she backed down.[31]

Dispossessed of its churches Arianism dwindled thereafter. Theodosius embarked on a long succession of anti-heresy laws over the following years, of varying clarity and severity but unmistakable in direction.[32] They were not and could not be strictly enforced, any more than could the draconian laws on army recruitment. The reiteration of the same prohibitions, and the almost casual threat of extreme penalties, indicate how erratic general enforcement was. Nor is there reason to doubt the view of contemporaries that Theodosius himself much preferred to persuade, cajole or threaten heretics into orthodoxy, rather than carry out the threats. But, taken together, they expressed the imperial will clearly enough and gave full license for zealous Catholics to hunt out heretical practices.

Nor should Theodosius be considered as a lone, untypical fanatic. Though more devout that any previous emperor he was nevertheless acting consistently with the Christian standards of his day: it was those standards that had changed significantly in the three generations since Constantine. Theodosius' Spanish homeland was staunchly Catholic, and this was well reflected in the kinsmen and compatriots who filled the prefectures and top government posts — men liked Maternus Cynegius, and his many relatives and protégés.[33] They naturally expected the emperor to use the full weight of the law against heresy, just as the bishops did. Some expected even more rigorous action, especially against the Jews, who were expressly protected from the anti-heresy measures.[34]

Among the lay governing classes in the East Christian piety was far stronger than in Constantine's day: they now endowed churches and monasteries, revered saints and relics, invested in the futures of their souls and those of their relatives and did not generally dispute the forcible reunification of the church. To the clergy also there was no merit or logic in toleration as a principle; Arianism would have enforced its own orthodoxy if it could. The earlier emperors' comparative toleration of rival Christian factions and their refusal to criminalise heresy outright had often been a matter of practical politics, but it had been toleration nonetheless. The policies of Gratian and, especially, Theodosius brought it to an end. It was a far cry from Constantine's emphatic rejection of coercion when he first adopted Christianity:

> No one should injure another in the name of a faith he himself has accepted from conviction. He who is quickest to understand the truth, let him try as he may to convince his neighbour. But if this is not possible, he must desist.[35]

Theodosius had brought the law centrally into differences of the Christian faith, conflated false belief with criminal intent, and obedience to the church with obedience to the state. He had reunited the split churches, made them define orthodoxy, and then used the imperial power to recall deviants to the fold or else cut them off totally. It was thus Theodosius, as much as the Council of Nicaea, who can be considered as the historic founder of the established Catholic church.

Towards paganism, his policies in the first period of his reign were more lenient.[36] Although pagan traditions and practices of all kinds were still very widespread they did not present any real threat to the church. Paganism had little or none of Christianity's crusading zeal and united, disciplined organisation. Even the emperor Julian's attempted counter-revolution twenty years earlier had been a failure. Except for the mystery cults, which were extremely personal, paganism was concerned with social rites and the traditional gods of the Roman state. Through priesthoods and ceremonies believed to be as old as mankind, Romans of social standing would reaffirm their ancestral links with the fabulous past. Pagans were still very numerous among the upper aristocracy who filled the top government posts, especially in the West: it was, after all, pagan classical learning which formed the core of what distinguished the cultured man from the rustic and barbarian.

As a devout Catholic, Theodosius disliked this state of affairs and hoped it would diminish, but as a responsible Roman emperor he needed the support of the partly pagan ruling classes no less than the Christians.[37] The only well-established prohibition was on sacrifice — the one rite Christians abhorred and perhaps feared. Exodus commanded, that 'He who sacrifices to other gods shall be destroyed', and the refusal to break this prohibition had been the central issue in the bloody persecutions of Diocletian, Galerius and Maximus. It was also connected in imperial eyes with divination and its dangerous echoes of conspiracy. Yet even this was not always effective, especially in Rome, where bishops complained that the smoke of sacrifice everywhere assaulted their nostrils.[38]

Theodosius reiterated the ban on sacrifice, but went no further. Incense, votive offerings, libations and similar rites were not illegal.[39] In one of his earliest enactments he protected a sacred grove at Daphne near Antioch against tree-felling. In 382 he expressly ordered a temple to be kept open since it had come to be a proper place for public assembly. The statues of pagan gods should not, he said, be considered offensive to Christians, since they may be valued as works of art, not idols. Nor did he curtail the traditional rites of the imperial cult, provided they did not include sacrifice.[40]

Churchmen were impatient with such lenience, but to pagan traditionalists Theodosius at this time presented himself as a tolerant, civilised Christian emperor. This was reinforced by his friendly relations with many of them, such as the philosopher and public servant Themistius, who became tutor to his elder son Arcadius. Another such friend, Libanius of Antioch, said —

after a decade of the reign — that apart from bloody sacrifices pagans are permitted all other rites. He argues, (fallaciously, perhaps) that since the law had singled out this one act for prohibition then, logically, it permits all others. He acknowledges that as a Christian the emperor would like to see pagans converted, but as a wise ruler he knows this cannot be done by force. Forcible conversions, he hastens to add, are valueless, and the Christians' own law condemns such violence.[41]

There is, however, a note of special pleading in Libanius, who is addressing the fears of his fellow-pagans. What they are fearful about is only too clear from his oration. Despite Theodosius' mild laws many other Christians, high and low, were eager for repression. In the East it was becoming common for fanatical mobs of monks to attack, destroy or loot temples. The practice accelerated alarmingly after 384, when the zealous Spanish Catholic Maternus Cynegius, a close associate of Theodosius, was appointed Prefect for the East. He positively encouraged the destructive mobs, who now rampaged with complete impunity.

The great temple of Edessa, near the Persian frontier, a monumental building with many fine works of art, was destroyed.[42] At Apamea the huge temple of Zeus was in effect besieged by armed troops led by the provincial governor, Deinias.[43] The building was so strong it had to be reduced by undermining the columns, using the techniques of military engineers against fortresses. The bitterly resentful population was cowed into submission by the soldiers.

Libanius vehemently deplores these outrages. Though not mentioning Cynegius by name he clearly implies that he is the culprit, and professes to believe that Theodosius has not authorised these illegal acts.[44] It is true he did not explicitly authorise them, but he obviously knew of them and did nothing at all to prevent them — in distinct contrast to his protection of synagogues against Christian mobs.[45] His 'toleration' of paganism at this time seems to have been a balancing act, expediently avoiding the hostility of influential pagan opinion, but privately condoning these assaults as long as the blame was not imputed directly to him.

None of this, then or later, altered his personal or official attitudes to individual pagans in the governing circles. Unlike the medieval Inquisition, and unlike his own policies towards heresy and Manicheanism, pagan opinion was not penalised: its poets, orators and philosophers continued to teach and write well into the Byzantine empire.

In the West anti-pagan zeal was forcefully represented by Ambrose who, as bishop of the imperial capital, had dominated the religious beliefs of Gratian, and after him, of Valentinian II. Ambrose's bold project was to attack paganism at its heart, in the elemental traditions and symbols of the Roman state. He intended to disestablish and if possible destroy the state cults, after a thousand years of veneration, and in the pious young emperor he had a pliable instrument.

Unlike Constantinople, which from its inception was a Christian capital for a Christian emperor and governing class, containing far more churches than temples, the emperor in the West inherited considerable baggage from the ancient state religion. As *Pontifex Maximus* his revenues automatically went to support the colleges of priests — the Pontiffs, Augurs, Flamens, Vestals and others — whose ceremonies had protected the Eternal City since the days of the kings. In the Senate House at Rome stood the winged statue and Altar of Victory, placed there by Augustus after the battle of Actium, not so much to commemorate that victory as to epitomise the eternal triumph of the Spirit of Rome over all its adversaries. 'As long as you revere the gods, you will rule': Horace's words contained the simple, central message of the Roman official religion, which had been so amply borne out by the City's unique and glorious history. The Altar of Victory was a focal symbol, to which senators had regularly burnt incense and made libations before their proceedings. The emperor Constantius had removed it, but his pagan successor Julian had naturally restored it, and Valentinian I, though a Christian, had let it remain.

Now, in 382, under the urgings of bishop Ambrose, Gratian not only removed the altar but abolished the age-old subsidies to the priesthoods. The Senate sent the eloquent and highly esteemed Symmachus to plead respectfully against these measures. He was refused an audience. The following year Gratian completed the disestablishment by formally repudiating the robe and title of *Pontifex Maximus*, but later the same year he was murdered and the uneasy throne at Milan was occupied by Valentinian II, a boy of twelve.[47] In 384 Symmachus was Prefect of the City, and some instructions to him from the new emperor — to punish the despoilers of temples — gave him and his colleagues some hope that the issues might be reopened. At the request of the Senate Symmachus composed a long letter to Valentinian, putting the case for restoration of the state cults and, in particular, the Altar of Victory. The exchange with Ambrose is one of the most celebrated religious debates in the Roman world.

Symmachus sincerely believes that the ending of the state cults will jeopardise divine protection of the empire, but he is naturally careful not to offend Christianity. So great a secret as the truth and meaning of existence, he suggests, eludes man's puny reason and cannot be attained by any one particular route. What practical rites each of us follows is perhaps of secondary importance. But, just as each man on earth is given an individual soul, so each city and people is given a special guardian spirit or genius. Man's knowledge of the divinity is obscure, but one acknowledged kind of evidence we can have is the consistent good fortune bestowed by the divine, whatever its ultimate essence. Rome has enjoyed this blessing down the many centuries when the rites were faithfully and correctly performed. Is this now a time to abandon them? Are we on such good terms with the barbarians that we can do without the Altar of Victory?

Symmachus then imagines the tutelary spirit of the City, Roma herself, addressing the emperors:

Best of emperors, fathers of your country: respect my venerable age, which has been gained by the faithful observance of these ancient ceremonies. I am surely free to worship in my own way? This worship has brought the whole world under my laws. These ancient sacred rites repelled Hannibal from my walls, and drove the ancient Senones from the Capitol. Have I lived so long, simply to be reprimanded for this in my old age? I do not understand this new system I am being asked to adopt, but I do know that it is always undignified and humiliating when youth tries to re-educate the ancientry.[48]

Ambrose, in bullying tone, threatened Valentinian with excommunication if he gave way. Instead, he composed for him a polemical reply against Symmachus, dealing with his arguments point by point. With considerable sophistry he even adopts the tone of a scientific sceptic when it suits him. Why, he asks, do we need to postulate any immaterial agencies to explain Rome's victories? They are fully accounted for by the strength and valour of her armies. The exaggerated reverence for the past is not wisdom but hidebound reaction, which inhibits progress and improvement, and can only lead men back to their original barbarism. It is not true that divinity can be approached by many routes. Christianity alone has received the truth from God, and is the only true doctrine and path to salvation. The polytheistic cults are simply deluded, and lead to eternal damnation.[49]

In these stark terms the Senate heard not just the rejection of its petition, but of all the background of Roman tradition which it had supposed still counted for something, even with Christian emperors. Rebuffed by such arrogant triumphalism, it pulled in its horns.

5

VICTORY IN THE WEST

Within months of the sedition at Antioch, in the autumn of 387, Maximus finally struck. It was too late in the year for Theodosius to move a full campaign army to Italy, and in any case the relative distances would always give Maximus the advantage. Even so, his invasion of Italy was carried out with alarming speed and was immediately successful. There was almost no resistance. Valentinian, his mother, family, and most of the court simply fled — first to Aquileia, then by ship to Salonica where they sought the safety and help of Theodosius. Ambrose seems to have remained at Milan.

The completeness of the collapse must have shaken Theodosius. It is still unexplained how Maximus' forces could have crossed the narrow Alpine passes so easily, for they were supposedly garrisoned against just such a move. Zosimus claims it was a ruse, but his version of events seems implausible.[1] In this story Valentinian's envoy to Trier, Domninus, was persuaded by Maximus to accept military assistance for a campaign against their shared enemies in Pannonia. The Alpine route was therefore opened to allow the passage of these supposedly friendly troops, who of course turned out to be the advance-guard of Maximus' main army. Such gullibility by Valentinian's generals seems scarcely credible, nor is it any more likely that Valentinian, a minor, would have ordered this move against advice. It is possible that it was accomplished by treachery of some kind: Maximus was popular, and very good at seducing the loyalties of troops — he even managed to turn some German troops whom Theodosius was enlisting for the war against him. Maximus had recently invested his own infant son, Victor, with the rank of Augustus,[2] and he remained to occupy the throne at Trier under the protection of the generals Nannenius and Quintinus. At this time they were heavily engaged with a Frankish invasion and subsequent expedition across the Rhine, which ended in a costly Roman defeat. Maximus could therefore count on no more reinforcements from Gaul.

Theodosius received the fugitive boy emperor at Salonica, and immediately began planning his restoration. Much has been written about Theodosius' eventual decision to fight Maximus, often influenced by the erratic and hostile chronicle of Zosimus writing a century later. He portrays Theodosius as a lazy, sensual, careless ruler who wanted to avoid the exertions of war if possible, and needed some powerful stimulus to spur him into action. In this case it was provided by the charms of Valentinian's sister Galla,[3] who entranced the recently wifeless emperor, and whose bride-price was the war on Maximus:

. . . As Theodosius listened to her he became captivated by the sight of the girl's beauty and showed in his eyes the striking effect she had on him. He deferred a decision . . . until, his desire for the girl growing more urgent, he applied to Justina for her daughter's hand in marriage . . . She replied that she would only consent if he declared war against Maximus to avenge Gratian, and restore Valentinian to his father's throne.[4]

Theodosius did indeed marry Galla, and there is no reason to doubt that he was strongly attracted to her, nor that Justina deployed her daughter skilfully in this political role. But effect should not be confused with cause: the marriage was the outcome of his commitment to the war, and its public expression in a dynastic alliance, not its reason.[5]

Whether or not Theodosius planned eventually to deal with Maximus we cannot know because Maximus struck first, and once that happened war was inevitable. The temporary loss of the Gallic provinces to a usurper might be sustained, but no emperor at Constantinople could tolerate an enemy in control of Italy, which was still the strategic heartland of the West, the key to control of the western Mediterranean, the granaries of Africa, and the vital communication routes through Illyricum to the East. With control of Italy and the central provinces of the empire Maximus was now in a position to threaten Theodosius' own security in the East.

From Salonica Theodosius completed his war preparations and made other dispositions for a long absence, filling the important government posts with a group of thoroughly loyal officials. Tatianus, after a long and distinguished career under several emperors, became Praetorian Prefect of the Orient,[6] and his son, Proculus, Prefect of Constantinople.[7] The fact that both were pagans, in contrast to their zealous Catholic predecessor Cynegius, indicates the prudence with which Theodosius moved. He had need of it: early in 388 a plot was uncovered among some German troops in Macedonia, who had been suborned by Maximus' agents. On discovery they deserted, and some survived as a threat to the security of Macedonia three years later when war broke out with the Gothic federates.[8] At Alexandria there had been popular demonstrations in favour of Maximus, and Theodosius thus felt it politic to station a sizeable force in Egypt.[9]

The army included a high proportion of barbarian troops, including Goths, Huns and Alans. Under the overall command of the emperor himself it was commanded by Promotus (cavalry), Timasius (infantry) and Richomer. Stilicho would have accompanied Theodosius as *Comes Domesticorum*. The strategy involved a two-pronged offensive, by land and sea. A powerful invasion fleet sailed for Italy, while the main army marched west into Pannonia. The aim was to attack Maximus from both directions and trap him between two armies if possible.[10]

Theodosius' preparations may have been slow and methodical, but now he moved very fast indeed and succeeded in taking his opponent off balance. Maximus' headquarters were at Aquileia, the gateway to Italy (map II). His main general Andragathius[11] was stationed with strong forces on the approaches to the Julian Alps, while an advance force had already been sent to occupy Siscia (modern Sisak) on the river Save, blocking Theodosius' line of advance towards Italy. On learning of Theodosius' naval expedition, Andragathius, on Maximus' orders, led a fleet into the Adriatic to intercept it, which he failed to do. The defensive preparations at Siscia were still incomplete when Theodosius' army, with its fast Hun and Alan cavalry, reached the area, immediately crossed the river successfully and defeated Maximus' forces outside the city.[12]

Maximus' main army was descending on them from Noricum, commanded in part by Maximus' brother Marcellinus. The two armies met at Poetovio (Ptuj). It was a major set battle, stubbornly contested: 'The enemy . . . fought with the desperation of gladiators. They did not yield an inch, but stood their ground and fell.'[13] Finally Theodosius' army prevailed and Maximus' remaining troops either surrendered or retreated south. The city of Emona (Ljubljana) welcomed Theodosius with loud protestations of loyalty, thus opening the route of the Julian Alps.

Maximus himself retreated in desperation westward to Aquileia, which he hoped could withstand a seige — perhaps until relief forces, if there were any, arrived from northern Italy. But his reverses had been too damaging, and the loyalties of his remaining troops soon crumbled. When Theodosius' advance guard arrived at the city Maximus was handed over. The small Moorish bodyguard who had remained loyal to him were executed on capture; Maximus was taken to Theodosius' camp three miles outside Aquileia, interrogated, and beheaded on 28 August. His head then went on a tour of the provinces.

The flattering Pacatus suggests that the humane, merciful Theodosius hesitated to execute Maximus, but was persuaded by his generals: he is represented as turning away in anguish as the soldiers drag Maximus out of his sight and to his death. This is all good panegyric, but quite preposterous as history. Theodosius' well-attested clemency could not possibly have stretched that far — especially since his next step was to despatch Arbogast to Trier with orders to kill the boy emperor Victor, which was quickly done. Maximus' general Andragathius was still at sea with his fleet, and on learning of the turn of events threw himself overboard.[14]

The incorporation of Maximus' remaining troops into Theodosius' army was straightforward enough, but the wider political task of securing the loyalty of Italy and the West now required much more care. Theodosius was forced to recognise that Maximus had been in many ways a strong and popular ruler, among the Hispano-Gallic aristocracy as well as the military. Britain had also been solidly behind the usurper, and may have bargained for reinforcement of its frontiers before acknowledging Theodosius' overlordship.[15] The inexperienced, ineffective Valentinian, now seventeen, could hardly constitute a credible successor in his own right: that would be running the risk of Gratian all over again, and it was a risk Theodosius was not prepared to take, whatever he may supposedly have promised his new wife Galla (now at Constantinople in the late stages of pregnancy).

Early in that same year, when Maximus had been at Milan and war imminent, no less a figure than the celebrated Symmachus had travelled to Milan for the celebration of Maximus' consulship, and there he had delivered a panegyric to the conquering emperor.[16] This naturally put him in a most embarrassing position after Theodosius' victory, only months later. It had been a political blunder of the first order, signalling to a now dead and disgraced traitor the approval not only of himself but, by implication, Italian senatorial opinion. In an earlier reign it could have cost him his property, even his life. According to one source Symmachus, a pagan, at one point sought sanctuary in a church, but in fact he was in no real danger.

Theodosius was merciful from necessity, policy and personal inclination. He could not possibly afford to alienate the Gallo-Hispanic aristocracy from which both he and Maximus had come; nor could he be seen to be any harsher in his rule than Maximus had been perceived as being. Having won, he was generally expected to forgive errors, conciliate and heal wounds, as after all he had done with his former Gothic enemies.

After eliminating Victor, and perhaps a handful of others, there was to be no further vengeance. The remaining family of Maximus was treated with conspicuous clemency: his daughters were given to Theodosius' own relations to rear, and his mother received a pension.[17] Maximus' former civil officials were allowed to retire gracefully in favour of Theodosius' nominees, mainly men who had served him well in the East. Trifolius, former finance minister, became Praetorian Prefect of Italy and Illyricum. Constantianus, formerly *Vicarius* of Pontica, became Prefect of Gaul, and Rufinus, Master of Offices.[18] Others in the West who had remained loyal to Valentinian, such as Messianus and Polemius, were singled out for promotion. The trusted Frankish general Arbogast was now promoted to *Magister Militum*. Although Valentinian was nominally Augustus Theodosius himself decided to remain in Italy for the present, with Valentinian safely under his wing.

It was now that Theodosius made the acquaintance of bishop Ambrose of Milan; and thus began a complex, turbulent, but also deeply personal relationship between the two men, that was to have profoundly important consequences. During the brief war, Ambrose had been in no danger, for the ultra-pious Catholic Maximus would hardly have harmed the bishop of his capital, but the fact that he did not flee enhanced his prestige. Indeed, he himself considered his moral authority to be second to none. He saw himself as answerable only to God, and thus his duty was to dictate to the conscience — hence the religious policy — of the emperor, by whatever means served this high end.

Ambrose expected, as a matter of course, to dominate Theodosius as he had Gratian and Valentinian, and the first confrontation was not long in coming. A mob of fanatical monks, spurred on by their bishop, had pulled down a synagogue at Callinicum on the Euphrates, in direct defiance of the law which expressly protected Judaism.[19] Theodosius instructed the military commander of the East to order the bishop to pay directly for the synagogue to be rebuilt. On learning of this Ambrose immediately wrote from Aquileia protesting at the rebuilding. He warned that if the emperor defended the Jews God would no longer give him victory over his enemies, as he had clearly done over Maximus, but would smite him as He had smitten the Jews throughout their history.

Theodosius had already modified his original decision, requiring the whole community of Callinicum to pay for the rebuilding and not the bishop alone. But this was not nearly enough to satisfy Ambrose, who considered that Jews should no more be protected by the law than heretics. Despite strong arguments by the general Timasius, who pointed to a long record of disorders by these monks, Ambrose now escalated the whole issue in public, enlisting his devoted and zealous congregation of Milan. From the pulpit of Milan cathedral he adopted the role of Nathan admonishing King David, and finally announced that he would not administer the holy sacrament of communion until Theodosius revoked the whole order to rebuild the synagogue and cancelled any official inquiry into the incident.

To the astonishment and dismay of Timasius and many others Theodosius climbed down. Ambrose was a demagogue, on his home territory and amidst his fanatical supporters — but with the important addition that Theodosius' agonised Catholic conscience could not flatly condemn these fanatical supporters, and Ambrose knew it. Imperial duty and Theodosius' Christian soul were painfully at odds and Ambrose, quicker intellect and dialectician, pushed his advantage relentlessly. Perhaps, too, Theodosius did not yet feel his authority in the West secure enough to stand an open breach with the bishop and people of the capital, but it was a grievous public humiliation nonetheless. No bishop would have dared talk to Constantine or Valentinian I like that.

The next step in securing the West was a triumphal visit to Rome in June 389. There were many diplomatic tasks to be accomplished here, and there is no doubt that Theodosius, with his consummate skill at ceremony, his affability and confident charm in every kind of company, succeeded in his aims and enjoyed the occasion of his first visit to the Eternal City. The Senate, still largely pagan,[20] and who had only recently been paying their respects to Maximus, had reasons for some nervousness. Theodosius dispelled any anxieties and entered with ease into the role of a traditional emperor: majestic in the official ceremonies, good-humoured at the popular games and spectacles, courteous and amenable with individuals, always observing the expected protocol of rank and position in each situation but, above all, always approachable. He also honoured individual senators by visiting them in their homes, leaving aside his military escort and adopting a deliberately civilian manner.

The political errors of those who had supported Maximus were forgotten.

Symmachus, after a tactful defence of his earlier panegyric, was forgiven and gradually allowed back into favour, being nominated for the consulship of 391. The religious differences were carefully put aside, although Theodosius almost certainly visited the great basilica of St Paul beyond the walls, now being rebuilt, and whose apse mosaic commemorates his work.[21] Many other prominent pagans were honoured: Nichomachus Flavianus[22] enjoyed the meteoric promotion to Praetorian Prefect of Italy, Africa and Illyricum for 390 to 392; Caeonius Rufius Albinus became Prefect of the City, and dedicated a group of statues to the emperors and the family of Theodosius.[23] His brother, Volusianus, even received the renewal of the rite of the Taurobolium, the cult of the Great Mother Cybele, in which the neophyte is initiated by being drenched with the blood of a sacrificial bull.[24] Such was Theodosius' apparent favour towards traditionalism that many believed, mistakenly, that he was adopting a policy of official toleration of the cults, but when Symmachus once more ventured to request the restoration of the Altar of Victory, he was firmly refused. The matter was closed.

The cultivation of the traditional senatorial aristocracy was a matter of policy. Theodosius needed their support, particularly for his evolving dynastic plans. His elder son Arcadius, already with the title and rank of Augustus, had remained at Constantinople, but his five-year-old brother Honorius was now brought to Rome and presented to the Senate as their future ruler. Valentinian, pointedly, was not presented to them but remained at Milan. This, plus the coin issues, made it clear that his rule in Italy was titular only. In practice, Theodosius now ruled the whole empire.

Among the ceremonies was a public panegyric in praise of the emperor, delivered in the Senate House by the Gallic pagan orator Latinus Pacatus Drepanus. The stylised adulation of emperors in the panegyrics is very foreign to our democratic ears, but they were composed with great care and behind the laudatory effusions contain subtly coded political messages, indicating both how the emperor wished to be seen, and also some of the specific concerns of his subjects. The roars of the mob in the Circus were one safe way the plebs could express their opinions and grievances to an emperor; for the ruling classes there were more discreet vehicles, and the panegyric was one.

Pacatus naturally praises Theodosius' birthplace (which gave Rome the emperors Trajan and Hadrian), his family and his heroic military exploits, but more particularly his clemency in present circumstances and the impression of easy urbanity, *civilitas*, that he has made on Rome. More delicately, as a Gallic noble Pacatus has both to damn Maximus yet somehow explain why he enjoyed such support. He paints Maximus in the stock colours of a bloody, rapacious tyrant, but suggests that Gaul supported him in the mistaken belief that he had Theodosius' approval; '. . . the miserable people who, while putting a misguided trust in the purple-clad butcher who was boasting of his kinship with you and of your good will, committed the gravest crime of all in a spirit of innocence.'[25]

Among other things the panegyric illustrates Theodosius' readiness — at least at this time and place, away from the hectoring of Ambrose — to live with the traditional symbolism of Roman paganism. The text of the oration gives very little hint that the emperor being addressed is a Christian, or even that any such religion exists. He is compared with the heroes Scipio and Alexander, and themes from classical mythology are strewn throughout the address. Even more surprising — and surely offensive to pious Christian ears — he is referred to at many points as divine, a living god, and compared with Jupiter and Hercules. Far from being offended, Theodosius rewarded Pacatus with the proconsulship of Africa.[26]

Christian or not, the cult of the divine emperor was one of the roles it was absolutely necessary for Theodosius to play. Sacrifices to his genius had been forbidden since Constantine,[27] but the late Roman emperor, beset on all sides by enemies, needed the elevated figure of the godlike monarch as a universal focus of loyalty: Protector, Father, Tower of Strength, *Basileus*.[28] Diocletian had claimed special kinship with Jupiter. Constantine had, if anything, carried the cult further with his elaborate court rituals and gigantic, almost Pharoanic statues. Theodosius also had to know how to act the remote, bejewelled demigod when demanded — especially to dazzle his new barbarian allies with the awesome, fabulous majesty of Rome.

This iconic status is well illustrated in the splendid silver missorium of Theodosius found near Merida, obviously a treasured commemorative dish of some high official returning from the East to his native Spain.[29] It shows the investiture of the official, whoever he was, by the emperor who is flanked by his junior imperial colleagues and his loyal Germanic soldiers. Ornamented by classical gods and cherubim, the figures are full-face, no longer with the relaxed postures and draperies of classical imagery but stiff and symbolic, dominated by the huge figure of the enthroned Theodosius, impassive and eternal, his filleted head surrounded by the heavenly nimbus.

Relations between Ambrose and the imperial court at Milan had become sensitive, partly because of Ambrose's regular receipt of leaked information from the confidential meetings of the emperor's Consistory, from which he doubtless resented being excluded. Even Ambrose seemed to have sensed for once that he was encroaching too far, but soon afterwards, in mid-390, an event occurred at the hippodrome at Salonica which shocked both religious and civil opinion in the empire, and eventually led to an extraordinary enhancement of Ambrose's authority over Theodosius, and indeed a zenith in the influence of Church over State.

Like those of most other great cities, the plebs of Salonica were extraordinarily addicted to chariot racing in the great hippodrome, a building capable of holding perhaps 100,000. At the time the city was garrisoned and policed by a small contingent of Gothic allies under the command of Butheric, one of Theodosius' favoured Germanic commanders. A star charioteer had been arrested and imprisoned by Butheric for a crime of homosexual rape, or something very similar, which had the most inconvenient consequence that he could not appear at the games, despite all popular entreaties. Deprived of their idol, the mob's indignation boiled over into a rampaging riot through the city.

We lack the precise details of this riot as we have them for Antioch, but the damage and consequences were incomparably graver. Perhaps the incident triggered a far wider ferment of anti-Gothic resentment that was common to Greek cities who had not forgotten the terrible pillaging raids a century earlier. Whatever the reason, the garrison was outnumbered and Butheric and several other officers brutally murdered and their corpses mutilated and dragged through the streets, to the greater glory of chariot racing (and perhaps, Greek vice against barbarian rectitude, for homosexuality in general was far more shocking to Germanic sensibilities than to Greek).

Not surprisingly the immediate reaction of Theodosius was of volcanic anger; but this time, unlike Antioch, in his choler he threw aside any inquiry or trial, and immediately sent secret orders to the new Gothic garrison at Salonica for a terrible, salutary bloodletting of the rebellious rabble. Accordingly, on a certain day when the people once again thronged excitedly into the hippodrome for the races, at a signal the gates were barred. Without pity, deaf to the screams and entreaties of the people (or even enflamed by them) the troops proceeded for several hours to butcher the spectators indiscriminately. According to Theoderet 7,000 people of both sexes and all ages were slaughtered.[30] Whatever the numbers, no Roman city had experienced anything like this in living memory: it was something only brutal conquerors did to captured enemy cities, and it put the emperor's Gothic troops in exactly that light. The moral shock throughout the empire was, if anything, accentuated by the general reputation Theodosius had for mercy and humanity.

It is reported that Theodosius' anger soon cooled and he revoked the order, but it came too late. This is plausible, given his swings of mood in other situations such as the Antioch riot.[31] Shortly afterwards, in August 390, he issued a law requiring all capital sentences to be delayed for thirty days before execution, to allow for possible review.[32] Doubtless this was a good law in itself, but if it was some gesture of restitution or correction it was painfully irrelevant. The slain at Salonica had not been convicted of capital crimes by due process of law, but were victims of an arbitrary massacre. That Theodosius was enraged and should immediately seek to mete out punishment was natural enough, but the appalling form his wrath was permitted to take was the most savage reminder of the mailed fist, the despotic power an emperor wielded over his subjects.

Where constitutional remedy fell short spiritual admonition now stepped into its place. There was nothing Theodosius could do to bring the dead to life, as he ruefully admitted, but he might still make his peace with God and save his imperilled soul. Ambrose was presiding over a council of bishops when the news reached him, and he immediately avoided Theodosius and left Milan for the country.[33] Unlike his strident public demands over the Callinicum synagogue issue he now addressed a careful private letter to the emperor, which clearly recognised his proneness to radical swings of mood and correctly assumed that his present mood was of deep and genuine guilt. Some Christian apologists of Theodosius have sought to shift the blame to Rufinus, the Master of Offices, who was probably involved in transmitting the order — and indeed there is a hint in Ambrose that others shared the responsibility. However the firm, but diplomatic tone of his letter points the accusation clearly at Theodosius.

He protests his friendship for the emperor, and his tone is one of grief. He acknowledges Theodosius' piety, faith and merciful disposition, but points out his impetuosity, which has led to this enormity. Once again he cites King David, who acknowledged his sin before the Lord and sought expiation in sacrifice. Theodosius likewise must humbly and publicly acknowledge his sin before God:

> I have written this not to confound you, but so that the examples of Kings may prompt you to take away this sin from your reign. You are man, and temptation has come to you: conquer it . . . Sin is only taken away by tears and penitence . . .
> . . . I advise, I beg, I urge, I admonish, because it is to my sorrow that you, who were an example of outstanding piety, who held the crown of mercy, who would not allow even individual offenders to be at risk, do not grieve when so many innocent people have perished.'[34]

Again Ambrose, in sorrow rather than anger, will not administer the holy eucharist unless the emperor either avoids the church — that is, excommunicates himself — or purges himself of his sin:

> I have no reason for obstinacy towards you, but I have cause to fear. I do not dare to offer the sacrifice if you intend to be present. Can that which is unlawful when the blood of one innocent is spilt, be lawful after spilling the blood of so many? I think not.

Ambrose had a shrewd pyschological knowledge of Theodosius, and his performance was subtle and masterly, unlike his earlier bludgeon tactics from the pulpit. Theodosius was tormented not just by moral guilt, but by a very real fear of eternal damnation. Thus it was that an astonished people beheld an extraordinary spectacle as the Ever-Victorious, Sacred Eternal Augustus, Lord of the World put aside his gorgeous imperial regalia, and for several months wept and groaned as a humble, prostrate penitent in the cathedral of Milan. It was all the more extraordinary in its stark, public contrast between the despotic and universal power of the emperor, and the grovelling abasement of that same power before the priests.

Eventually, by Christmas 390, he was restored to the community of the faithful and permitted once again to take communion from the bishop of his Western capital. Ambrose rose enormously in stature. No earlier bishop, such as Eusebius, would have demanded public penitence from emperors such as Constantine and Constantius for their blatant fratricidal murders. Ambrose had become, to his lasting fame, the mouthpiece of public conscience, justice, and the moral equality of souls before God. But what was most striking, and a portentous sign of the times, was that his pleading was in exclusively Judaeo-Christian terms. His famous epistle does not appeal to the traditional Roman virtues always expected of an emperor — clemency, humanity, justice, prudence, government of himself. It does not invoke the common maxim that a ruler must be bound by his own laws, as Seneca might have done, or insist that the highest quality in a ruler is *philanthropia*, as Themistius would have done. Instead it is piety and fear of the Lord that a king must have. The strongest weapon of persuasion was now the dreadful threat of excommunication from the mystical lifeline of the eucharist.

If it was a victory for humanity and decency, it was every bit as much a victory for the prestige of Church against State. However sincerely they deplored the massacre at Salonica many pagans must have been deeply dismayed by the public humiliation of an emperor before a bishop, the trampling of the office of their supreme magistrate in the mud, and the clear signal that in religious matters the church could now have its way. They may have recalled the tired old prejudice, that the main reason Constantine had embraced Christianity was that it was the only religion that was prepared to wash away his murders with a sprinkling of holy water.[35]

The church was not slow to press its advantage. In February 391, barely a year since his successful rapprochement with the traditionalist senators at Rome, Theodosius obliged the church with a new and far sterner law against paganism. The ban on all sacrifice, public or private, was reiterated, and all access to temples now prohibited. It was followed by yet further laws with detailed prohibitions of purely private rituals. All this was taken by zealous monks as tacit permission for a new campaign of temple-smashing.[36]

Perhaps it had always been Theodosius' intention to move against paganism when the time was right, and he was now simply casting off an ill-fitting mask of conciliation. Whatever the truth, there is no doubt that it partly undermined his newly-established support in the West. Just as the Salonica massacre had badly damaged his general reputation for clemency, so the new edicts rudely shattered the earlier impression of toleration of pagan traditionalism, and undid much of the good work he had done in Rome. The timing of these edicts was so maladroit that it is difficult not to see them as the direct consequences of the Salonica affair. The face Theodosius now presented to the Western ruling classes was not the urbane ruler mixing easily with senate and people, but the persecuting fanatic, priest-ridden to the point of puppetry. It is difficult to identify the emperor portrayed — to his own satisfaction — in the panegyric of Pacatus, with the fierce voice of the anti-pagan laws that now issued from his Consistory.

Unlike any of the previous Christian emperors, Theodosius was racked by a deep and genuine conflict between his position as a statesmanlike, conciliating ruler in very difficult times, and as a devout son of an intolerant church which was not of this world, and which alone held the keys to his own eternal salvation. The whole appalling business of Salonica had tipped this balance decidedly in the Catholic direction. Ambrose, on the other hand, with a more educated intellect, had no such inner conflicts at all.

In April 391, apprised of an open breach at Constantinople between his son Arcadius, now fourteen, and his wife Galla, now mother of a baby daughter Galla Placidia,[37] Theodosius and his court began the long journey back to the Eastern capital. Before doing so he put into operation his plans for the division of the Western government. Valentinian II, who was now nineteen years old and had languished as a mere figurehead at Milan, was sent to rule the Gallic provinces from Trier in his own name, with his own palace, court and regalia. His *Magister Militum* and unofficial regent was Theodosius' trusted Frankish general Arbogast. Through him, Theodosius would indirectly manage Gaul, as well as directly ruling Italy and the East from Constantinople.[38]

It may have seemed a reasonable solution. Certainly it avoided the rivalries and factions which had characterised the earlier court at Milan. Theodosius knew well the enormous difficulties of one man ruling both Italy and the East, but he was the sole emperor with real power, authority and experience, who could command the loyalties of civil society, bureaucracy, army and Germanic allies. His two sons, still children, had been invested with symbols of imperial status,[39] confirming as publicly as possible that the purple now rested with the Theodosian dynasty, but it would be many years before they would be capable of ruling in their own right. As for Valentinian, he had, after all, been restored to a kingdom of sorts. Theodosius had honoured his debt to the earlier dynasty, but he could hardly be expected to put it before his own.

Yet, ironically, his settlement in the West was almost an inadvertent compliment to Maximus. If the latter's propaganda against Theodosius had any message, apart from self-justification, it was roughly this: a boy cannot rule a beleaguered sector of the empire. It must have a powerful warlord, and is it not better to have a Roman warlord than a barbarian one? It was a lesson Theodosius never entirely learned. Consistent with his pro-Germanic policy he now entrusted a Frankish warlord to rule the north-west through a puppet emperor — unintentionally creating what was to prove a dangerous precedent. This is, of course, unfair to Arbogast, who had served the empire loyally and was to prove more successful than Maximus in defending the Rhine frontier. But the fact remained that a Frankish leader could not command the same civil loyalties as a Roman one, and could not aspire to the purple himself.

What stands out starkly once again is the lower priority Theodosius accorded the Gallic provinces. After such convulsions any prudent emperor would have considered it imperative to visit Trier with his court and army, to reassure the provincials of his dedication to their defence. It was barely a decade since Valentinian I had spent years defending, refortifying and consolidating the Rhine defences in person.[40] Theodosius did none of this, even despite his own Spanish origins. He did not indeed make any conscious division between East and West — this came later — but in the besieged empire his policies and repeated decisions began to mark a distinction between those provinces that constituted vital imperial interests, as understood at Constantinople, and those that did not. Italy, Africa and Illyricum were clearly in the first category. Gaul, Spain and Britain, any official would be forgiven for thinking, were in the second.

Theodosius left behind him a West ostensibly pacified. Gaul was under the control of a trusted general, and the civil administration of Italy in the capable hands of the Prefect, Nicomachus Flavianus, who owed his rise entirely to Theodosius. It was now thirteen years since the disaster of Adrianople, and nine since the settlement with the Goths. For all the continuing difficulties, Theodosius had some reason for satisfaction compared with the perils of those years. His Gothic federate allies had largely kept their part of the bargain, supplied troops for the war against Maximus and had not taken territorial advantage of his absence in the West.[41] He had rebuilt the armies from their shattered and demoralised condition, with a large infusion of barbarian manpower; he had multiplied the number of *magistri* in the East, balanced between Roman and Germanic. Any earlier impression that the Danube frontier was an open door for the new Gothic migrations had been dispelled by the defeat of the Greuthungian attempt in 386.[42] Given time and careful management there seemed no reason why the settled Visigoths should not be integrated into the empire as others had been. The civil war had been costly, but not nearly as costly as he had feared. Now the empire was united, as the church was united.

Theodosius was to be the last sole ruler of a unified empire of East and West. The crises that followed soon after his premature death were so momentous, that historians, ancient and modern, have naturally traced their causes back to the weaknesses of his state, and seen them as consequences of his policies – particularly the treaty of 382 and the general policy of conciliation with the barbarians. It is as if the authority and stability he reestablished was illusory, resting on a deceptively smooth surface of thinning ice which must sooner or later crack. Before we can assess any such judgements we must step back from this beguiling picture of historical inevitability, and examine in some detail the conditions, constraints and options in the empire which Theodosius inherited and ruled.

PART II
THE CHANGED
BACKGROUND

*'The introduction of barbarians into the Roman armies became every day
more universal, more necessary, and more fatal.... As they freely
mingled with the inhabitants of the empire, they began to despise their
manners and imitate their arts. They abjured the implicit reverence which
the pride of Rome had extracted from their ignorance, while they
acquired the knowledge and possession of those advantages by which
alone she supported her declining greatness.'*

Gibbon, *Decline and Fall*, Ch. XVIII

6

THE WAR MACHINE

Since Gibbon,[1] historians have commonly assumed that the Roman army of the late fourth century, which faced the Goths at Adrianople, was distinctly inferior in fighting ability to the traditional legionary army of Augustus and Trajan; and that this was a major cause of the eventual collapse of the Western empire under the pressures of barbarian invasions. Various reasons for this supposed degeneration are put forward, of differing sophistication and plausibility: a loss of 'Roman martial spirit'; the mistaken reforms of Constantine, which supposedly split the legions into smaller units and favoured cavalry over infantry; the 'barbarisation' of the army; the effects of population decline and manpower shortages; the chronic corruption in army and bureaucracy, which left units under strength and let the incompetent bribe their way to higher commands; and many others.[2]

These claims have to be examined critically. It is significant that by far our best contemporary source, Ammianus Marcellinus, does not bear out this picture of a degenerate, poorly organised or unwarlike army. As well as being a perceptive historian of acknowledged honesty, Ammianus was himself a professional officer who served in the campaigns on the Rhine and in the East in the 350s and 360s.[3] His histories contain numerous accounts of battles and sieges, victories and defeats, but in his explanations of these there is hardly any reference to a lack of fighting skills or failure of weapons or equipment. Just as in earlier centuries there is an undented confidence that Roman arms must always prove irresistible in the end: 'We know, both from experience and from literature, that while the Roman cause has occasionally lost battles, it has never lost the final outcome of any war.'[4]

It is easy, but misleading, to think of the Roman imperial army in terms of a single, earlier ideal (doubtless in the more prosperous, polite first or second century) from which things then degenerated. One imagines standard equipment, standard legionary organisation as attested by Josephus,[5] or on Trajan's column[6] and the Corbridge armour.[7] But in fact there was no one standard. The Roman army was continually changing, and had been since its distant origins as a citizen militia. Certainly there were phases of consolidation and of more radical change, but neither army nor state were ever static. The legendary success of the Roman military system over the centuries lay not just in its famous discipline and superb logistic system, but equally in its constant, intelligent flexibility. It was always readier than others to adopt the weapons or tactics of foreigners, if they proved effective (the 'typical' Roman sword, the *gladius*, was adopted from Spain);[8] to assemble carefully composed task forces of different weapon units for specific campaigns (dromedary camelry, mounted light archers, marines, armoured cavalry, etc.); and to adapt its organisation to fulfil different kinds of tactical and strategic roles.

A corrective picture to the formalised, ceremonial monument of Trajan's column is that of Adamklissi, at Tropaeum Traiani on the eastern Danube, which shows a great diversity of equipment and styles within a campaign army.[9] There were also differences in army composition and equipment in various parts of the empire, to meet local requirements. As the weapons, armour and unit organisations developed and altered to meet the requirements of the time and location the overall nature and appearance of the Roman army changed, and the developments which took place in the fourth century were only the latest in this long process of evolution. In addition to such gradual or localised changes there were also phases of deliberate reform, but the constant feature of the army through all of its development was the expectation that Roman arms would ultimately prevail.[10]

Major changes in the military system were usually associated both with changed strategic problems, and particular emperors whose reigns were long enough to tackle them systematically. Augustus, who began the process, had inherited the huge armies raised for empire-wide civil wars, and over forty years he successfully turned them into a standing professional force designed to control and defend the enormous territories Rome had acquired in the late republican period and during his own reign.

Hadrian's task was to abandon and avoid useless new conquests, establish rational and permanent frontiers for the empire, and overhaul the army to defend and manage them against potentially aggressive, potentially Romanisable tribes outside. Septimius Severus (193–211) reformed the status of the army in Roman society, emphasising its role in the continuance of empire, and opened up the command structure to career soldiers. Gallienus (254–68), who faced the disintegration of the empire under breakaway power bases in east and west, along with major threats from the Sassanid Persians and Germanic tribes on the Rhine and Danube, established a mobile force based in the north of Italy — the centre of his remaining authority. This force consisted of detachments of legions, and other infantry, and — most significantly — an extensive cavalry corps of new style and status, which later ranked with the legions in seniority. Command of this force was given to a professional officer corps, which later supplied many of his successors to the throne.[11]

The problems of the late third-century emperors were far graver. By now they were faced by a continuous arc of hostile and powerful Germanic tribes all along the 2000-mile Rhine and Danube frontiers, as well as a more powerful, expansionist Persia under the Sassanids (since 226) on the Euphrates. The frontiers had been repeatedly breached, the provinces ravaged, fighting was continuous, and with strained communications the armies would readily support their own regional general in a bid for the purple. Barbarian invasion and civil war together had all but wrecked the empire.

The strategic response to this prolonged crisis was one major element in the comprehensive reforms of the state by Diocletian and Constantine, who between them ruled (with various colleagues) for fifty-three years and were responsible for the general shape of the later empire. Common to both emperors, and those who followed them, was a new and heavy investment in frontier fortifications.[12] New designs of fort appeared, with higher, thicker and shorter walls, projecting artillery bastions, moats and heavily defended gateways, built to hold out alone for long periods if need be — and quite unlike the conventional 'playing-card shape' forts common since the late first century, which were essentially barracks for troops who were intended always to take the initiative.[13] Towns and cities, including Rome itself, were provided with similar walls, and exposed frontier farms converted into strongpoints.[14] Diocletian steadily reinforced the old Hadrianic frontiers with a system of defence in depth. Instead of a distinct linear frontier from which any external threat could easily be anticipated and met well in advance, there was now a shallow obstacle zone with a network of well-garrisoned strongpoints, which could contain a small-scale incursion, and at least impose a considerable delay on a larger invasion, giving time for a larger force to be assembled and to concentrate in the invaded area.[15]

The major change in the structure of this main army was the creation of permanent, mobile field forces, the *comitatenses*.[16] Prior to Constantine a large field army would be assembled for a major campaign (such as the Persian war of 297–9), and then most of its elements dispersed again to different locations.[17] But Constantine, after his final civil war against Licinius in 324, kept these great forces in being, partly as a political insurance, but also as the main strategic component of an empire-wide defence system. Much of his field army derived from the Western forces he brought with him from Gaul in his campaign against Maxentius in 312, and its continuing existence must also have owed something to the need for a permanent force in being throughout the civil and foreign wars of Constantine's reign. He also added an essentially new command structure, with the appointment of two senior commanders — the *Magister Peditum* and *Magister Equitum* (Masters of Infantry and Cavalry) — who were the supreme military officials, answering only to the emperor and ranking with the civilian Praetorian Prefect as the highest officials in the empire.[18]

The *comitatenses* were usually billeted in strategic cities, and contained first-class cavalry and infantry as well as all the specialist troops. They were essentially aggressive striking forces for rapid deployment anywhere in the empire — against external or internal enemies. They would support the first line of defence, the frontier garrisons in the forts and walled towns. Thus there grew up the distinction between the first-class forces, the *comitatenses*, and the second-class static border garrisons, the *limitanei*, with lower pay and status.[19]

Constantine has been criticised both for leaving immediate frontier defence to the *limitanei* (and, by implication, weakening the frontiers), and for splitting the traditional self-contained legions into smaller infantry units, but this account tends towards caricature. The conventional legions had been splitting into smaller, ad-hoc units for a long time. Whole legions had repeatedly proved insufficiently mobile and flexible to meet the rapidly changing threats of the third century. Thus vexillations (detachments) of several cohorts or whatever required size and composition would be siphoned off for some particular task — a practice that went back at least to Marcus Aurelius. There was nothing revolutionary about this: the cohort, not the legion, had always been the basic tactical unit.

But by the end of the third century, many vexillations never returned to their parent legions. In Diocletian's army in Egypt we find a number of units, indifferently called legions or vexillations, each of between 1000 and 2000 men.[20] Constantine was thus continuing and formalising what had long been common practice.

It is too readily assumed that there was a strict apartheid between the elite field army and the frontier troops, who degenerated in quality and morale through neglect and isolation, while the field army's primary role was to protect the emperor, not the frontiers. It is true they had different roles, commanders and official status. But then the Roman imperial army had always traditionally been divided into legions and auxiliaries — a distinction which had become near-meaningless when almost everyone in the empire was a 'citizen' and high-valued specialist troops such as 'Moorish' light cavalry[21] cooperated with legionary infantry on a fully equal basis. Ammianus does not suggest any failure of morale or military competence on the part of the frontier troops he describes in action, especially in the Eastern wars. A further indication of this is that *limitanei* were raised to the field army on occasion, with the title of *pseudocomitatenses*.[22]

While it is true that without regular support from, and interaction with, the field armies the mainly static *limitanei* would decline in fighting quality (and this no doubt happened in certain areas), this was the result of emergencies and expedients as the system attempted to deal with the stresses facing it. For most of the fourth century the structure was one of flexible cooperation and it worked: the constant failure of the barbarians to exploit their successes were in no small measure due to this Diocletianic/Constantinian system in its developed form.

Traditionally it had always been the auxiliaries who did whatever frontier fighting had to be done, supported by the citizen legions only if absolutely necessary or on major campaigns. Under Diocletian there was undoubtedly a trend towards reinforcement of the frontiers, not only through his programme of fortification but also by dispersing to these garrison points and frontier towns some of the elements of his *comitatus*, his inherited mobile force which originated under Gallienus. This brought the highest class of legions and other units to the frontier armies, and may have contributed to the emergence of smaller units as they were broken down into suitably-sized garrisons.[23]

Although Constantine did recruit part of his field army from the western provinces early in his reign, he also raised new units and increased the overall size of the army. While Diocletian had significantly increased the overall size of the army (possibly doubling it), Constantine's reign saw the emergence as a major element of the army of new infantry units called *auxilia*, who seem to have been mainly raised in Gaul. Their titles suggest a Germanic origin, either recruited from across the Rhine or from Germans settled in the western provinces. These were, however, regular units of the Roman army and not groups of barbarian irregulars. They are matched by cavalry vexillations with similar names, and the overall effect may have been to increase the total size of the army by another 25 per cent from the Diocletianic total.

The size of the late Roman army has always been a contentious issue. The *Notitia Dignitatum*, a listing of the military and civil authorities of the empire, gives a confused picture of the state of the armies. Its lists are not of one date (the Eastern lists refer to the position *c*. 395, the Western to the 420s), and they were obviously updated haphazardly and at different times for different provinces and commands. Along with other sources it does, however, allow some reasonable guesses to be made about the size of the army as it developed through the fourth century.

The third century had seen almost continuous foreign and civil wars, with consequent heavy losses among Roman troops. This included some major disasters, such as the destruction of Decius' army by the Goths in 251[24] and the defeat of Valerian by the Persians in 259. At the beginning of the third century the army under Severus had contained thirty-three legions, and with a roughly equivalent number of auxiliaries the total numbers may have been in the region of 330,000 men. John Lydus[25] gives a total for some point in Diocletian's reign of 389,000. This is likely to be a low figure by the early fourth century after Diocletian's reforms. The increases in the number of legions by Diocletian and in the cavalry numbers since Gallienus, may have resulted in a Constantinian army of some 500,000 men. Agathias, writing in the sixth century, suggests a total force of 645,000 men for the whole empire, and Jones has suggested that this may be a reflection of the official count based on the *Notitia* and other sources, while admitting that it probably bore little resemblance to the true numbers available for the defence of the empire.[26]

Whilst the figures given above for the strength of the late Roman army have often been criticised[27] as grossly exaggerated, it is undeniable that there was a significant increase in the total size of the army under Diocletian and Constantine. There is ample evidence that units of the later army were not of the uniform size suggested by Jones, and that they were substantially under-strength at times. If some allowance is made for this, then the calculations made by Jones produce a revised figure for the whole empire before Adrianople of some 450,000 men.[28] Given the very expensive civil wars between the descendants of Constantine, the constant campaigning on the Rhine and Danube and the Persian conflicts, this figure is not far removed from those above for the size of the Diocletianic and Constantinian armies.[29]

The difficulty lies in understanding how such large forces could be reduced to relative impotence by the end of the fourth century, with reliance instead being placed on large and increasingly unruly federate forces. The answers lie in a combination of the internal and external changes which had to be faced.

Through the fourth century there was a tendency for the *comitatenses* to be split into smaller, regional groups. This began under the multiple rule of Constantine's sons, each of whom had a field army, and was compounded by the need to establish mobile response forces for particular frontiers or provinces as threats dictated. Constantine had also essentially completed the split between military and civil posts,[30] so that military officials with the rank of *Dux* held the frontier provincial commands. The title of *Comes Rei Militaris* emerged for those higher officers who commanded the smaller detachments of the field army, and the *Magistri Militum* were also multiplied to command the major regional armies (usually with the title *Magister Equitum*, indicating that cavalry was still seen to be the 'junior' branch of the service).

Over time, there was an inevitable tendency on the part of all elements of the army — *comitatenses* as well as *limitanei* — to become tied to their region, where most of them had their origins, their homes and their families. This led to the mobility of the army becoming limited, taking place within a region, unless an exceptional situation or leader could command a greater effort in pursuit of a particular goal — perhaps a major campaign for glory (and booty) in Persia, or a bid for the purple and the favours that a successful general would bestow on his loyal troops.[31]

There was also a need to maintain a minimum level of security on a frontier, which required the presence of an adequate garrison: the history of the empire is full of occasions where barbarians took advantage of temporarily weakened frontiers when troops had been withdrawn for major campaigns elsewhere. This again limited the disposable strength which could be released from any area to contribute to a campaigning army, or to face a particular threat.

The greatest limit on the disposable manpower of the late army was undoubtedly the static nature of the *limitanei*, who accounted for over half of the total strength. This meant that, although the cities and other 'hardpoint' defences were generally secure from the raiding barbarians, as our sources frequently demonstrate, the field army which could be disposed of on a major campaign was already being drawn from the smaller component of the total force. Instead of questioning why an army of 450,000 men could not defeat a barbarian horde we have to consider, for example, how much of his total field army of perhaps 100,000 Valens could redeploy from their other tasks to face the Goths at Adrianople. Given the distance of the Egyptian garrisons, and the need to leave a strong defence of the eastern frontier, it is not at all surprising that Valens faced the Goths with a force which may have been not much greater than that of the barbarians, if at all.[32] Permanent threats on all frontiers deprived the emperors of the flexibility, enjoyed in the early empire, which had allowed huge armies to be assembled.

In command structure and officer quality the post-Constantinian army was probably better than anything before.[33] Of sheer necessity the third-century emperors had broken with the tradition whereby higher commands were reserved for senatorial amateurs as a step in their aristocratic careers. Promotion was henceforth by merit, and the high commands opened up to a far wider pool of talent. Civil and military lines of authority — and hence careers — were now clearly separated by Constantine. All officers were fully professional, although there were still avenues of favour through which individuals could achieve promotion beyond their merits. One of Julian's most popular announcements to his troops in Gaul was that he would stamp out such corruption in the military career structure, and the lower ranks would have a fair hope of rewards for their achievements.[34]

There were opportunities for promotion on the basis of long service and merit within units of the army, and the experience of such individuals must have been invaluable. Some would have been promoted to the corps of the *protectores*, which functioned as an officer training school. These individuals served as staff officers attached to various senior commands, and performed a range of military administrative functions such as the processing of recruits, and the control of transport, and military and political duties. After gaining experience in this body these trained officers would be given their own unit commands.

Some of the *protectores* were stationed at court in attendance on the emperor, and of these (distinguished by the title *domestici*) many were directly recruited from the families of high-ranking officers or barbarian nobles. By the early fifth century this corps had become more of a means to acquiring rewards and status, rather than the officer training school which it once had been. Theodosius did attempt to reform it in 392 by dismissing those who were not actively carrying out their duties, and this reform was extended to the *protectores*, for a while restoring the function of the corps.[35]

After serving as commander of a unit (*tribunus, praepositus* or *praefectus*),[36] an officer might rise to one of the higher, regional commands such as *dux* or *comes*, or even *magister*. Many senior appointments, however, went to members of military families (such as Theodosius himself) or increasingly, as the fourth century progressed, to barbarian nobles who had a proven record as military or charismatic figures.[37]

In a period of unending warfare the higher commanders were subject to the most implacable process of natural selection. The incompetent were quickly weeded out by failure, and there were always others ready to take their places (unless, like Romanus, they had powerful friends at Court).[38] Military careers might be brilliant or tragic, but they usually moved fast.

The so-called barbarisation of the armies (leaving aside the echo of civilian prejudice) had been going on for centuries. The army had always been a multi-national force (the empire would not have survived long otherwise), and the recruitment of Germans, either as mercenaries or regular soldiers, was standard practice. The armies of Diocletian and his colleagues, which raised the equivalent of about fourteen full legions (about 70,000 extra men), included Franks, Saxons, Alamanni, Vandals, Quadi, Juthungi, Sarmatians and others. But at that time, before about 310, higher commands still went predominantly to officers from the Danube provinces (*Illyrici*) who had formed the backbone of the Roman military recovery and supplied all the great soldier-emperors, including Aurelian, Diocletian and Constantine. Although steadily crystallising apart, top commands were still partly combined with administrative posts requiring at least some education and legal knowledge. Diocletian's Praetorian Prefects were professional generals first and foremost, but they still had to deal with justice, administration and finance.[39]

Constantine finally separated these powers. Praetorian Prefects were the supreme civil magistrates under the emperor, but no longer had military functions. Conversely, *Magistri* no longer needed Roman birth or education to command the armies. The way was thus open for Germanic officers to reach the top, and they performed very well. Arbitio,[40] who had enlisted as a common soldier, eventually became *Magister Equitum* and in 355 was actually honoured with the consulship, however shocking to senatorial opinion. Germanic soldiers could reach commands through this rather long career ladder, but many came into the army at higher ranks and progressed rapidly due to their favoured backgrounds. The *scholae*, which had emerged under Diocletian and became the elite troops of the empire following Constantine's disbandment of the Praetorian Guard, also favoured the recruitment of Germans and provided a rapid route to the top for favoured and successful barbarians.[41]

The warlike Germanic tribes were an excellent reservoir of fighting manpower, as every Roman commander recognised, but with a few exceptions they were certainly not recruited as tribal units to fight with their own weapons in their own ferocious fashion. Whatever their unit names might suggest, they were enrolled, trained, equipped, disciplined and paid as Roman soldiers within a Roman structure of command. Some of their specific tactics or weapons, as well as their dress styles and ornament, were adopted by the army, but the essential structure, as always, was a Roman one, whether its soldiers bore Germanic names or not. At the battle of Strasbourg in 357, where Julian overwhelmed the whole army of the Alamanni, the war-chant of the elite legions was of Germanic origin; but their steady shield-to-shield discipline which finally decided the battle was as distinctly Roman as any tactics of Scipio or Caesar.[42]

To be *barbarus* denoted one's origins beyond the frontiers, not one's present nationality or allegiance. As time went on, many Germanic soldiers had never seen their ancestral homes in the forests: their fathers had been settled in Roman lands as *laeti*, served in the armies and perhaps retired with honourable status. Germanic generals like the Frank Nevitta, the Alamann Dagalaif, or the Goth Arintheus[43] saw themselves not as mercenary tribal warriors in an alien land, but as loyal, high-ranking Roman commanders, members of the Roman ruling classes — which is just what they were. Whatever the attitudes in literary circles there is no sign of anti-German prejudice in the armies. Everyone with power and responsibility made a fundamental distinction between the Germanic tribes beyond the frontiers and those of German ethnic origins serving in the armies, and this distinction was reciprocated by the external enemies themselves.[44]

Of course one's background culture counted, of course one could not simply shed all the values and attitudes of one's tribe, but the primary loyalties of the soldiers, and especially the higher officers, were never in doubt: it was to the emperor, to Rome, and to a prestigious military system which offered them high honours. Frankish generals would fight other Franks, or Goth fight Goth, without the slighest hesitation. The case of the Alamannic general Hortar, executed by Valentinian for treasonable correspondence with his former kinsmen, is almost unique.[45]

It is true that Germanic generals, like Roman ones, were involved in various intrigues, rebellions and civil wars in this period, which in their positions they could hardly avoid. But they knew, as the emperors and courtiers knew, that their non-Roman origins and (usually) lack of education and culture, precluded them from ever aspiring to the purple themselves. One exception — the usurpation of the Christian Frank Silvanus in 355 — was a single act of sheer desperation, forced on a loyal general trapped in a vicious court intrigue. At one stage in his plight Silvanus actually contemplated deserting back to his Frankish kinsmen, but a fellow Frank, the Tribune Laniogaisus, told him, as a friend, that they would either sell him back to the Romans or kill him outright. They had no use for traitors; Germanic generals, having crossed the divide, had nowhere else to go. In the course of the whole murky affair the Frankish commander of the *gentiles*, Malarich,[46] protested vigorously in the emperor's Consistory that men devoted to the empire should not be made victims of cliques and intrigues.[47]

A larger discussion of the German influence on Roman society and institutions is in our next chapter. Other strategic questions which concern us here are the scale of the external Germanic threat in the late fourth century, the effectiveness of the Roman armies deployed to meet it, and the unrelenting demands on military manpower and resources to supply these armies.

Unfortunately we lack any really authentic account of the Germanic peoples, their outlook, ambitions and aspirations, told from the German side.[48] All our accounts of them are through Roman eyes, and when Germans speak to us through the sources they are already half-Romanised, like Athaulf.[49] With a few rare exceptions, like Tacitus, the Romans were not interested in cultural anthropology. Their interest in the Germans was purely instrumental: how do we manage and control them, what do they want, will they make good soldiers and farmers and can we use their endless inter-tribal warfare to Rome's advantage? Consequently there is no Germanic counterpart of Jomo Kenyatta or Credo Mutwa, who undertook to explain, from the inside, Kikuyu and Zulu people to an urban civilisation.

In the second and third centuries the barbarian tribes beyond the Rhine and Danube had proved capable of amalgamating into larger units, constituting a formidable force for raiding and conquest under war leaders whose authority was charismatic and dependent on their continued success. This had been serious enough, especially in the case of the Gothic kingdom which emerged north of the Black Sea in the early third century.[50] The Goths and Heruli had rampaged through Greece, plundering city after city including Athens. The Franks, Alamanni and Burgundians had repeatedly overrun much of Gaul, and the Alamanni and Vandals had invaded Italy and threatened Rome itself. Devastating though these expeditions were, most of them were at least partly opportunist. Even the great Gothic invasions of the Eastern and Danubian provinces in the 250s and 260s were expeditionary raids on a huge scale rather than literal migrations of peoples — that would come later. As they were defeated by Roman armies in the recovery of the later third century many were then settled as *coloni* or taken into the army. It may have been through this process that the settlement of barbarians as *laeti* emerged.[51]

As each tribal group and subgroup had to fight others continuously to maintain its territory it was a natural temptation to move instead into Roman lands, either as suppliants or invaders. Pressures on scarce land and resources, and the imperative demand that young males have proven warrior status and booty before they could marry, sent them naturally into the war-bands.[52] Despite their major successes of the mid-third century, and other, local victories, it was still generally true throughout this troubled period that Roman arms prevailed over the adventurism of the warrior societies.

Having secured the ascendancy the Romans, like any great power, practised an active diplomacy among the peoples beyond the frontiers. They could offer controlled settlements, money subsidies, trading advantages, or military assistance to one tribe against another; and they became a party in tribal power struggles and helped to create or depose chieftains. In the 280s, for example, Maximian helped the deposed Frankish king Gennobaudes recover his territory and installed him with great ceremony as king and ally of Rome, enabling him to demand the homage of many lesser chiefs. Constantine, and later Constantius II, intervened on several occasions in the affairs of the Sarmatians to support one or other group striving for ascendancy, and Constantine is said to have settled 300,000 of them in Thrace, Macedonia and Italy.[53] Both emperors also concluded agreements with the Gothic tribes, as did Licinius in his struggles with Constantine.[54]

Roman–barbarian relations were thus a complex affair, and the Romans had considerable influence in changing tribal society, some deliberate, some unintended. What Rome wanted most of all were reasonably stable, settled tribal states instead of wandering, marauding warbands. This required leaders with control over their warlike people, with whom Rome could negotiate realistically — in a word, kings. Tribal rulers in turn soon found that their relations with the Romans affected their relations with their own people. Rome was thus instrumental in fostering what was perhaps a natural development from mere charismatic war chiefs to hereditary tribal kings, with other than purely military functions, supported by a kin aristocracy replacing or counterbalancing the restless anarchic equality of the warriors' assembly (over which 'republican' literary figures were inclined to sentimentalise, at a safe distance). The pressures of dealing with dominant Roman influence, and the competitive structure which this engendered, must have assisted in the emergence and importance of hereditary leadership, such as that of Athanaric.[55] The redistributive economic effect of Roman influence and subsidy, channelled through the nobility with whom Rome concluded treaties, was also an important factor emphasising the role of successful leaders, reinforcing hierarchies and helping to stabilise and encourage more sophisticated barbarian nations.

Of course Rome still wanted, if possible, to keep the tribal groupings of modest size — in effect, its ideal was something like a mosaic of small but orderly and disciplined kingships which it could manipulate, much as it had done with the Hellenistic and oriental kingdoms in the past, but this did not generally happen. Agglomeration into great federations was already going on, and Rome's active promotion of kingship and hierarchy actually helped cement the process, as with the great and menacing Alamannic alliance under king Chnodomarius.[56]

Largely as a result of their long experience of Rome, for both good and ill, tribal organisation was now displaying greater sophistication and greater capacity for planned and sustained cooperation. The Franks, Alamanni, Burgundians, Carpi and Vandals were federations of this kind. The greater Gothic kingdom which had developed in the early third century, and been destroyed by Roman victories under Aurelian, Claudius and others, had been superseded by two great groupings of Tervingi and Greuthungi. They had come to dominate the great river systems of the Dneister, Dnieper and Don, and occupied the former Roman province of Dacia (Romania), threatening the Sarmatians in the Hungarian plain. Both groups were polyethnic confederations in which the Goths were the dominant element, and amongst their nobles and lesser kings were royal families which supplied their warleaders.[57]

By the 370s these great confederations were on the move as never before, levered out of their spacious territories by the seemingly irresistible cavalry onslaughts of the Huns and their allies, the Alans. This was a true migration of peoples on a huge scale, peoples whose simple imperative was land within the empire — or extinction as independent nations.

If anything, the external threat facing the empire in the late fourth century was potentially greater than that of the third, owing to the new migration pressures of the Goths, and the greater size, unity and sophistication of many (though not all) of the Germanic nations. We say 'potentially', because their kingship and unity were of course desirable to Rome, with their greater opportunities for durable treaties and selective alliances, but when this diplomacy broke down, or was sabotaged, as it was by Lupicinus in 376, the declared enemy was now a more united and dangerous one.

The effective numbers of any of the external Germanic peoples, as of the Roman army itself at any one time and place, are among the most vexing questions to historians. We cannot make pronouncements with any certainty, but four broad conclusions seem to be secure.

First, the Germanic nations were not the myriad hordes of legend, swamping the empire like human waves. The total Visigothic population admitted to the empire was probably in the region of 100,000 and the Alan/Greuthungian groups must have been considerably fewer in numbers, given the nature of their flight from the Huns and their role in the warfare of the next five years.

Second, as essentially warrior societies (which usually controlled their population structures through strictly enforced late marriage rules, as did the modern Zulu nation before the battle of Ulundi), the proportion of physically strong fighting males would be very high. A gross population of 100,000 could still mean as many as 20,000 soldiers.[58] By contrast, Roman soldiers amounted to at most one per cent of the empire's total population.[59]

Third, the figures for Roman army strengths extrapolated from the *Notitia Dignitatum* err heavily on the high side.[60] And fourth, even before the disaster of Adrianople deployable Roman military manpower was a more scarce commodity in the late fourth century than hitherto.

It is a commonplace that ancient writers, especially those without military experience, greatly exaggerated military numbers in their accounts. Tens of thousands easily become hundreds of thousands. Among some modern historians also, there has been a tendency to assume that every legion or cohort was always automatically up to full strength, but in any army continually at war many of its units will be below strength at any one time. Improvisation is inseparable from military skill. We have seen that certain types of unit, such as *vexillationes, cunei, numeri*, were of indeterminate size.[61] When units did change permanently in size and function, they retained their old status titles as well as their individual names and symbols, just as modern regiments do. For all Theodosius' suppression of even the most innocent pagan images, we still find the proud symbols of Jove and Hercules on the shields of the leading units, although these were no longer 5000-strong legions but small infantry formations, no longer recruited from the *Illyrici* but from wherever they were stationed, or from barbarian groups, and quite probably Christian to a man.

We hear of new units being raised, but rarely of any being disbanded, although splitting and amalgamation were undoubtedly going on all the time. Whether through simple inertia, or political deception, it is near-certain that many of the formations which proliferate so abundantly in the *Notitia* existed largely on paper only. It is where we have actual pay records, such as those for Egypt, that numbers become mercifully more definite (vexillation of Legio II Traiana, 1109 men; Legio III Diocletiana, 1716 men). Yet even here, if MacMullen is right, the real or effective numbers may have been less, if corrupt local quartermasters had been concealing losses and wastage and pocketing the difference.[62]

Although some of the units in the *Notitia* probably existed in name only, this need not imply a picture of feeble, degenerate shells of former units dotted all over the empire. It could equally mean that the disbanding and amalgamations were not being recorded in that copy of the document which has come down to us. The army was probably distinctly smaller than has been conjectured from the *Notitia*, but that does not tell us that its actual units were ineffective. At least in the period of which Ammianus is writing — up to 378 — the indications seem to be otherwise. The army of Julian defeated a far larger army of the Alamanni (Ammianus' figures are 13,000 Roman troops against 35,000), and he had other successes against the Franks. Constantius II was acclaimed for his victories over the Sarmatians and other Danubian tribes in several campaigns, although in the east he was less successful, suffering the loss of Amida, but only after a prolonged, subbornly contested siege by the main Persian army led by the Great King himself. Julian's great Persian expedition ended in failure following his questionable strategic decisions, but was never defeated at the tactical level and retreated in good order. Valentinian and his generals again inflicted great defeats on the Alamanni across the Rhine, and the Quadi north of the Danube, and Valens had of course campaigned successfully against the Tervingi prior to their admission to the empire.

It is true that there are many instances of incompetent generalship, desertion, bribery and other failures. Ammianus is relating near-contemporary events, many of which he witnessed at first hand, and he is determined to transcend other chroniclers by telling the unvarnished truth. Unlike Caesar he has no political reason to exalt his own role or conceal awkward facts. He is a great admirer of Julian, and sometimes his eye for the dramatic scene dominates his concern for factual detail, but it is undisputed that as a historical source he is of the first rank.[63] In the great majority of battles that he describes the Roman troops are warlike and resourceful, their artillery and other machinery as effective as ever and their commanders generally skilled and energetic. Where there are failures it is either attributed to corrupt appointments, or poor generalship — and when the poor general is the emperor with the whole field army at Adrianople the failure is all the more serious.

Corruption there undoubtedly was, very probably more pervasive than in the early empire, but MacMullen's suggestion that it resulted in widespread and crippling diminution of the manpower strengths and fighting ability of the army raises several unanswered questions. It was in the interests of quartermasters and civil officials to falsify returns and milk the pay and rations at various points on the supply chain; it was in the interests of lower officers to take bribes for excusing men onerous duties; but in a time of continuous fighting, and rapid promotion and demotion of higher officers, it is difficult to believe that any *comites* or *magistri* wanted to give battle with seriously understrength units, nor that these malpractices by lower commanders in the field army could easily be concealed from them.[64] Military discipline was quite savage. Lupicinus squeezed the Goths, rather than try to manage an orderly immigration, because it seemed to him a safe option, but for any high commander victory in the field meant honours and rewards, defeat or negligence meant demotion or sacking, and conviction for corruption, death. They could only get away with such abuses if they avoided fighting or benefited from Court politics.

The long stream of rescripts covering recruitment, conscription, deserted land and the chronic shortages of rural labour leave little doubt that both military and agricultural labour was becoming more scarce as the fourth century progressed.[65] Diocletian and Constantine had increased the overall size of the army and manned it by new forms of conscription, by a manpower tax on landowners, by insisting on hereditary military service and by tapping the barbarian populations heavily. Despite all this it still became more difficult to raise men.

In his classic essay Boak has argued an absolute decline in the populations of the West; MacMullen has stressed the hugely distorting processes of bureaucratic waste and corruption at all levels; Ste Croix and many others have pointed to the greater burden of oppression on the rural poor, leading to flight, brigandage and even desertion to the barbarian invaders.[66] While not wasteful of men the early and mid-fourth-century emperors were engaged in a series of very large civil wars involving the field armies, carried on at a time when external enemies still had to be fought every campaigning season. After the collapse of the second Tetrarchy we have major civil wars of Galerius against Maximian (307), Constantine against Maxentius (312), Licinius against Maximinus Daza (313), Constantine against Licinius (324), Constans against Constantine II (340), and Constantius against Magnentius (351 and 353). Though far less frequent, these wars were generally larger and often far bloodier than the endless round of revolts and power struggles in the third century: indeed, it was the institution of the mobile field army that made them possible. The battle of Mursa, for example, was prodigiously costly in men, and Ammianus bemoans the losses in civil wars at this time.[67]

After this very large field armies could still be assembled — as for Julian's abortive Persian war of 363 — but it seems to have been genuinely more difficult.

Our conclusions are these. The Roman field army before 378 was changing in organisation, as always, but there is no convincing evidence of a significant decline in fighting quality. Indeed, its officer corps was as good as or better than at any other time. Properly led and commanded it could count on being able to defeat, immediately or eventually, any of the enemies confronting it. If there was any decline in quality it was probably among parts of the *limitanei*, who had been neglected or drained of men for the field army.

However, the field army was probably smaller than that of Constantine.[68] For reasons to be discussed later the continual supply of men needed to fill the ranks was now drying up. At the same time the external threat to the empire was greater, owing to the huge Gothic migrations and the greater coherence and sophistication of the other tribal federations. Thus the margin of strategic superiority, the reserve of usable resources to meet great emergencies, was less. Serious defeats were comparatively rare, and usually due to incompetent generalship, although when imperial generalship failed — as in the case of Valens, and Julian in Persia — it was more difficult to repair.

It is a mistake to suppose, as many have done, that because the Roman army was defeated at Adrianople this army was tactically of low quality. Valens was out-generalled by Fritigern but, even so, the Roman army, surrounded as at Cannae, kept their discipline and fought on for many hours, and even then about a third of them managed to break out of the encirclement and escape in reasonable order. In the conditions of that collapse it was remarkable that so many of the army managed to escape, largely due to their determination which prolonged the fight until dusk.

Theodosius then had somehow to rebuild this shattered army in the most adverse conditions. His great shortage was of men, not officers. As his recruitment policy shows he clearly had to accept a decline in standards of physical fitness and training, as well as hiring and enrolling Goths and other Germans in large numbers and on more relaxed conditions, and probably weakening the frontier garrisons too.[69] Nonetheless time, battle experience and good officers can bring low-quality units up to standard. Ten years later, relying substantially on his Visigothic allies, the Gothic recruits now part of the Roman army, and other barbarians (especially Huns), he was able both to repel a new Greuthungian invasion on the Danube (386), and march westward to defeat Maximus with ease (388)[70].

Again in 394 Theodosius' Eastern army, bolstered by a large Visigothic force of *foederati* and other barbarians, fought a successful campaign against Arbogast and Eugenius.[71] His army had obviously developed to the stage where it could campaign successfully against the most formidable opponent — another Roman army. However these two victories for the

Eastern forces must have undone much of Theodosius' good work since Adrianople. The Western army had not seriously suffered in barbarian wars, but had now been heavily defeated, especially in 394 when casualties on both sides were high. Together with the loss of confidence of the *foederati* in the empire due to their high casualties in the front line of Theodosius' army, the losses in these essentially avoidable campaigns seriously weakened the army which Theodosius had struggled to rebuild after 378, and damaged the capacity of the West to respond to future threats.

One other change which arose in these years was in the command structure of the army, again a product of Theodosius' policies in the West. Due to his dynastic intentions, and the need to keep Valentinian II under control, Theodosius had essentially created the powerful position enjoyed, and later abused, by Arbogast. Despite this he continued the approach, and clearly intended Stilicho to command in the West on behalf of Theodosius himself, and of Honorius after him.

Conversely in the East, after the defeat of Maximus, Theodosius reorganised and broadened the command structure. He multiplied the number of *Magistri* to five: two were based at Constantinople (*in praesenti*), and three led the field armies of Illyricum, Thrace and the Orient. All were nominally equal, but the two close to the Emperor naturally had greater influence and hence status.

The army, therefore, and its command in 395 were very much the personal creation of Theodosius — partly through his deliberate choice of style of Western rule, partly through his two civil wars and their outcomes, partly through the necessity to reach an accommodation with the Goths — and so Stilicho's inheritance as the effective successor to the emperor was the result of Theodosius' actions, deliberate or enforced.

THE BARBARIAN SETTLEMENTS:
FROM *LAETI* TO *FOEDERATI*

In a justly famous essay, Machiavelli advises the Prince on the two possible ways to treat a conquered enemy. Either crush them so completely that they can never again be a threat to you. Or, dictate firm but moderate peace terms that avoid humiliation and permanent grievances, and work for reconciliation so that the next generation will have more to gain from friendship than enmity. But above all, do not fall between the two stools: do not injure and humiliate your beaten enemy yet still leave them strong enough to wage a war of revenge at some future time.[1]

Occasionally, as at Carthage or Corinth or Jerusalem,[2] Rome did the first, but overwhelmingly, since the earliest history of Rome's wars with the other Latin cities, it had turned defeated enemies into allies. This was one of the great qualities of Roman statecraft, which the Greek city states, for all their superior culture, never accomplished: in their long and mutually exhausting war, both Athens and Sparta had the greatest difficulties holding conquered cities to their alliances.[3]

Partly because it was land-based, with better communications and a growing rural population, Roman expansion was able to overcome these problems. A defeated enemy would lose its right to conduct foreign relations, and be accorded a subordinate but well-defined status in relation to Rome. Rather than a money tribute what Rome demanded was its young fighting men. This both robbed the city of the means of revolt, and recruited its warriors to fight alongside the Romans against their next enemy, and to share naturally in the spoils. That this process would inevitably erode the strictly Roman identity of the expanding state was generally accepted, and over the centuries Roman political institutions evolved to accommodate this. The mechanisms of gradual assimilation extended, not without crises, first to Latium, then the whole of Italy (the so-called Social War of 91–89 BC, in which the Italian cities combined against Rome, was not at all a war of independence but, on the contrary, a struggle for full Roman citizenship rights: they wanted to opt in, not out).[4] By the early empire it had extended to favoured provincials: within a century of Caesar's bloody conquest of Gaul, Claudius enabled Gallic nobles to hold the rank of Roman senators.[5]

It was therefore no radical innovation to take in Germanic peoples, as soldiers, farmer-settlers, or both. It had been done in one form or another since the beginning of the principate, when Tiberius settled 40,000 Suevi and Sugambri west of the Rhine. Later, Marcus Aurelius made settlements in Dacia, Pannonia, Moesia, Germany and Italy.[6] By the third and fourth centuries the practice was far more widespread, and with good reason. The growing threat from the Germanic tribes on the Rhine and Danube was matched by the rise of the powerful Sassanid Persian empire on the eastern frontier after AD 226. It was a period of intense frontier war and its accompanying diplomacy, and the empire badly needed bargaining levers to manage the external tribes, get deserted land under cultivation again, and replenish its own armies.[7] The scale of the absorption is indicated by the settlement of 300,000 Sarmatians in Thrace, Macedonia and Italy by Constantine in 334 (even if the numbers are exaggerated they still indicate a very substantial immigration).[8]

Similarly, Rome had always recruited temporary forces from tribes beyond the frontiers. They served either as allies for the duration of a campaign (usually in adjacent territories), or as levies supplied through treaties arising from earlier wars. Goths were found in this role as early as 242, when Gothic and Germanic contingents served under Gordian III in his Persian campaign,[9] and on several later occasions. There was no hesitation on the part of Rome in using barbarians rather than Roman troops, and by the reign of Theodosius it could be a matter for boasting that barbarian contingents were a large part of the army.[10]

In its military recruitment, the Roman empire had long been experiencing what later empires were to encounter in their turn — that the very spread of its peace, civilisation and urbanisation to more backward provinces made these people less willing to choose military careers than their fathers had been, and less suitable as soldiers. It was nearly always the more rustic, semi-tribal peoples, whose warlike traditions were still alive, who made the readiest recruits — as in the very high proportion of Highland regiments in the British army after about 1800.[11] From Italy and southern Gaul Roman recruiting grounds had shifted emphatically to the Danube provinces in the third century. By the fourth the army had to look further afield, to the Germanic peoples to whom continuous war, external or fratricidal, was still the natural and proper way of life for every young male.

The steady 'barbarisation' of the armies since Constantine has to be seen in this light, as does Theodosius' own policy before and after 382, of tapping Gothic manpower on a large scale. Barbarian tribal and subtribal groupings would continually fight one another with or without Roman encouragement, and Rome sought to harness and direct these aggressive energies for its own purposes, to use barbarians to fight other barbarians.[12]

Though the great Germanic federations — Franks, Alamanni, Burgundians, Vandals, Tervingi, Greuthungi and others — were undergoing great changes due to their contacts with Rome, there was still a considerable gulf, economically, technologically and especially politically, between the two societies, as their own kings and chieftains often acknowledged. Their vision of Rome — whose rule, they knew, extended to utterly remote and alien lands — was of boundless riches, fabulous cities, magnificence and power. The dignified German nobleman, who in AD5 was granted permission to cross the river and see and touch the Caesar Tiberius, declared: 'I have today seen those gods, whom until now I had only heard tell of... Our young warriors are foolish to try to defeat you, instead of gaining your trust.' Much the same was said by Athanaric when Theodosius impressed him with the splendours of Constantinople.[13]

These tribal federations consisted of farmers, with a mixed arable and livestock (usually cattle) economy. In his frequent descriptions of Roman raids into Alamannic territory, Ammianus recounts the destruction of crops, the killing or driving off of cattle and the burning of the timber homes of the Germans. The territory of the Alamanni largely coincided with the former Roman lands beyond the Rhine and Danube, and Ammianus does not seem to have felt the need, as he did with more distant or obscure peoples, to describe their customs or society to his readers — they were probably not unfamiliar. They lived in settled villages, within the more fertile areas such as the river valleys or forest clearances, and, although their agricultural base was adequate for normal circumstances, the depredations of the Romans could reduce them rapidly to starvation and capitulation. There was a heavy dependence on trade with the empire to supplement the production of their own lands, and also to supply the status goods (wine, glassware, jewellery, etc.) which served to identify and enhance the social stratification of their societies. The importance of these links is emphasised by the frequent use of grant or denial of trading rights by the Romans to secure the compliance of barbarians.[14]

The Alamanni were divided into a number of cantons (*pagi* in Ammianus), each of which was ruled by its own king (*rex*), and which represented the individual tribal elements which went to make up the wider confederation. There were apparently different levels of this 'royal' authority, with sub-kings (*regales*) also being mentioned as ruling territories. In either case these rulers were attended by a number of nobles (*optimates*), who constituted the next rank of society and provided a noble warrior class, and envoys and hostages to the Romans. Each ruler would also have a band of retainers, or sworn companions, who provided his following in peace and war and to a large extent reflected his status, prowess and ability to maintain them. The distribution of wealth and status goods downwards through this hierarchy reinforced it, provided stability to it and was also one of the principal motivations for trade in high-value items with the empire. The precious metals and goods which were given by Rome through treaties and as gifts were distributed by those who concluded the treaties — the 'kings' — and underpinned the social order.

The residences of such rulers might consist of more elaborate timber buildings than those of their subjects, or in the case of some of the Alamanni, Roman-style buildings which were probably reused villas.[15] One further indication of the organisation of society by these rulers is the reuse of hillforts dating from the pre-Roman period, as strongpoints dominating an area or as refuges in times of trouble. The fortification of such sites, and the social organisation involved in this work and the population movements, indicate a fair degree of authority being exercised, as do the establishment of boundary markers used to delineate tribal territories.[16]

The highest expression of authority lay in the occasional emergence of a confederal leader of several divisions of the Alamanni, such as Chnodomarius, who led their army to face Julian at the battle of Strasbourg in AD 357. He was a charismatic warleader, who had been able to assemble his large army (supposedly 35,000 strong) through a combination of personal prestige, mutual support between various tribal divisions and the promise of financial rewards. The structure of the hierarchy can be seen through the listing of Chnodomarius, and his nephew Serapio, (mentioned with him but clearly junior to him) as 'kings higher than all the rest in authority', followed by five *reges*, ten *regales* and many *optimates*. Such charismatic authority was, however, dependent on continued success and not a permanent or inherited position: defeat, or inability to command respect, would depose such a leader, as might the lack of any external cause which served to unite people across their local, tribal or cantonal lines.

Politically the tribes and the wider confederations were still fragmented, with their society based on kinship and the obedience commanded by the nobility as leaders of their individual groups and territories. There was no institution of monarchical authority, with a coercive apparatus by which control could be imposed on a whole confederation. There was not, for example, the centralised, tyrannical and disciplined regimentation by which Shaka managed to weld the Zulus into a supra-tribal military nation.[17]

The Sarmatian groups (and some Germanic tribes which had adopted similar customs) also lived in small settlements with timber houses, although they were much more dependent on their pastoral wealth in cattle and horses. They do not seem to have reached the same degree of political sophistication and cohesion as their Germanic and Gothic neighbours, perhaps due to their semi-nomadic lifestyle, but they still represented a significant military threat to the empire due to the strength of their cavalry and the mobility in warfare it provided.[18] Their volatility and frequent internal wars contributed to their lack of cohesion, and provided opportunities for Rome to intervene in the empire's interests: Constantius II appointed rulers for Sarmatian tribes after success against them on campaign.[19]

Among the Burgundians there were distinct offices of priest and king (*sinistus* and *hendinos*), with the priests being appointed for life, whereas the kings were charismatic and could be deposed after defeat in war, or for failure of the crops. This religious function of kingship is not known for other Germanic rulers, but the similarities between Burgundian hierarchies and the rest are closer than this difference. Ammianus refers to them as having several 'kings' (*reges*), and the office of *hendinos* might be simply a variant on the role of overlords such as Chnodomarius.

Gothic political structures were similar to those of their Germanic neighbours, and were to be of great significance in their relations with the empire. The earliest references to the Goths (as *Gutones, Guti*) suggest that they differed from their neighbours in one respect: they had a more developed form of royal authority, with a body of retainers forming a 'royal' warrior army. Archaeologically, too, they can easily be distinguished from their neighbours since their burials do not contain weapons. With this authority they broke free from the domination of their more powerful neighbours, and established themselves on the Vistula river by the second century AD. These kings may have combined the powers of the hereditary tribal ruler and of the prestigious military/religious figures we have referred to above.[20]

In the second and early third century Gothic authority became established in the Ukraine, and finally reached the Black Sea. They emerge into Roman history as a powerful threat, leading barbarian invasions and securing concessions from the empire (in return for providing soldiers), in 238. In 250, taking advantage of Roman distraction in yet another of the third century's civil wars, the Goths under their king, Cniva, led a number of barbarian tribes under their authority into Dacia and Moesia. He held sufficient authority to lead contingents from several tribes, who may have been by now subject to the Goths, organise a competent military campaign and even survive occasional defeats without being abandoned or deposed. The great Gothic expeditions, or raids in force, across the Black Sea and into Greece in the 250s and 260s also suggest considerable organisation and authority in leadership.

However, this leadership seems to have been shattered by the Roman victories under Claudius and Aurelian, and in 291 the Tervingi appear as a division of the Goths fighting to establish themselves against rivals north of the Danube. The Greuthungi also emerge as a division of the Goths, and until they are mentioned fighting Valens in 369 they seem to have been occupied in establishing their control over the lower Dneister and the lands to the north of the Black Sea.

Among the Tervingi there emerged a pre-eminent 'royal' line, which seems to have had hereditary authority over the whole federation in certain matters, such as concluding binding treaties with the empire, ruling on religious matters or organising joint defence of their homeland in times of danger. However, the kings (*reiks*) of the several tribal groupings retained their authority over their own clans, who could pursue their own policies and wars. These kings also could form a confederal council, which may have called the authority of this greater figure (*iudex* is the title used by Ammianus) into being when required, or even challenge it. Athanaric is the prime example of the *iudex*, and Fritigern and Alavivus of the *reiks*.[21]

Kingship thus had no uniform meaning, but usually involved nobility, military leadership and other functions, such as arbitration in disputes between lesser nobles, and sometimes religious status as well. The broader tribal structure was based on family and extended kin, under patriarchal nobles (*optimates*) and elders of villages or clans. Among the Goths a great deal of real power was concentrated in these second-tier clan leaders. Cutting across these hierarchies was the institution of the tribal assembly, which traditionally distributed land, elected or deposed leaders, and decided on peace or war. Though no longer dominant, its sanction in some form usually had to be sought by kings for any important decision or enterprise.[22]

As we have seen, Roman diplomacy penetrated these tribal relations in many different ways: through wars and treaties, trade, political support in kingship rivalries, conspicuous cultivation of nobles and their sons, recruitment of fighting men and grants of territory for settlement. Treaties took many forms, but always Rome was the dominant partner (which was not always so in relations with Persia). With the Germans they usually reflected the conditions of Roman ascendancy, such as whether it was a voluntary strategic agreement or the outcome of outright military defeat; but in every case the propaganda represented it as 'submission' to Rome.[23]

Possibly the most important treaty was Constantine's settlement of 332 with the Tervingi. He had campaigned extensively north of the Danube, against the Sarmatians, Taifali and Tervingi, and was prepared to extend Roman involvement in the settlement of political affairs amongst the barbarians; the client or allied status of these peoples and their leaders amounted to a virtual Roman protectorate, with military assistance against their enemies being extended to them following Constantine's victories. In return they had to provide hostages (including the father of Athanaric), and a supply of soldiers. Favourable trading arrangements and gifts to the barbarian leaders helped to confirm the arrangements. Although Roman literature refers to them as subjects, almost as if they were a fully conquered province, they certainly were not: their status was that of a semi-independent client kingdom outside the empire's frontiers.[24].

Constantius II had also intervened in the political settlement of the Sarmatian groups north of the Danube, through his campaigns in 358 and 359, when he appointed their kings, allotted territories and attempted to settle large numbers of them within the empire. In these campaigns the Taifali assisted the Romans in answer to their treaty obligations. Constantius also settled large numbers of Christian Tervingi in the Balkans, where they remained steadfastly loyal to the emperor and his successors, even during the wars of 378–82 and 395–7. They had been driven out of their territory in a Gothic civil conflict. Aoric and his son, Athanaric, persecuted Christian Tervingi.[25]

Rome also made territorial concessions in the course of its settlements with barbarians. Aurelian followed up his own great successes, and those of Claudius II, by withdrawing from Dacia north of the Danube from a position of strength. The Tervingi were left to struggle with various rivals for supremacy for many years, and this contest resulted in large-scale admissions of barbarians (Carpi, Bastarnae and others) to the Danube provinces over the next three decades.[26] The development of new defences in depth within the Belgic provinces of northern Gaul may relate to the settlement of Franks on both banks of the lower Rhine. The *Agri Decumates* — the lands in the angle of the upper Rhine and Danube — were abandoned and became a settlement zone for the Alamanni, with Roman military ascendancy being maintained from the new river frontier. All these settlements were conducted from a position of Roman strength, by successful military emperors such as Aurelian and Probus, and so were considered as deliberate attempts to secure long-term stability and allies rather than *ad hoc* expedients.

Settlements of barbarians within the empire also had many variants.[27] One natural form was, of course, foreign veterans, as when 5500 Sarmatian auxiliary cavalry, provided to Marcus Aurelius under treaty, were posted to Britain; on eventual completion of their service they settled there and had families, rather than return to their remote Hungarian homelands. These were a self-contained military formation, an integral part of the army whose retired veterans became civilianised. By contrast, barbarian prisoners of war had no rights at all and might still be sold as slaves, but more usually, in the treaty following a decisive victory, barbarian captives and family groups could be assigned land as *coloni*. They were often distributed in small groups over large areas to counteract any potential for trouble. As *coloni* they were subject to tax, rent and military conscription as individuals. If possible, emperors preferred to settle them on imperial estates, which — at least in theory — would cut out a major middleman in the process of fiscal exploitation.

Where an enemy had submitted voluntarily, rather than been defeated, or even where land pressures were threatening the frontiers, a common form of settlement was to place them in groups on agricultural lands as *laeti*. These communities were intended to enhance the productivity of lands which had often been abandoned, and they became freeholders of their territories, unlike those settled as defeated enemies. They were given land, and the means and encouragement to work them with the assistance of the Roman government. The dominant reason for their settlement was, however, to provide recruits for the army.[28]

We know of settlements of Alamanni, Sarmatians and Alans in Italy, and Alans, Sarmatians, Franks, Taifali, Suevi and Alamanni in Gaul; a further series of groups in Gaul carry names of peoples who had been part of the empire for centuries — Batavii, Nervii, etc. — and they may represent the settlement as *laeti* of former provincials who had returned from barbarian captivity or domination to be allocated public lands. The land for these settlers was not always deserted, and there must have been a significant amount of movement of existing provincial populations to provide coherent territories within which to plant these groups. The scale of settlements under Probus and Constantine must have entailed considerable movements to accommodate them. The *terra laetica* so established is only known in Italy and Gaul, but we know of very significant barbarian settlements in almost every other part of the empire, and it is likely that similar institutions prevailed elsewhere (possibly under the designation *gentiles*, or foreigners). The emperor was involved in every settlement of *laeti* that we know of, suggesting that they took place on public lands, but the territory remained attached to its local *civitas* and was originally organised by its decurions.

Numbers are, as usual, impossible to estimate with any accuracy, but the constant references to barbarian settlements, mention of *laeti* in contemporary sources, and growing archaeological and place-name evidence suggest that the process resulted in a significant part of provincial populations arriving from outside the empire. The terms under which these settlements were made may have varied, but they were all intended to fulfil the joint aims of agricultural and military supply. This does not mean, however, that the *laeti* formed military units: they were farmers with a particular duty to supply recruits to the army, who would then be allocated to units as necessary. They were not communities in arms since, like all Roman civilians, they were not permitted to carry weapons.

Their status was permanent and hereditary, and each settlement was organised as a public corporation with a liability to supply men for the army. The groups were under the authority of a Roman official, a *praepositus laetorum*, who might be in charge of several such settlements. He was responsible for the administrative, legal and political organisation of the groups, and no doubt also for ensuring smooth assimilation and good relations with their neighbouring provincial populations. The social organisations within the groups may have persisted from their time outside the empire, with their own nobles exercising traditional functions. The community would retain its customs, essential kinship structure and land apportionment among families. The overriding authority, however, lay with the Roman administration and the *praepositi*. There are no real indications of conflict between these two traditions, and in this lies an indication of the success of the whole process.

The arrangements were anything but tidy, or harmonious, or precisely regulated. It was hoped and vaguely expected that the group's *tribal* identity would be eroded in time, but this was secondary to their great value as a source of soldiers. Roman and barbarian communities lived in friction, mutual suspicion and prejudice, especially in the Greek East, but after a generation these hard edges inevitably blunted. A veteran returning after service in the army would have been introduced into a military culture very different from that of a tribal warband. Far from looking down on him, the army honoured his strength and bravery, trained him in far more complex tactical skills and weaponry, and gave him not the comradeship of the mead-hall, but the powerful regimental traditions of those who served the great Caesar Augustus. He could gain honours and promotion, and certainly enjoy the respected social rank of all soldiers: *honestiores*, who had the right to wear the gold ring which was denied to a mere peasant or artisan. The case of Arbitio, who rose to become *Magister Equitum*, is of course exceptional (how many private soldiers ever rise to Field Marshal?), but the steady proliferation of Germanic names among the lists of *tribunes, protectores, duces* and *comites* surely indicate something of the opportunities open to Germanic soldiers of ability. Many of these officers were of noble background, recruited directly into senior positions and bringing with them their authority and experience of leadership and command in battle. However the process of integration applied at all levels.

The Germanic soldier's attitude towards things Roman would thus have changed greatly by the time he retired honourably, either where he had served, or to his home community. This community too would have had considerable interchange with urban society: using its currency, adopting its farming practices, building and other techniques, and trading items of all kinds, including, of course, language and religious ideas. Nor was this traffic in one direction only: via the armies fine Germanic metalwork and ornament became generally popular, as did some of their colourful styles of dress. Given the honoured status of soldiers, whatever their ethnic origins, intermarriage was a viable option from comparatively early on.

It is important not to compare the Germanic settlements with modern immigration into European nation states that are ethnically and culturally more homogeneous. The Roman empire had always been a conglomeration of distinct nationalities, in which Greek despised Egyptian, Gaul looked down on Italian, and so on. Latin and Greek were the universal languages of law, military command and government; but the 'vernacular' was a salad of indigenous languages and dialects as diverse as modern India. Germanic peoples added several more national cultures to this collection. To ask how far and how quickly they became 'Romanised' is too simple a question, for *Romanitas* meant many different things and the Germanic tribes were in any case not a uniform society. Militarily and politically the adaptation occurred quickly, with their allegiance to the army and through it to the emperor; educationally and legally, only in the ruling classes and very gradually even there; in religion, slowly but steadily, especially with Christianisation. In all this they were not very different from many other traditional communities — Celts, Berbers, Copts, Dacians — who counted as 'Roman'. By the second or third generation the *laeti* were less alien bodies within the empire, than more of its many nationalities — with neighbour problems, like most of them.

Hostility and prejudice there certainly were. Anti-Gothic sentiment was strong among many Greek cities, reflecting not just perennial Hellenic contempt for all barbarians, but also long memories of the very destructive Gothic sack of so many cities in the third century, and shorter ones of the Visigothic depredations after Adrianople. The Western civilian aristocracy too was inveterately hostile to the Germanic upstarts, clothing their resentments in an exaggerated Roman patriotism. They hated these successful barbarians who were favoured by the emperors, who commanded his armies, attended his Consistory and even received the honour of the consulship — men not even of Roman family, let alone good family!

A law of Valentinian I prohibited intermarriage between Roman and barbarian, but it was probably little more than a sop to aristocratic feelings, which needed placating.[29] Ever since Augustus attempted reform of public morals, emperors had inherited the vague duty of legislating not only for religious piety, but also for traditional Roman propriety, whatever that might mean in practice. Even Valentinian himself was privately scorned by the Italian senatorial aristocracy for his rustic Pannonian origins. The law did not prevent the children of Bauto, and then Stilicho himself and his children, from marrying into the imperial family, and it probably made little difference to current practice. Fravitta received specific permission to take a Roman wife, and among the nobility this may have become just another device to bestow favour on barbarian or *semibarbari* leaders.

Many modern scholars have inherited this classical dispute over barbarian recruitment and settlement. They range from Gibbon, Bury and Piganiol to whom the policy was a catastrophic mistake, to other historians, such as Seeck, Ensslin and Vogt, who seem to see their early compatriots as brave newcomers infusing new blood into an exhausted empire. It is unnecessary to play this futile game. There were pro-Roman and anti-Roman barbarians too, but as in any large, long-term strategy the balance of risk and benefit depended not so much on the inherent goodwill of the parties, but on certain boundary conditions holding.

Whatever the specific pattern of barbarian settlements, one essential boundary condition was abundantly clear on both sides: they were carried out under conditions of Roman supremacy (or at least could be represented as such), and this underpinned their success. But in the confused war situation in the years following Adrianople this condition began to unravel, and was never fully restored. Theodosius' eventual settlement of the 100,000 or more Visigothic enemies in Thrace, Moesia and Scythia under the treaty of 382 was a distinctly new departure, and he knew it. No doubt it was the best that could be achieved in the circumstances, but it was far from a continuation of the normal settlement policies which had preceded it.[30]

There was only one model for the treaty of 382 with the Visigoths, and we have even less information about it. While Theodosius and his generals were seeking to regain the initiative against the Visigoths in Thrace, Gratian was dealing with the forces of Alatheus and Saphrax: in 380 he concluded a treaty with them and settled them in Pannonia as armed *foederati*, where they provided a strong defence of the upper Danube area, and contributed to the success of the armies of Theodosius, Gratian and Stilicho. They continued to fight as cavalry under their own leaders, who seem to have still been the two *duces* mentioned above,[31] and were a significant element of Theodosius' forces in his two civil wars.

The Visigoths were settled not as a community of *laeti*, but as a semi-independent nation in arms; not under a *praepositus*, but under their own kings and nobles; not as subjects of the emperor, but led by Visigothic leaders who had merely entered into a personal treaty of alliance with the emperor. Their soldiers would fight for Rome not as individual recruits or small units within a Roman command structure, but *en masse* as a Visigothic national army under its own leaders (although they would only have the subordinate command of their own warriors, and not any high Roman office). The underlying moral and psychological precondition of recognised Roman military ascendancy was now much more doubtful. It was equally open to the Visigoths to regard the treaty of 382 as a national victory they had prised out of Theodosius after the long struggle since Adrianople, and some did. Among them the pro-Roman and anti-Roman factions were still very much alive in the followings of Fravitta and Eriulf. Their continued adherence to this treaty was not a foregone conclusion. Their very success could also lead to fragmentation, and variable acceptance of the terms of the treaty, since they no longer needed national solidarity in the face of Roman military hostility.

Ironically, it was the consistent Roman policy of encouraging hierarchical Germanic kingdoms ruling definite territories that now helped bring all this about. The Visigoths now had an assigned territory, and their leaders' authority over their followers was enhanced and clarified in the process (despite there being no recognition of one supreme King — the Goths did not have one, and in some ways the emperor now filled this higher role, which had been partly taken by the *iudex* outside the empire). The goal of Roman policy — tractable, orderly German quasi-states with whom to do business — had come about, but *inside* imperial territory. In effect, all the familiar contingencies of frontier diplomacy had now been transferred to within Roman frontiers. *Foederati* were no longer external client tribes or buffer territories but, implicitly, states within a state: alien political bodies in a way that *laeti* were not.

Of course, the Gothic settlements were made of necessity, and perhaps they need not have set a precedent. The traditional, controlled immigrations could still be managed, and Theodosius himself settled Greuthungi as *coloni* in Phrygia after defeating their Danube invasion of 386. He may well have hoped that in time the Visigothic quasi-state could be reduced, perhaps through manipulating its internal divisions, to something nearer *terra laetica*, with a less pronounced national consciousness.

There was a certain rough symmetry in the way both sides sought advantage from the treaty arrangements. Theodosius needed this reservoir of warriors, especially in his great civil wars against Maximus, and later, Eugenius. Indeed, this extra reserve may well have been crucial in his decisions to fight, and in private he and his generals could not be displeased when Gothic lives rather than Roman ones were being sacrificed. The potential threat of the Huns to the north of the Danube must also have recommended the settlement of so many warriors to face them.

To the Goths it was difficult to feel binding loyalty in purely internal Roman quarrels, and equally natural to want to conserve their nation's fighting manpower — their only ultimate safeguard against Roman bad faith, which they had experienced so often before. However they did fight for Theodosius, since he was the *thiudans* figure (the higher monarchical leader) with whom their lesser kings had concluded a treaty. They also sought joint security with the empire against the Huns, and the payment and supplies which would enable them to settle again after their wanderings.

The step taken in 382 could not be reversed. The emergence of *foederati* did not assist, but retarded the natural tendency towards assimilation and integration of the *laeti*. Henceforth, Germanic leaders came to realise that there were other, preferable conditions of settlement for their peoples, and status for themselves, within imperial territories. It was not in any way inevitable that they would decline political integration, or turn against their Roman allies. Many prominent leaders, such as Athaulf, Fravitta and Sarus, were to become enthusiastic pro-Romans. But now, they had much wider options, which the earlier Germanic communities had never possessed. Their ambitions had scope to expand.[32]

As military emergencies continued into the next decades, and commanders had to raise whatever troops they could at short notice, the fraying bargaining conditions came to favour the barbarians. Local, *ad hoc* treaties would be resorted to if only so many fighting men, under their own leaders if need be, could be supplied quickly. Long-term strategic advantage came to be sacrificed to immediate and pressing need. There had always been individual arrangements with barbarian groups, and these continued to be made in terms that favoured the empire (such as the admission of Athanaric and his followers in 381). Rome was not applying strict immigration rules, but in the early fifth century the disintegration of its army in the West brought such pressures that further *foederati* settlements became inevitable and commonplace, and contributed to the fragmentation of the empire. The precedent had been set by Theodosius and Gratian in 380/2, but the dire consequences (for the West especially) did not follow until long after the structures which they had put in place had collapsed. In their lifetime the settlement was a success.

8

THE TOPHEAVY EMPIRE

The effective defence of the empire by war and diplomacy naturally depended both on imperial unity and stability, and on a total resource base of manpower and wealth. At a period when the external threat was graver than ever, the state's total tax burden was very many times greater than in the earlier, more secure empire of Vespasian or Hadrian.[1] In that vanished period the newly pacified provinces could still be parted from much of their indigenous wealth, to the benefit of the Italian heartland and the older provinces, so that both actual and perceived taxation was modest, at least among the classes who counted. Although that empire had fought its wars, it had not been required to face continuous war, decade after decade, on two great frontiers simultaneously; nor was it equipped for it.

Now, in the besieged fourth century, all these conditions were gone: there was far more fighting to be done, far more troops and supplies constantly demanded, but no great conquests and booty to offset the great expense. It is also argued by many writers that the resource base itself had seriously diminished; that there had been, for example, a great shrinkage in the area of productive land, and a significant population decline, especially in the West.[2]

To assess the position we must distinguish genuinely independent constraints from those that resulted, perhaps unintentionally, from the state's own actions; between the potential resource base of the various parts of the empire and the usable wealth that could actually be raised; between the total tax wealth raised at source, and the proportion that was in fact applied for its proper purposes at the time and place it was needed.

The comprehensive reforms of Diocletian at the end of the third century, completed by Constantine, had succeeded in stabilising the empire after over fifty years of near-anarchy. They had resulted in a greatly enlarged, more autocratic state machine which attempted to mobilise all the resources of the empire for the allotted tasks of administration and military defence. A detailed account of the interlocking elements of Diocletian's grand plan is given in other sources.[3] Here we sketch only the framework in order to understand the underlying resources that Theodosius inherited.

Diocletian had expanded the armies and civil service, subdivided the provinces into smaller administrative units, refortified the shattered frontiers, and overcome the dangerously separatist tendencies of regional military commanders by multiplying the number of imperial rulers, first to two, then four. The economic cost of this hard-won stability and security had been a high one, and it was paid for by a revolutionary overhaul of the tax system which bypassed the chronic monetary inflation. The part-barter economy and the military requisitions in kind, which were often little different from arbitrary plunder, were legitimised and regularised, in theory at least, by the comprehensive annual assessments of all usable goods and services, on a scale never attempted before and resembling Domesday Book in thoroughness.

People, estates and all productive land, slaves, livestock, living space, transport, manufactures, labour and services of every kind were measured in abstract units of wealth (*iuga* and *capita*), interchangeable and payable to the state in whatever form required. Traditional unpaid public services and labour duties were likewise forcibly integrated into the system. Trade guilds and agricultural communities were tied down into compulsory, hereditary corporations, including shipowners, builders, weavers, bakers, dyers and the rest, collectively responsible for the tax and public service deliveries of each of their individual members. Military industries, such as the arms factories, were directly managed by the state. Constantine had added new taxes, particularly on urban commerce of all kinds. The legal basis of economic life remained private property and freedom of contract; but in reality the state tried to extend its fiscal tentacles into every area, and legalised compulsion, regimentation and enserfment to keep production and delivery going.[4]

In practice this rational and supposedly equitable system suffered all the distortions, crudities, inertia and venality that were to be expected, given the slowness of communications and the tenacity of custom in the ancient world. Certainly, much was achieved. The armies were expanded.[5] Many long-neglected functions were revised, from roadbuilding to land reclamation, temple restoration (later, church-building) or regular access to law courts. Administration was undoubtedly more thorough, definitely more populous. Far more detailed legislation was issued, intervening in every sphere of life. Local and regional discretion was severely curtailed, civil and military lines of authority strictly separated, official posts and tiers of regional government multiplied, all in the interests of a more obedient, clearly departmentalised apparatus of government. The system served most of its intended purposes for a good half-century after Diocletian's retirement in 305. Despite the great costs entailed by several major civil wars, the new armies and frontier defence systems had been so well designed and constructed that on all fronts — Rhine, Africa, Danube, Egypt and Euphrates — Roman power was once again clearly dominant and could dictate terms to its foreign neighbours.[6]

But several dysfunctional developments soon appeared. The chains of transmission of power, resources and information between the centre and the periphery grew longer, clumsier and more attenuated. The bureaucracy was hugely enlarged: four prefectures, twelve vicariates, about a hundred smaller provincial governorships, all with considerable staffs, plus of course the separate and partly parallel structure of the military establishment.[7] All this was not just very costly but rapidly self-proliferating: the distended officialdom that retarded the arteries of government thereby acquired such opportunities for embezzlement in all its forms that the real cost of the civil administration must have been many times that of the official salary rolls.[8]

Emperors could and did appoint officials to punish corruption and abuse of office, but this meant yet more bureaucracy, more salary charges, more points in the ponderous chain at which resources could be diverted. Thus we find a senior official in Egypt rebuking his subordinates who are allowing swarms of superfluous men to invent new titles for themselves, such as secretaries, administrators, superintendents, solely so that they can then draw a state salary. Added to all this was yet a third parallel bureaucracy, that of the church, which was both unproductive and legally exempt from taxation or compulsory public services, and which therefore attracted a steady stream of novices eager for holy orders.[9]

Diocletian's new tax machine had invented, or stumbled across, the wonderful device of an annual budget.[10] The state's total needs were calculated, then apportioned down to each province and city according to their taxable wealth in its various forms. Unlike the earlier, untidily traditional percentage money taxes which inflation had made meaningless, this was now entirely adjustable from year to year. Unsurprisingly, wealth now flowed abundantly into the state's coffers. Equally unsurprisingly, successive governments assessed the state's 'needs' ever upwards, as if this superior machine of exploitation was a magical key to unlimited riches, instead of a more efficient fiscal toll entirely parasitical on a healthy economy producing a surplus.

The rich and powerful passed on as much as possible of this great burden downward to the poor and defenceless. Peasant smallholders were not merely squeezed by the official tax collectors; they were terrorised and maltreated without effective redress, and trapped by debt and dependence on the larger landowners. Often their only options were flight to the big anonymous cities that offered a dole to their idle proletariat,[11] or even to the growing bands of brigands who lived by marauding;[12] or acquiescing in the powerless, serf status of a tenant farmer (*colonus*) to a larger landowner.[13] Many ended up in the last category. Even so, there is a persistent complaint from landowners, including the bailiffs of the imperial estates, about the chronic shortage of agricultural labour — witness for example, the almost universal preference for money payments instead of supplying army recruits, and the readiness to harbour deserters. Military service was, in many regions, the least attractive option for the destitute peasantry, nor did the armies look to them except *in extremis*.[14]

In classical civilisation almost all land was formally attached to a city, small or great, and men above a certain basic property qualification formed a legally defined order from which was constituted that city's ruling council (*Curia, Decuria, Dekaprotoi*).[15] It was their task not merely to keep order and collect taxes, but to perform all the other unpaid public services (*munera, liturgia*) such as building and repairing roads, aqueducts, theatres, temples, fora and other public buildings, providing municipal services such as street cleaning, sewerage, baths, lighting, entertainments, representing their city in legal petitions, and so on. In earlier, more placid times prospering men gladly accepted these kinds of obligations in return for the honoured social rank the *curiales* enjoyed in every city. This order of men, with their conspicuous endowments of their native cities attested in so many inscriptions and dedications, had been a mainstay of the empire's civic prosperity and municipal pride in the first and second centuries.

By the late third and fourth centuries, with all their calamities, curial office had become a crushing and unmitigated burden which everyone sought to avoid. Since the whole *curia* was collectively responsible for its own city's total assessed tax returns, with each man's own property as surety, and since the assessments rose ever higher and were compounded by the illegal extortions of a powerful officialdom, curial office could now easily mean financial ruin. Diocletian had bluntly ruled that even illiterates, or men of illegitimate or slave birth, must serve as *curiales*, provided only that they possessed 25 *iugera* of land.[16] Nor were they permitted to leave their city to avoid that duty.

But, naturally, many did. In the decade following Constantine ten imperial laws attempted to prevent decurions deserting their cities: of these, eight concerned the West. In the Theodosian Code, covering the next century until 438, there are 192 laws covering the position and duties of decurions. Decurions migrated or bought their way into the clergy or the lower bureaucracy (rarely the army) — anything to avoid the ruinous expense of public office. Having wrung money out of their own *coloni* until they could wring no more, they were now wrung in their turn, equally mercilessly, and with the full concurrence of the state's officials. Their depressed condition is illustrated by the fact that after 376 they could legally be flogged — a degrading penalty appropriate to slaves and *humiliores*, from which their social rank had previously protected them, at least in theory. In a famous exchange the emperor Valentinian, enraged at some real or alleged crime, ordered three decurions to be executed in several Gallic cities. He was asked drily by the Prefect Florentius, 'And what if the city does not have that many decurions?'[17]

The curial order had never been homogeneous, and in the fourth century it became more sharply stratified. The gulf between the struggling small landowner and the provincial city bigwig grew immensely. The rich, powerful and influential, the *honorati*, those who could cultivate the upper circles of power and awe their provincial peers accordingly, gravitated into a class of their own, using their wealth and influence to avoid their own civic obligations, and pass their tax burdens on to weaker shoulders. They did so not by flight, but by, for example, procuring some prestigious government rank or post which exempted them from curial obligations (these *principales* were eventually acknowledged in law as a distinct order). Better still, they would buy or bribe their way into the senatorial order, even at enormous expense: there, at last, they might enjoy sufficient standing and connections as to be secure from intimidation from government officials, and beyond the reach of their own *curia*'s right and duty to compel tax defaulters. Except at the highest levels it was most unwise to antagonise a man of such overweening rank and influence, in the lawcourts or anywhere else.[18]

This pitiless polarisation of wealth and power is partly illustrated by the enormous size of the incomes of the Western upper senatorial nobles, many of whom now had vast, multiple estates in Italy, Gaul, or Africa, yielding perhaps five times the wealth they had enjoyed in the first century. A typical senatorial income has been estimated at about 120,000 *solidi*, compared with about 1000 for the salary of an upper government official, and five for a peasant. At the very top of this pyramid a noble like Symmachus could afford to spend the colossal sum of 2000 lb of gold (about 140,000 *solidi*) to celebrate his son's praetorian games.[19] This did not of course constitute a personal, private income: it had to support an enormous number of dependants and clients, and the public celebrations were indeed redistributive. But the figures indicate just how much power, leverage, patronage and influence someone like Symmachus enjoyed and just how many humbler people were utterly dependent on his favours.

Such enrichment and aggrandisement had certainly not been the intention of the emperors who had constructed the new order of things. Diocletian, a military man of the very lowest social origins (possibly even of slave birth), had sought to make the rich pay an equitable share, and had incurred their animosity by bringing the Italian senatorial estates into taxation for the first time and systematically excluding the old nobility from government posts.[20] Although deprived of their traditional political offices, the great Western senatorial families were not dispossessed of their wealth, and through intermarriages and skilful dynastic politics had consolidated their positions so well that, by the time of Theodosius, most of Gaul and Italy was legally owned by twenty or so great families, who had once again insinuated themselves and their clients into the topmost posts at court.[21] Money and family prestige talked, ever more loudly. It is no exaggeration to say that the great senatorial clans, such as the Anicii, Caeionii, Valerii and others, regarded Italy as their private fief, and the state as a convenience designed to safeguard it and provide them with the prestigious offices to which their birth and rank entitled them. Senatorial tax evasion on a quite gigantic scale — possibly 50 per cent or more — was thus easy and normal, and a substantial proportion of the West's real resources was denied to the imperial government, however urgent its needs or draconian its threats.[22].

In modern industrial societies soaking the rich may make little difference to state finances, whatever its ideological attractions, but in the late Roman agricultural economy, with its radically different wealth distribution, there is no doubt that full taxation of the Western senatorial estates would have put much greater wealth at the disposal of the emperors and their armies. Such a huge, single cause of distortion of the fiscal process did not dominate in the East, where government was more pervasive, landholding more widely distributed, and the 'senatorial' class more recent.[23]

The East, however, shared other distortions. Since Diocletian and Constantine, the supposedly meritocratic new civil service mandarinate had become a career elite with quasi-senatorial titles and ranks (*Illustris, Spectabilis, Clarissimus, Perfectissimus*, etc.) which aped the older aristocracy of birth and family and amassed money in order to buy itself land.[24] In a way that had not generally been true of the earlier principate, money, class, social status and effective power (legal or illegal) came to coalesce. Rank and office could be purchased, and was purchased primarily in order to be in a position to tap even greater wealth from the public treasury. If this sounds like a Victorian morality tale, so much the better. There was a dangerous erosion of institutionalised ethical values, to which we shall return later.

Closely allied to this is the constant theme, in the third and fourth centuries, of the migration of wealth, especially in the West, away from all but the great metropolitan cities. City life in the more modest provincial centres was economically more precarious. Civil wars, barbarian incursions, the billeting of rapacious soldiers in towns and, above all, spiralling taxation had inhibited trade and the incentives to invest or risk.[25] The prosperous provincial landowner in an earlier age, though a far smaller figure than the great nobles of Rome, would willingly endow his native city with baths, temples, public festivals and handouts, acquiring gratitude and honours thereby. If he could not run to that, he would share with others of his peers to restore or supply some municipal service or monument, recorded in a suitable inscription. This kind of ostentatious civic spending was what mainly kept the self-governing *municipia* going, dependent as they inevitably were on the productive base of the countryside.[26]

By the fourth century many landowners had cut loose entirely from town life, withdrawn to the countryside and consolidated their wealth in rich villas. In such times of severe fiscal oppression they could and did buy up poor, struggling farms quite cheaply. Landholdings became concentrated into bigger and fewer units. Towns, always dependent on the surrounding countryside, suffered accordingly. It is a development we seen in southern Gaul, and southern Italy, Pannonia, and especially Britain, whose wealthier classes underwent a rural heyday in the villa economies of the early and middle fourth century. By contrast, almost all the British cities except London were in visible decline after about 370.[27]

In their villas these greater or lesser *possessores* might not entirely evade the fiscal demands of the state, but as lords of the region, on whom all lesser folk were dependent, they could certainly negotiate with government officials from a far stronger position. And indeed, government itself approved and encouraged the development of larger landholdings, worked by landless tenant *coloni*. Many laws of the Constantinian period confirmed the unfree, serflike, semi–slave status (*inquilini*) of these tenant farmers, forbidding them to leave the estates.²⁸ Such tying of labour followed logically from the general immobilisation of labour in the trades guilds. The great estate and its magnate became, from the state's point of view, one more fixed corporation whose productive surplus supplied its strategic needs. That this entailed greater oppression and a tyrannical, irredressible servitude for the legally free peasantry, was simply part of the price.

Various emperors issued many laws and instructions aimed at helping and protecting the poorest classes. Constantine, Julian, Valentinian and Gratian all decreed various measures to reduce taxation, combat corruption and abuses, and protect the poor against the rich and powerful. Valentinian, for example, established a free legal service to defend the Roman plebs, improved the doles and assigned a doctor to each district of the City; but these piecemeal acts could make very little difference in the face of the inexorable, pervasive coalition of interests between the state and the great landed magnates — cemented more firmly by the fact that most of the government's own higher officials, from the court magistrates downwards, were themselves landowners intent on increasing their wealth.²⁹

The global price in fact grew greater. The great villas and their tied *coloni* maintained agricultural production, but their emphasis was now on local self-sufficiency, on independence from the cities and the centres of governmental power. They set up or effectively controlled their own local workshops, potteries and factories, brick kilns and building facilities, clothing factories, metalworking, and eventually, when the state would or could not provide security, their own defensive perimeter walls and unofficial private militias.³⁰ They traded less. The cost of land transport had always been high, even in good times. Now barbarian raids, brigandage and the sheer insecurity of travel confined their markets to smaller localities. Among many other consequences, this meant that local crop failures or famines, to which an agricultural economy is always prone, were less likely to be relieved from surpluses elsewhere.

Hence, the considerable wealth generated in all its forms by the villa economy circulated far more tardily, if at all, into the wider regions of the province or the empire. Regional economic differences became more pronounced — especially in the north-west and western Danube provinces. Wealth, labour and trade did not beget more wealth as they normally had done in the more secure first and second centuries, when they had flowed abundantly through the cities, marketplaces and smaller townships. The city artisan classes suffered a slump in their trade. The total of real, available resources in all forms was slowly diminishing, simply through the sluggishness and unpredictability of trade, investment, circulation and all their usual multiplying effects in confidence and the commercial exchange which it engenders.³¹

Naturally the pattern was anything but uniform. In the huge metropolises, such as Alexandria or Antioch, trade was as brisk as ever, wealth circulated rapidly and people gambled recklessly on the eternal chariot racing as always. In the strategic cities and their satellites along the great highway systems — Trier, Arles, Ravenna, Milan, Aquileia, Vindobona, Mursa, Sirmium and the rest — the economic effect was the reverse of that in the insecure areas mentioned above. Emperors, courts and armies there spent freely, giving a great boost to the cities and the hinterland economies of what had been beleaguered frontier provinces. But such prosperity, although real enough, did not always extend very far, and even — as in Italy — drew off wealth from other regions. It was generated by the great stimulus of imperial spending, not original wealth generation. If this were to be withdrawn the result could be near-collapse of the regional economy, as in the great Gallic imperial city of Trier after the government eventually migrated to Arles in the fifth century. Around them, many lesser Gallic cities had long languished into impoverishment and decay.[32]

Thus the vertical polarisation of wealth was being compounded by a regional, geographical polarisation, and a reversion to more local, rural economies, as a result of insecurity, economic oppression, and the diminishing returns of trade and communications. There were many regional variations in this pattern, but the general trend can be seen that the Western provinces of the empire suffered more due to their greater levels of insecurity. At the same time, from the fourth century onwards, there was a rise in the population and apparent wealth of most of the Eastern provinces.

There may have been an overall decline in population in the West, as suggested by the abandonment of land which appears in our sources as *agri deserti*, and the availability of land for frequent settlements of barbarians. However, this pattern was not uniform and some areas continued to prosper, such as Spain and parts of North Africa into the early fifth century.[33]

The urban decline was sharpest in the West, where the cities had always been crucially dependent on the countryside. The regions that survived best were Italy north of the Po, based on Milan, Ravenna and Aquileia, and North Africa, where Carthage, Djemila, Timgad and other cities continued to enjoy prosperity through the export of grain to Italy, despite a shrinkage of cultivated lands. Southern Italy, Gaul, Spain, Dalmatia and the upper Danube provinces all experienced fairly severe urban and agricultural depression in the late fourth century. In some areas, such as northern Pannonia and the Rhineland, repeated fighting and occupation by invaders led to general abandonment of villas and farms.[34]

The East had suffered the same great tax and liturgy burdens, as well as the great destruction from the six-year Gothic war up to 382, but it was more resilient. There were more and larger cities, a closer imperial presence, better and more defensible strategic and mercantile communications. The cities supported a greater middle class of traders and manufacturers, and were not so completely reliant on the countryside. The landowning pattern was of more numerous, modest-sized holdings (in Syria there was even a breaking up of the very large estates).[35] Wealth was not so drastically polarised, and the ruling aristocracy was unable to acquire the paralysing, near-monopoly of economic power its counterparts enjoyed in the West, which may have been partly due to its more recent emergence. There was certainly economic depression in Thrace, where the war had been most damaging, and in Egypt also, but against this Asia Minor, Syria and, especially Palestine, continued and even increased their prosperity.[36]

Corruption, particularisation and the greater atomisation of self-interest and sheer survival cut all across this picture. The closer identification of wealth, status, class and power was both cause and effect of a significant change in the character of public service since the more secure and prosperous first and second centuries. MacMullen, more than any other, has traced with some care the way that mercenary abuse of office in all its forms was so much more pervasive, more commonplace, more acquiesced at in every level of government, that it became, like the black market in a tottering modern command economy, not so much a perversion of the system as an alternative system replacing it.[37]

The earliest principate had been flexible and economic in its civil service, though it had never been meritocratic. The main considerations in reaching high or middle office had been birth and social rank. A man might aspire to proconsulship or prefecture because of the grand public dignity it conferred on him and, above all, his family. Anchored in this were complex social networks of obligation (*clientelia*), involving family, kin, city, guild membership, or simply the readiness to acknowledge a patron in return for the protection and advancement this promised. These networks were publicly acknowledged, unashamed, and enduring. People knew where they were and what they might reasonably expect.

By the late fourth century this subtle network had largely been broken. Ties of social and personal obligation had increasingly been replaced by an impersonal market of naked self-interest in which almost everything had its cash price — government posts, bishoprics, judicial decisions, exemptions from tax and service obligations. In the notorious case of Count Romanus, who was abusing his military command in Africa on a huge scale, the very official first sent by Valentinian to investigate complaints was himself bribed into reporting that they were groundless. Similarly, Palladius recounts quite casually how the bishoprics of Egypt and Asia were up for sale to those desperate to avoid curial obligations.[38]

Naturally some corruption had always occurred: the change in norms was one in which scale and perception were crucial. If there is no other practical way to get what one wants or needs, if most people at every level are seen to be methodically lining their pockets, it becomes only rational to do likewise, whatever one's personal misgivings. It takes the unusually brave and honest to stand out against it, and these, by definition, are a minority.

However, it does not automatically follow that everyone who was profiting from their role in government was necessarily ineffective in their job. There were many professional and effective officials in both civil and military posts, and we should not lose sight of the fact that the empire did recover from the trials of the third century, and survive those of the fourth, in no small part due to these professional classes. The East went on to prosper through the fifth and sixth centuries relying on the same basic administrative systems.

The reasons for this change to institutionalised corruption are an extremely important question, though peripheral to this book. The reconstructed government and military machines of Diocletian and Constantine had filled their posts, less according to social rank, than merit and professionalism; but this had come to be steadily dominated by the cash nexus as time went on. Official positions rapidly became fixed social ranks, a process which was enhanced by the establishment of grades within the administration corresponding to military posts, with the privileges and status associated with them. The denser, more anonymous bureaucracy, the proliferation of extremely detailed imperial legislation, the quartering of troops in towns, the weakening of custom and tradition, the relative social rootlessness of the bureaucrats — all have been suggested as factors in this insidious process.

The separation of civil and military responsibilities had also created a career group of men whose access to, and control of, the economic processes of government was unprecedented. Without military demands and expectations of them, they had an obvious interest in personal advancement through those areas under their control: land, money, politics. This could also lead to destructive conflicts between court officials and military officers, who were both competing for the emperor's attention and favour. The intrigues which arose must have restricted the potential of many competent officials.[39]

Like the decay of civic life and the polarisation of wealth, this development had profound effects well beyond the merely economic. The earlier, elitist service ethic was dissolved, but not replaced by another. Earlier obligations, loyalties and patriotism, which had counteracted the forces of sheer private avarice, had been gravely weakened. Imperial government, though wielding despotic power over those within its immediate reach, was less able to impose its will on events. Emperors were more securely in command of their thrones, but also more insulated in their courts and palaces. The translation of their commands into effective action at the distant points where it was needed now involved more dissipation of power into a thousand private channels. No wonder their edicts combating corruption, drafted by the very men against whom they were directed, were a dead letter.[40]

Alongside the government edifice, of course, was that of the church, which Constantine had unwisely exempted from taxes or public services. The landed estates he settled on the church yielded some 30,000 *solidi* annually, but these grew steadily in the next century.[41] The numbers of monks and clerics grew into hundreds of thousands, the great majority from the poorer classes who would otherwise have been producers. By the sixth century, if not earlier, each city had a bishop with an official salary equivalent to that of a provincial governor. Of course, charitable activities provided some badly needed redistribution and the building of churches and monasteries itself provided work and stimulated some commerce (for example, in the vigorous church-building in the cities around Carthage). Nevertheless, the dominant effect of the growth of the church was decidedly away from the main arteries of productive, commercial society. Monasteries and convents took people completely out of the economic cycle, devoting themselves to as isolated and self-sufficient an economy as possible, and considering it sinful to produce a profitable surplus. Whereas the rich would once have endowed great public buildings and services in their native cities, naturally stimulating confidence, markets and commercial growth, now their benefactions went more to churches, monasteries, baptistries and martyria — all essentially unproductive.

Monasteries were only the most obvious effect. In offering an escape from all kinds of worldly hardships — primarily, of course, taxes and curial duties — the clergy was becoming almost a rival institution to the state. Unlike the army and civil service it contributed very little to the political survival of the empire. Its possible unifying effects, in the fourth century at least, were badly offset by the endless splits and schisms. Unlike the pagan state cults its great religious promises were directed to another world, not the defence and preservation of this one. The time had not yet come when the miraculous icons of Christ and his Holy Mother would march at the head of Byzantine armies, and those honest and capable administrators whose talents were so sorely needed by the corrupted state — men like Ambrose, John Chrysostom, or Jerome — were instead princes of the church.[42]

We can now perhaps sketch the overall position. First, there is little reason to suppose that the total potentially available resources of the empire had shrunk dramatically: what had altered most were the patterns of exploitation, distribution and use. There were some exceptions: areas of Africa had suffered climatic changes and soil erosion, independently of the political insecurity which diminished cultivation; around the Rhine estuary a small rise in sea level took much land out of use; and the declining output of the Spanish silver mines suggests exhaustion rather than political causes. The loss of the eastern trade routes to Persia after the treaty of 363 must have affected the flow of luxury goods into the Eastern provinces.

It is also plausible that native populations fell in some areas. Impoverishment, flight, loss of stable livelihood and expectations tend to reduce the number of marriageable males, while increasing infant mortality. It is also likely that many of the poor who fled the land for the anonymous cities, or enserfment on large estates, did not live long nor replace themselves demographically, but had their numbers replenished only by continued migration. This again seems to follow a regional pattern, with the population of areas such as Syria increasing steadily while the north-western provinces were suffering from insecurity and population shifts. Against this, of course, were the new Germanic immigrants into the empire, who were largely settled in those areas which had suffered most from insecurity.

The problem was not so much a low population as a maldistributed one; not loss of fertile land *per se*, but its abandonment due to insecurity and fiscal oppression. Too many people were outside the productive process, heavily parasitical on it or refugees from it, despite — or even because of — the state's clumsy efforts to tie them down by compulsion. Among the greatest parasites were the government's own agents themselves, the political ruling classes whose oppression of the lower orders (now including the *curiales*) had become so heavy, so naked and so ubiquitous that it eroded basic economic incentives and with them, the real productive base.

Government's legitimate demands — naturally high owing to the expansion and professionalisation of army and civil service — were magnified many times further by the widespread corruption which deflected and diluted government's own effectiveness. When the state attempted to correct some of its mistakes, for example by ending the too generous levels of tax and service exemptions, it found its own power thwarted and evaded at every turn. The decay of the town infrastructure meant less wealth generation and greater social, economic and geographical polarisation, as the middle levels of society and wealth disappeared, and some regions reverted to more local, rural economies. This made it genuinely more costly and difficult for government to recruit, assemble, supply and move armies to new areas where they were needed. After Adrianople, regional military threats tended to tie down the surviving major army groups. This in turn deprived some areas of security, leading to all the downward economic effects already described. Support for a regional warlord, banditry, uprisings against the rich, and even siding with the invading barbarians, are all common responses in this period.

Conversely Government would, by gravitational pull, come to concentrate more on the central regions where communications were good, cities numerous and defensible, wealth and recruits plentiful and frontiers manageable. Strategic priority regions were emerging, usually corresponding with the economically stronger ones: Italy, with its imperial prestige and military bases, and Africa, its granary; Greece, Illyricum and the Danube provinces, backbone to East–West communication; Asia Minor and Syria, with their close network of roads and rich trading cities; Egypt, the breadbasket of Constantinople.[43] The regions beyond the Alps — northern and southern Gaul, Spain and Britain — were, from an imperial point of view, more remote, more difficult to defend, less urbanised and increasingly less secure.

Faced with these difficulties, Theodosius did appoint to his senior administrative posts men who had acquired experience in other positions in the East, but he also relied very heavily on officials recruited from the West, either known associates and supporters or officials from the Western government. Along with Gratian he embarked on a series of revisions to the senatorial class, and of all the ranks below, which resulted in further expansions to the already privileged groups who contributed to the weight of government as we have seen above.[44]

He also had to deal with the considerable losses in revenue brought about by the devastation caused by the Gothic wars, remitting taxes on occasions, and was severe in his pursuit of income from other areas. This even affected his relations with the church, since he refused to allow *curiales* to take holy orders unless they surrendered their property and made provision for their duties to be carried on. It would seem that despite his attempts to foster the recovery of the East from the disasters of the years 376–82, Theodosius was not capable of preventing the undermining of the process by the corrupting elements which we have reviewed. The civilian character of his government in the East did provide a better administrative and financial legacy to Arcadius than that inherited by Honorius (and Stilicho) in the West, where most of the problems discussed above were more extreme, and compounded by the relative neglect of the Western provinces by Theodosius.

After 395 the West, under Honorius and Stilicho, could spare little time or resources for the more peripheral provinces when the heart of the empire in Italy was threatened, and the political situation meant that there was no prospect of support from the wealthier, more secure East.

PART III
CONFRONTATION

'Tell the King: on earth has fallen the glorious dwelling!
The god has nothing left, no hearth, no roof, no home.
In his hand the prophet laurel is withered,
And the water spring which spoke, is choked and dead.'

Alleged answer of the Delphic oracle to the Emperor Julian on the future
of paganism. *Vita S. Artemii* (Swinburne)

9

CONTRA PAGANOS

In the spring and summer of 391 Theodosius and his Court began the long return to Constantinople, after three years of direct rule in the West from Milan.[1] Italy and the Gallic provinces were ostensibly pacified after the victory over Maximus. The formidable and trusted *Magister Militum*, Arbogast, effectively protected the north-west of the empire from Trier,[2] through the overt imperial authority of the youthful Valentinian II, now nearly twenty but without serious political or military experience.[3] In Italy, the senatorial nobility, still largely pagan, had been forgiven their compromises with Maximus, carefully conciliated and brought over to support Theodosius and his dynasty. The very influential pagan aristocrat, Nicomachus Flavianus, had been honoured and entrusted with the multiple Prefecture of Italy, Africa and Illyricum — perhaps the highest position of rank and authority possible for any minister in the West.[4]

Yet, as early as February 391, Theodosius' apparently successful *modus vivendi* with pagan traditionalism was abruptly ended by his radical new law, not only reiterating the ban on all sacrifice, public or private, but for the very first time forbidding all access to shrines and temples.[5] This was followed by three others, even more repressive and aimed at erasing every vestige of pagan ritual, custom or gesture. The face Theodosius now presented to the Italian pagan senatorial classes was no longer the tolerant, urbane ruler, but the fierce, religious bigot. The whole religious balance he had carefully constructed, he now seemed to upset at a single stroke.[6]

There are many opinions about Theodosius' sudden apparent change of religious policy at this time.[7] It is suggested that it was part of a systematic programme of tackling heresy first, then paganism, and he was now free to put the second part into operation;[8] that he had now shed any last superstitious reservations about the efficacy of the ancient Roman state sacrifices, which had hitherto inhibited him;[9] or that the new influence of his forceful Catholic minister Rufinus, Master of Offices combined with that of Ambrose, now impelled him to extreme measures.[10]

All of these may be true, but what is surprising and uncharacteristic is his political clumsiness in the timing and occasion of these laws. The first, of 24 February 391, would certainly have been debated in the Consistory at Milan with the Prefect Flavianus, a leading representative of senatorial paganism, who would then be required to broadcast and enforce laws to which he was bitterly opposed.[11] The second, issued from Concordia on 9 June, was addressed directly to the same Flavianus, now deputising for his emperor.[12] This is not Theodosius the adroit diplomatic ruler, but Theodosius subject to some other imperative. King remarks: 'It is a measure of Theodosius' greatness, laziness or duplicity that he was able to continue a policy which held together two mutually contradictory ideas' — namely, the broad imperial toleration of Constantine and Valentinian I, and the root-and-branch persecution advocated by Ambrose, Cynegius and the marauding monks who were illegally destroying temples throughout the Eastern provinces.[13]

Most of Theodosius' policies in every sphere were, of necessity, difficult balancing acts: his frontier and foreign policy, his top military appointments; but what is happening here is not part of any deliberate balance. Theodosius is being pulled abruptly in different directions by warring influences which he — as a statesman, a Catholic soul, a legislator — no longer really manages to juggle successfully. It is almost impossible not to see here the traumatic effects of the Salonica affair and the consequences of the readmission of the penitent emperor into the Catholic fold.

Theodosius had never actually accepted toleration of paganism as a principle. Libanius' oration on the subject, prompted by the illegal Christian fashion of temple-smashing, delicately reminds the emperor of Constantine's maxim of toleration: that if persuasion fails, compulsion should not be attempted. However, after half a century of Christian dissension and schism Theodosius had already used legal coercion to suppress heresy (and Maximus had also taken this to extremes with the execution of the heretic Priscillian and some of his followers.[14] There was no logical reason why he should not do the same to suppress paganism, equally offensive in God's eyes. Only considerations of political pragmatism held him back and, after Salonica and Ambrose, these gave way to the Will of God and his own stern duty to impose Catholic Christianity on his subjects.

It is possible, but difficult, to find greater examples of intolerance and fanaticism than in the spirit that animates these new laws. It does not just discard the symbols of paganism but actively demonises them, even down to the most ordinary domestic rites. The first law, *Nemo se hostiis polluat*, firmly prohibits all sacrifices, including — for the first time — the traditional state ceremonies still practised at Rome. It goes on to rule, 'No person shall approach the shrines, nor walk through the temples, nor revere the images formed of mortal hands.' Men of higher rank who transgressed were to be fined fifteen pounds of gold.

This is the state's adoption of the stern Mosaic view of idolatry: that these images were fetishes being worshipped in and for themselves. Every educated person who moved among the shrines, including cultured Christians like Ausonius or Petronius Probus, knew that most pagans did not literally worship artefacts, but treated them as visible symbols of their gods.[15] The traditions and myths of Hellenistic polytheism, the common property of classical culture, were now officially effaced by the more primitive Hebrew revulsion for the blasphemous idols of their ancient tribal enemies. This was the Christianity of the monks and the mobs, expressed in the language of imperial law; inspired not by a sober policy of desirable religious aims, but the ruler's dread of damnation and need for magical prescriptions to counteract the juju. Having been baptised in 380, and thereby cleaning his soul, Theodosius must have dreaded the consequences of further sin.

The law of 9 June expressly forbids apostasy (from Christian to pagan), which is to be punishable by loss of testamentary rights. The law of 16 June repeats the February law expressly for Egypt, where Alexandria, like Rome, had long enjoyed special privileges for its cults, including sacrificial ceremonies.[16] Like the divine protection such rites secured for the Eternal City, these were widely believed to ensure the continued rise of the fertilising Nile and the consequent productivity of Egypt.[17] Libanius had earlier pointed out how, in effect, Christian rulers had still not ventured to abolish these two cardinal sacrificial ceremonies out of wariness over the possible divine consequences.[18] Acknowledging this challenge, Theodosius now explicitly banned them both.

It is not clear how rigorously or universally this legislation was actually enforced. Lukewarm prefects and magistrates, many of them pagan, might have their hands forced by zealous bishops and mobs. At Rome the official state sacrifices, which had ensured the safety of the City for a thousand years, now ceased (they would have dwindled in any case, following the ending of state finance for the cults and priesthoods). By no means every other ceremony or offering ended, as is indicated in the use of temples, the continuing votive inscriptions, and other ritual tokens.[19] It would have been impractical to prevent all personal gestures of veneration at temples or shrines, short of shutting or destroying them — which was left to a later period. Private houses increasingly became the locations of pagan worship, just as they had once been for Christian. Sincere pagans such as Symmachus and Libanius, after all, believed that the gods required incense, libations and other offerings, and would hardly abandon these rituals provided they could be enacted discreetly.[20]

Nonetheless, it was a bitter blow to the aristocratic pagan circles in Italy, who so recently had experienced the seemingly tolerant urbanities of Theodosius, and who had, in their confidence, in the last two decades attempted a conscious revival of pagan thought and worship. The leaders of the movement, later idealised in the dialogues of Macrobius' *Saturnalia*, included Vettius Agorius Praetextatus,[21], Symmachus, Nicomachus Flavianus, Rufius Albinus[22] and the philosopher Eustathius.[23] Numerous inscriptions up to the year 390 at the shrine near the Vatican, the Phrygianum, record priesthoods to the official state cults as well as to Magna Mater, Mithras, Sol, Hecate, Liber and Isis. All this was now under threat.[24]

In the countryside very little changed immediately, especially if there was no strong clerical presence in the area. Shrines were maintained, temples visited. In Britain there are examples of Romano-Celtic temples being built as late as the 380s: at Maiden Castle in Dorset, Lydney in Gloucestershire and others. Convivial gatherings or 'festivals', while avoiding the technical illegalities of sacrifice, easily became occasions for religious ceremonies. Nor was this necessarily a conscious avoidance of the law: traditional rituals so pervaded the activities of everyday life, urban and rural, that it was most natural for them to continue, even if in an attenuated form.

At Alexandria the message of the third edict was read only too clearly, and prompted a new campaign of temple-smashing led by the bishop Theophilus. Its central target was the great temple of Serapis, the powerful Graeco-Egyptian sky god who combined the attributes of Zeus and Osiris, and on whose favour the Nile flood depended: until recently it had contained the ceremonial Nile Cubit, measuring the annual rise. The temple was generally recognised as one of the architectural wonders of the world, as Ammianus relates:

> ...Feeble words can only belittle it, but it is adorned with such vast columned halls, statues so lifelike they almost breathe, and so many other works of art, that second only to the Capitol, by which Rome raises herself to eternity, the world contains nothing more magnificent.[25]

Its central effigy was a colossal statue of the god which had originally been transported there from Sinope by Ptolemy I some six centuries earlier.

After some minor provocation rioting broke out among rival pagan and Christian mobs, as rioting so very easily did at Alexandria. The pagans were besieged within the great temple, where they butchered some of their Christian hostages. During a truce in the disorders advice was allegedly sought from Theodosius himself. His reply, according to the Christian historian Rufinus,[26] was in delphic tones: the slain, he says, are holy martyrs; their murderers should be spared, but the offending cause of discord — the worship of images — should be completely removed. This was eagerly taken as permission for destruction, and the Christians, led by their bishop, Theophilus, the Prefect, Evagrius, and the military, set to work with a will.

Rufinus claims that even then some hesitated to attack the great statue of the god, for fear of some terrible divine retribution. Then bishop Theophilus himself allegedly struck the first blow, and no such consequence followed. The statue was then smashed, and the mob went on to pull down the temple itself, or as much of it as they could. As often elsewhere, their demolition techniques were not fully equal to such a task. Where they failed in demolition, relates Eunapius bitterly, they made up for it in smashing and looting precious objects, and would have removed the floor too if the flagstones had not been too heavy.[27] This was all a far cry from the earlier ruling of Theodosius that pagan temples and statues should be preserved as secular buildings and works of art. Reportedly the pagans were dejected and the Christians jubilant when the Nile rose again in the normal way.

Attached to the temple was a great library, one of the finest in the world. It seems to have survived as a building, but the fate of its many thousands of volumes is unknown, presumed destroyed. Perhaps there is little point in speculating how incomparably richer we might be if they had survived. Libanius pleaded:

> Temples are the very soul of the countryside. They mark the very beginning of a settlement, and have passed down through countless generations to the present one. In them are placed all the hopes of a rural community — for husbands and wives, for children, for their animals, for the soil they sow and plant. An estate robbed of its temple has forfeited the hope and confidence of its peasants, who believe all their labour will now be fruitless without the god to prosper it.[28]

He was pleading increasingly in vain. Temples had been attacked or destroyed at Petraea, Areopolis, Canopus, Heliopolis, Gaza and elsewhere without any imperial disapproval. In Gaul a similar campaign of purification was begun by Martin of Tours.[29] The episode of the Serapaeum was rightly seen by both sides as an important milestone. After a decade of uneasy toleration, or at least truce, paganism was again in ragged retreat in the central regions of the empire. Certainly it still had many representatives in the cultured governing classes, where pagan opinion was not penalised, nor pagan aristocrats as yet disadvantaged in public appointments: both Theodosius' most powerful Prefects for 391 in East and West were pagans.[30]

Emperors could ill afford such discrimination at this time, even had they wished. Intellectual culture was quite inseparable from pagan and Hellenic tradition: the only education available was a classical one, based in pagan myth and history, and its best teachers were usually pagans. Not only Christian aristocrats but great churchmen such as John Chrysostom and Gregory of Nazianzus, were taught by pagan rhetors. The great noble families may have been divided between Christianity and paganism, but this difference was far smaller than the powerful common social links that united them as a class and an order, and it would have been most imprudent for Theodosius or any other emperor to try to drive a religious wedge between them.

Pagans in influential circles such as Symmachus, or even in the highest positions such as the Prefects Flavianus or Tatianus or Albinus, could not automatically protect the shrines, temples and cults among the wider population that were suffering violence. They could personally delay or thwart the enforcement of the laws, and protect individuals against prosecution or injustice, but in the longer run they were powerless against determined, organised mob vandalism by bishops and monks who knew they had the tacit approval of the emperor himself.

The fourth law, of 8 November 392, was totally uncompromising.[31] In its assault on vernacular traditions it was as if today an authoritarian atheist regime were to criminalise Easter eggs, holly, Christmas cards, Halloween pumpkins, first-footings, and even such universal gestures as the drinking of toasts.

The law declared all sacrifice and divination, by whoever of whatever rank or order, for whatever purpose, punishable by death. Every other identifiable pagan symbol, item or expression was now prohibited. The house in which they occurred was to be confiscated; decurions were ordered to inform and governors ordered to investigate each case on pain of crushing fines. Altars, votive offerings, libations, burning lamps, the simple domestic gods of the hearth and the kitchen, hanging wreaths or garlands, placing fillets on trees — all were now forbidden, anathematised as the filthy pollution of evil spirits, instead of the harmless social customs they very largely were. In this global ideological war of Light against Darkness there were no 'harmless' practices. Ambrose, of course, exults in this extirpation, which he ranks among Theodosius' great achievements:

> ...Theodosius who, after the example of Jacob, supplanted perfidious tyrants and banished the idols of the gentiles; who in his faith wiped out all worship of graven images, and trampled down their ceremonies.[32]

As Gibbon remarks, all this was the more ironical in view of the complacent ease with which, very soon, the bishops adopted and renamed local gods as saints, shrines as reliquaries, rustic festivals as feast-days, without too much painful soul-searching.[33]

The point was, as always, the gulf of radical incomprehension between the spirit of the Old and New Testaments and the spirit of Homer and the Olympians. As Tertullian arrogantly demanded, 'What has Athens to do with Jerusalem?' Pagan traditions were accommodating and flexible, could accept new deities — including Christ — and allow for shifts of identity. If Apollo merged with Helios, Baal with Jupiter, Tanit with Juno, this was undisturbing, for the gods had many roles in heavenly and human society, down to the localised protective deities. From that perspective, the gradual assimilation of these spirits to saints with similar attributes could be accepted smoothly and without great upheaval in the rhythms of life. But the exclusive worship of the omnipotent and jealous God of Abraham demanded unconditional war on these heathen practices, not just an easy extension of various godly names and attributes. At least officially, Christianity thus had to disown and deny the many missionary compromises which were obviously and naturally taking place.

It is of course quite wrong to think of paganism as if it were a coherent religious movement in any way symmetrical with Christianity. On the contrary, it had no such disciplined church organisation, no such doctrinal and scriptural base of authority. Its roots and strengths were ancient, cultural, traditional, customary and eclectic. The last serious attempt to reverse the tide of militant Christianity, by the short-lived but vigorous emperor Julian, had been a disappointment. Even his friend and devoted admirer Libanius had realised this. Julian had sought to dragoon the 'Hellenic' cults into some kind of rival campaigning and proselytising organisation, and failed. The unified, messianic, intolerant and fasting or fighting religions of the Judaeo-Christian-Manichean-Islamic mould were a quite distinct and novel development (if anything in religion can be novel), and paganism, for all its fears, could not model itself on its enemy.

Faced with the combined force of emperors, laws and militant clericalism, outraged pagan traditionalism could not organise the kind of resistance Christianity had done to the Diocletian persecutions. Membership of the body of Christ had counted more than Roman citizenship and status for most of the persecuted church, but to the still mainly pagan upper classes under the Theodosian screw there could be no such distinction: their social standing and family identity was inseparable from their religious traditions. As Libanius makes plain, they could not with clear conscience resist constitutionally established law, however much they personally resented it.[34] Theodosius, however, was moving logically towards a position where for the great mass of the population (pagan upper classes gracefully excepted) membership of the Catholic Christian church was almost coextensive with Roman citizenship.

However, the last anti-pagan law of 392, issued from Constantinople when there was already a grave crisis of a difference kind in the West, precipitated an untypical, perhaps despairing reaction. It has been depicted and celebrated by many historians as the Last Stand of Roman Paganism, and even been cast in similar tragic mould to the noble death-throes of the Roman Republic.[35]

Theodosius' settlement in the West was an improvisation, as it had been since the overthrow of Gratian. He was sole ruler of the empire at a time when strong imperial colleagues in its two halves were needed more than ever. He and his ministers had plenty of opportunity to reflect ruefully on the grave handicap of immature rulers. Arcadius was fourteen, Honorius seven, and Valentinian, who expected to rule in his own right after the crushing of Maximus, still only twenty.

It is easy to see that the position was unstable and dangerous, less easy to see what else Theodosius might have done after 388. Having disposed of Maximus he was left with an embarrassing power vacuum. He ruled from his own court at Milan for three years, decided the legitimate succession and put his most trusted nominees in the key positions in Italy and Gaul,[36] but this was still less than a real Western *imperium* — less in fact than Maximus had constituted. Conceivably, Theodosius might have dropped Valentinian altogether and adopted as emperor a powerful military colleague from outside his own family, just as he had been raised up by Gratian in the emergencies of 379.

This had been done before: Diocletian, who had no son, had even tried to make a regular system out of it. With the wisdom of hindsight into the disastrous reigns of boy-emperors manipulated by others all this might have been a risk worth taking, but Theodosius was no constitutional innovator. His own strong family loyalties, and the naturally expected dynastic ambitions of every emperor and usurper since Constantine, excluded such possibilities. Whatever the disadvantages — and they were obvious —

dynastic succession was recognised as the primary rule of orderly transfer.[37]

It was unavoidable that the restored Valentinian should remain a nominal emperor (a fact signalled by subtle conventions on the coinage). He had received no military apprenticeship (unlike Gratian), and at Milan had been little more than a cipher of the conflicting elements of the Court — Justina, Ambrose, the Prefect Petronius Probus and his successors, and generals. His headlong flight in the face of Maximus, however understandable, had done nothing at all for his public prestige. He remained decidedly a minor in action and in public perception. The new arrangement in Trier was a simple *de facto* regency which firmly excluded rival influences: Justina had died,[38] and Ambrose remained at Milan. Flavius Arbogastes, of Frankish origin, was a first-class military commander with a fine record, very popular with the army and wholly loyal to the houses of Valentinian and Theodosius. He had served as *comes* under Gratian, assisted Theodosius in his Gothic campaigns, succeeded Bauto as *Magister Militum* at Milan after 383, and recently taken a leading part in Theodosius' war against Maximus, capturing him and despatching his son Victor.[39]

Arbogast's titular position was *Magister Militum in Praesenti*, that is, commander of the armies in attendance on the emperor. Unlike the corresponding position in the East, where there were five equal *magistri*, he had no military peer to counterbalance him, even in Italy: he controlled under his own command virtually all the effective military force in the West, except for Africa.[40] He soon established his position as undisputed ruler of Gaul, Spain and Britain in the legal name of Valentinian, but actually subordinate only to Theodosius.

This was the clearly understood relationship and Arbogast grasped it confidently and fully, placing his own nominees in key posts in the government and issuing instructions to Valentinian's officials. He campaigned successfully on the Rhine frontier (against his own Frankish kinsmen), imposed a favourable peace on the defeated enemy and restored the strategic fortress city of Cologne — the last time a Roman army would ever occupy the east bank of the Rhine.[41] Yet, within a short time of his regency, there occurred a new political crisis with all the symptoms of blunder, misunderstanding and accident which now bedevilled communication between the two halves of the empire. It was to lead to another incalculably costly civil war between East and West which, on the evidence we have, appears as tragically unnecessary.

The problem which Arbogast mishandled was Valentinian himself, who was becoming restive in his gilded cage. Such princes have to be reassured, flattered, humoured, encouraged. Born in the purple, he had been continually tricked out of his imperial birthright: deposed by Maximus, sold short by Theodosius, and now blatantly ordered about by one of his own ministers. At this age his brother Gratian had been commanding armies in battle, whereas he was still being treated as a child. Allegedly, he sent urgent and pathetic messages to Theodosius and Ambrose for their help.

It was obviously in Arbogast's interest to placate and manage the young prince, but this was becoming difficult, perhaps even impossible. Possibly Arbogast, a barbarian, had not the skills or qualifications for this delicate task. Trust between them had disappeared. Perhaps by now Valentinian would be satisifed with nothing less than full imperial power, which meant his own appointees replacing those of Arbogast. The opportunity for a smooth power-sharing, which might have allowed Valentinian some palpable authority without wrecking the whole alliance, seems to have been missed. Things had gone beyond that stage when, according to Zosimus, there was a public confrontation between them at Vienne. From the throne Valentinian handed Arbogast a letter of his own dismissal, but the general retorted that Valentinian had not bestowed on him this command, and could not therefore deprive him of it.[42] This was indeed the true political position, but it caused a crisis by being displayed in this naked fashion. Valentinian was worsted, humiliated, powerless and friendless. Shortly afterward, on 15 May 392, he was found hanged in his quarters. Arbogast claimed it was suicide.[43]

A great deal of modern argument has gone on around this event, which has become one of history's murder mysteries. The textual accounts are conflicting and inconclusive, but the known events and circumstances of the case make murder problematic at least. Gibbon, following Zosimus, assumes a conspiracy: 'Whilst he was universally esteemed as the pillar of the state, the bold and crafty barbarian was determined to rule, or to ruin, the Empire of the West.'[44]

Against this, Arbogast already effectively ruled the north-west with the full approval of Theodosius, and his predominant military influence spread to Italy too. As a Frank he could not aspire to the purple himself, and thus it could not be in his interest for Valentinian to be removed, even by an impeccably natural death. True, the youth was intractable, but nonetheless all power was securely in Arbogast's hands, and even keeping Valentinian isolated was preferable to having him die. Unless he contemplated from the outset a break with Theodosius and probable civil war, Arbogast could have no assurance that any new arrangement would be more favourable.

If he did contemplate war from the outset he went about it in a very strange way indeed. It was four months before he finally adopted a new imperial candidate, and almost a year before he extended his power into Italy. This was quite unlike the premeditated, lightning revolt of Maximus. If Arbogast had intended to disguise his murder of Valentinian, perhaps in the hope that Theodosius would accept the situation, then a subtler ending such as poison or contrived accident would surely have been appropriate.

As it was, Arbogast continued to protest his innocence and loyalty, issuing coinage in the names of Theodosius and Arcadius.[45] The body of Valentinian was conveyed with due ceremony to Milan where, amid the lamentations of the dead youth's sisters Julia and Grata, Ambrose pronounced a funeral oration which could be taken to suggest foul play.[46] At the court of

Theodosius the news of the supposed suicide created a bad impression, as well it might. The version of events may easily have altered on its way to Constantinople. Perhaps under the influence of Galla[47] Theodosius was sceptical, but for months he did and said nothing, possibly genuinely uncertain of the situation.

In the East a poisonous power struggle was going on in which Tatianus, the Praetorian Prefect of the East, and his son Proculus, Urban Prefect of Constantinople, were arraigned on fabricated criminal charges through the machinations of the Master of Offices, Rufinus. He had come to acquire a considerable influence with Theodosius, which rightly alarmed many others at Court as he used it ruthlessly to further his own ambitions. Already he had won a confrontation in the Consistory with the general Promotus, which had ended by Promotus being removed from Court by Theodosius' order.[48] Now, by manipulating judges and witnesses and relying on the almost uncritical confidence Theodosius placed in him, he secured the exile of Tatianus and the execution of his son. He promptly succeeded him as the new Praetorian Prefect of the East, which post he retained until after Theodosius' death, when he met his bloody nemesis.

Rufinus stands out in all our sources as cruel, avaricious, domineering and voracious for personal power to an exceptional degree, even by the debased political standards of his own time. Extremely energetic, and a resourceful administrator with a tireless capacity for detail (as well as a zealous Catholic), he obviously presented himself as a pillar of support for Theodosius who needed just such qualities in his ministers. The emperor has been reproached on many sides for his trust in Rufinus, who was suspected of encouraging him to the Salonica massacre.[49] Zosimus portrays Theodosius as being at his best in wars and emergencies, but casual and relaxed to the point of lethargy over the routine mechanics of government: as soon as the war is over and the enemies crushed or conciliated, Theodosius abandons all the wearisome tasks and decisions to others, and retires into his luxurious palace as the benign father of his extensive family and friends.[50]

This is no doubt caricature, but perhaps not beyond contemporary recognition. Theodosius was a warm and emotional character, prone to remarkable swings of mood which directly affected his public decisions. He was open to influence by other powerful personalities such as Ambrose, so long as they kept in his presence. He did not show the driving determination to control everything, and supervise it in detail and in person, which we see in other great military emperors such as Julian and Valentinian.

It was perhaps these traits that Rufinus was able to turn to his advantage. As Praetorian Prefect he was now in the most powerful position of being able to influence or directly manage all politically important judicial cases, and filter the myriad channels of information reaching the emperor, at whose side he took care to be. He became unquestionably dominant after 392, courted, hated and feared throughout the government of the East.

In these circumstances it is perhaps not surprising if Arbogast received

1 The missorium of Theodosius, dating probably from 388. He is flanked by
Arcadius and Valentinian II, and his Germanic soldiers. Below is Tellus, the eternally
fertile Earth.

2–3 *Left:* The obelisk of Theodosius in the Hippodrome at Constantinople, erected in 390 by the City Prefect, Proculus.

2 *Top:* Theodosius, flanked by Arcadius, Valentinian II and Honorius, receives the tribute of the Persians and Dacians.

3 *Bottom:* Theodosius, from the Imperial box, presides over the chariot races.

4 Coin of Valens, Emperor in the East, who was killed in the disastrous Battle of Adrianople in 378. The reverse shows him with his powerful and protective brother – emperor Valentinian I. (All imperial coin portraits at this time are idealised icons, rather than naturalistic portraits.)

5 Coin of Gratian, Emperor in the West, son of Valentinian I. The reverse shows him still as *Princeps Iuventutis*, overshadowed by his powerful father.

6 Coin of Theodosius. The reverse shows the personified deity of Constantinople, helmeted, with spear and shield.

7 Coin of Magnus Maximus, overthrown by Theodosius in 388. The reverse shows two brother-emperors, indicating that Maximus was seeking recognition by Theodosius. The coin was probably minted in London (then named *Augusta*).

8 Bishop Ambrose of Milan, the foremost churchman of his age, and a powerful influence on Theodosius.

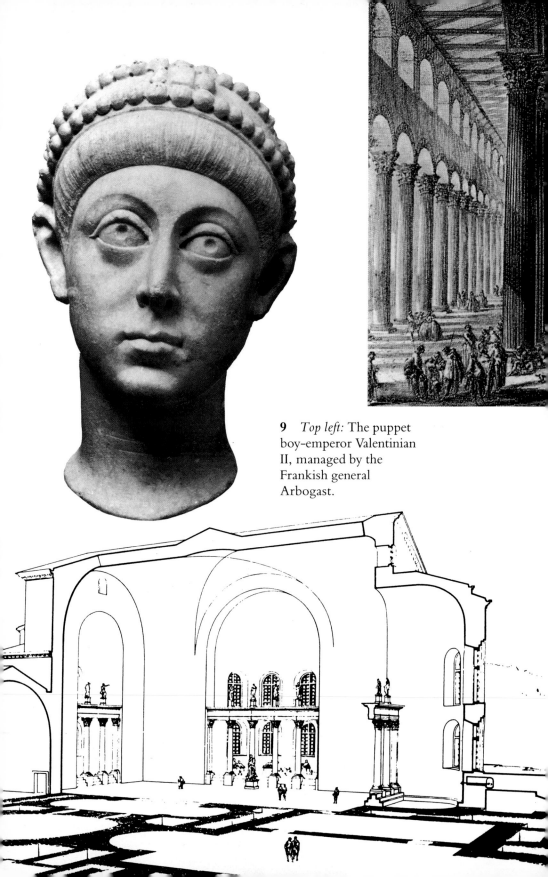

9 *Top left:* The puppet boy-emperor Valentinian II, managed by the Frankish general Arbogast.

10 *Left:* Reconstruction of the Imperial baths at Trier, the Western capital of Gratian and Valentinian II.

11 *Above:* The basilica of St Paul in Rome, partly rebuilt by Theodosius. A drawing by Piranesi.

12 *Right:* The sarcophagus of Junius Bassus, showing Christian themes rendered entirely in Hellenic style. Above, Christ between Peter and Paul; below, his entry into Jerusalem.

13 *Above left:* Pagan aristocratic art. In this ivory of the Symmachi, a priestess offers incense at an altar of Jupiter. It probably celebrated the wedding alliance between Symmachus and Flavianus.

14 *Above right:* Emperor Honorius, during whose reign the Western empire was dismembered.

15 *Right:* Flavius Stilicho, the 'barbarian' son-in-law of Theodosius and the protector of Honorius. His efforts to hold the West together ultimately failed. On his shield are the images of the boy emperors Honorius and Arcadius.

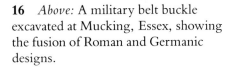

16 *Above:* A military belt buckle excavated at Mucking, Essex, showing the fusion of Roman and Germanic designs.

17 *Below:* Gemstone of Alaric, the 'allied' Visigothic king, who disrupted the empire and sacked Rome in 410.

18 The end of Roman Britain. This rich coin hoard from Hoxne, Suffolk, includes thousands of gold *solidi* of Honorius, which the owner never returned to unearth.

19 Reconstruction and photograph of the great land walls of Constantinople, built by the Prefect Anthemius in the early fifth century. They resisted all sieges and assaults until 1204.

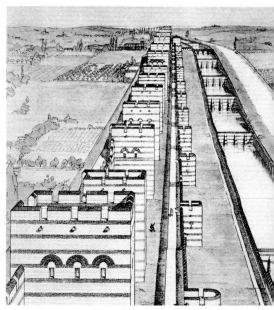

little clear response from Constantinople, and soon felt that his channels of communication with Theodosius were being obscured or frustrated. This left him in an untenable position. As ruler of the Gallic provinces, with the full support of the armies, he had to carry on the government yet at the same time avoid giving any suggestion that he was edging himself into the imperial position. He could not, of course, issue valid instructions, edicts or rescripts in his own name, only that of a legitimately acclaimed emperor. In the absence of a definite command or signal from Theodosius, and aware that his own authority could not be suspended indefinitely, Arbogast finally took the next logical step, irrevocable but not yet necessarily bellicose. On 22 August 392, he had a new Western emperor, Flavius Eugenius, officially proclaimed at Lyons.[51] This was still not legally treason, for there was no Augustus in the West. Almost immediately Eugenius sent a peaceful and fraternal embassy to Theodosius.

Eugenius seems at first sight a strange choice. A second-rank civil official, formerly a teacher of rhetoric, he had the qualifications of classical culture, but little of the standing of the great senatorial dignitaries with their prefectures and consulships. Arbogast's uncle, Richomer,[52] had introduced him to imperial circles, and he had come to the court of Valentinian II as *Magister Scriniorum*, Chief Secretary to the emperor. He was a Christian, but of a moderate kind and not likely to alienate potential pagan supporters.

His elevation signalled at least two things: that Arbogast remained firmly in real power, with Eugenius his civilian partner; but also that the regime was no barbarian army coup but legitimate, legal, Roman and civilised, deserving the serious support of the senatorial aristocracy. Arbogast himself being a pagan, Eugenius' Christianity might also have been a useful conciliatory flag to Theodosius, and especially to Ambrose at Milan, with whom Eugenius was acquainted. How willing Eugenius was to accept this dangerous honour we do not know: Zosimus claims he was distinctly reluctant. Probably he was out of his depth and had little real choice, but Arbogast protected and trusted him, and the two were now bound together in a common fate.

At least two distinct embassies went from Eugenius to Theodosius, one composed of Christian clergy: at this stage Eugenius had not broken with Ambrose. Both sought accommodation and friendship, and both were firmly and legally in the name of Eugenius Augustus, without mention of Arbogast. Both received ambivalent replies, and were sent away without achieving their purpose. Eugenius' coinage continued to recognise Theodosius and Arcadius, and in Western titulature he officially shared with Theodosius the consulship for 393 — a gesture that was pointedly not reciprocated by Theodosius, who shared the consulship with his general Abundantius.[53] Then in January he gave the clearest signal of repudiation by raising his younger son Honorius to the rank of full Augustus, implying the illegality of Eugenius.

Though the messages were now at last clear, the mutual appraisal of intentions up to this point seems to have been anything but. Theodosius had tolerated, or at least coexisted with, Maximus, an open murderer and usurper, for three years. Then why not with Arbogast, who was claiming nothing more than he did not legitimately have, and was vigorously defending the Rhine frontier in their common interest? In all this ungainly drift towards war it is difficult not to see, as a contributory cause, Theodosius' uninterest or at least vagueness towards the north-west, despite his own Spanish origins. All the mistakes and omissions of the Maximus revolt seem to be glaringly repeated. Had Theodosius believed Argobast's innocence, or merely wanted to temporise, he could easily have confirmed his general's *de facto* rule of the north-west in his own imperial name, or that of his son: this would have bestowed nothing that could not be rescinded, and prevented Arbogast seizing any greater power without declaring rebellion.

If Theodosius believed Arbogast aimed at dominating all of the West, then his apparent failure to do anything to buttress the position in Italy — which at the time had subordinate military status and fewer available troops — is almost incomprehensible after the events of the Maximus revolt. Of course, there are many elements and complications to the situation that we shall never know. Did Rufinus distort Theodosius' judgement, and if so, how and why? Did Theodosius actually suspect that Arbogast, whom he knew so well, was ultimately aiming at the purple himself? Was he perhaps genuinely undecided or misled in the early months, then saw the elevation of Eugenius as the irrevocable challenge to his dynasty? The last thing Theodosius can have wanted was yet another hazardous and enormously costly civil war if it could be avoided: and all the evidence that has come to us suggests that it was indeed avoidable, at least for the immediate future, whatever Arbogast's intentions.

By spring 393 the breach between Trier and Constantinople was complete, and in April Arbogast and Eugenius at last moved into Italy without resistance. Of the major political figures only Ambrose left Milan, for Bologna. At Rome, especially, pagan senatorial opinion was reeling from the shock of the ferocious edict of November 392, which left them nothing at all of their traditional symbolism, public or private. Aware that Arbogast was a pagan, they had nothing to lose from a regime which could not in any case be resisted militarily. Needing their support the regime responded, though cautiously at first. Ever hopeful, the senatorial pagan party in 391 had yet again petitioned Valentinian II (unsuccessfully) for the restoration of their cherished Altar of Victory, and now they petitioned Eugenius. After two refusals he finally agreed to the restoration, and other concessions followed. Although he did not formally restore state support for the official cults he provided private funds to revive the ceremonies.[54]

It was only with Eugenius' reappointment of Nicomachus Flavianus as Praetorian Prefect of Italy, that this cautious toleration became a full-blooded pagan revival, which swept Eugenius along with it. As the spiritual leader of the pagan cause since the death of Praetextatus, Flavianus' obligations and loyalty towards Theodosius — which he had expressed by dedicating a work of history to him — had been strained to breaking point. Disgusted by the grovelling abasement of an emperor before the bishop of Milan, alarmed and offended by the anti-pagan laws which he himself was expected to enforce, he was now asked to cooperate in nothing less than the total extinction of his ancestral religion. No wonder he grasped this new lifeline eagerly. Though not by nature militant, paganism was goaded into active defiance of Theodosius. It attached itself to the open political rebellion, whose emblems were now taken over by those of the old gods.[55]

Under the vigorous leadership of Flavianus (and perhaps the embarrassment of Eugenius) temples were rapidly restored and rededicated, festivals punctually celebrated, sacrifices correctly performed and the mystery cults revived. Flavianus himself was involved in the cults of Vesta, Sol, Mithras, Hecate, Isis, Serapis and others. His own son, Nicomachus the younger, became Prefect of Rome and rededicated a temple to Venus. At Ostia the temple of Hercules was rebuilt. The tradition continued of dedicatory gifts carrying strong pagan propaganda themes: for one's social peers, the fine ivory diptych styles with classical gods; for wider circulation, including the crowds at the games, were the many medallions celebrating pagan emperors, gods, heroes and classical mythology. Through these and other devices the regime came to be associated with the 'senatorial' cause, which in turn was portrayed as almost synonymous with paganism.

The celebrations and games reached their height at Rome in the spring of 394, actively directed by Flavianus. The festival of Attis was celebrated in March, with the god's sacred pine trunk being dragged into the City. This was shortly followed by that of Cybele, whose sacred effigy entered Rome in a chariot drawn by lions, Flavianus holding the silver reins. The festival of Flora and the Megalensian Games followed. It was many years since Rome had seen such religious spectacles.[56]

Of the principal pagan leaders, only Symmachus adroitly distanced himself from the regime, having burnt his fingers once with Maximus. He continued his polite, social contacts with Eugenius, and especially Flavianus, even to the extent of uniting their families by the marriage of his daughter to the younger Nicomachus, celebrated in the famous ivory diptych showing priestesses of Magna Mater, Liber Pater and Jupiter. Ambrose of course fled the whole horrid scene, and addressed reproachful letters to Eugenius from Faventia. His charge is not Eugenius' political treason but his apostasy as a Christian, especially in the charged matter of the Altar of Victory. Indeed, he addresses him by his imperial title:

> Even if imperial power is great, consider how great is God...Was it not your duty, Augustus, to refuse what was so injurious to Holy Law?...I had to look to my own welfare, since I could not look to yours.[57]

Thus Ambrose both explains and excuses his absence from his See, without laying himself open to treasonable charges from either side. As with

Symmachus, such was the delicate political etiquette among the civilian aristocracy that he ran no real risk by merely acknowledging the 'rebel' emperor, so long as he avoided active and gratuitous support.

Through early 394 both sides prepared for war. Arbogast concentrated his armies from all over Gaul and Italy, while Nicomachus appointed new officials to Africa to ensure the corn supply to Rome. In the event, this was not endangered. In Africa, Gildo, Theodosius' appointee, was now promoted by him to *Magister Utriusque*, of similar status to Arbogast. He was loyal to Constantinople, and could have blockaded Rome if commanded, but Theodosius planned a land invasion through Illyricum as before and an interruption in supplies to Rome would have done little good. Theodosius appointed as *magistri* in charge of the campaign Timasius and Stilicho (Richomer having died shortly before), and in subordinate commands the Goth Gainas, the Alan Saul and the Iberian Bacurius.[58] The proportion of Germanic troops was very large, especially from the Visigothic *foederati* serving under the 382 treaty, and led by their chieftain Alaric;[59] there was also a sizeable Alanic and Hunnic contingent.

Since Eugenius' open celebrations of paganism Theodosius had no difficulties (in contrast to the Maximus revolt) in seeing this as a Holy War, and enlisting the full armoury of fasting, prayer and ceremonies of supplication, the Christian counterpart of Flavius' festivals in Italy. As he had once before, he piously sought the prophetic advice of the holy hermit John of Lycopolis, who had dwelt fifty years in a remote mountain cell in Thebais.[60] John's prophecy was double-edged: that Theodosius would be victorious after great slaughter, but that he would die in Italy. Theodosius now received a more concrete blow to his spirits (whether or not seen as a sign) when on the very eve of the war his young wife Galla died in childbirth, together with the baby. For one as warmly emotional and devoted to his family as we know him to have been, the wound must have been cruel indeed, but we are told he followed the Homeric rule and allowed himself one day's mourning, then marched off to the war. The Prefect Rufinus remained at Constantinople with the boy-emperor Arcadius.

Arbogast, with the imperial figurehead Eugenius, concentrated his forces at Milan. He was joined there by Flavianus, who had consulted all the sacred entrails, which proved favourable. Pagan morale was also raised by the publication of an oracle explaining the advent of the 'Great Year' at the end of each mystical cycle of 365 years, when measured human destiny enters a new epoch. Calculating from AD 29 this brought matters neatly to 394, and clearly signalled an end to the term of Christianity.[61] As he travelled off Flavianus boasted that on his victorious return he would draft monks into the army and turn the holy churches of Ambrose into stables.[62]

For all the uprush of fervour and oracles, it was not realistically possible for Flavianus and his allies to undo the Christian change to any great extent. This was not an attempted pagan counter-revolution, but merely a defiant gesture of aristocratic traditionalism which had been lucky enough to find a political vehicle. Even had Arbogast's army won (which it very nearly did), the very most that could have been hoped for was toleration for pagan practices and support for the state cults (which had been the position even under Constantine). The established organisation of the Christian Church could not now be abolished, and even the most zealous pagan emperor would have been mad to try. Arbogast, who had many Christians in his army, was fighting to survive and rule — not to stable his cavalry in the nave of Milan cathedral.

Since both sides were so strongly affected by signs and prophecies the victors, in the shape of Christian writers such as Ambrose, Paulinus, Rufinus, Augustine, Theodoret and others, have readily given the conflict more religious significance than it perhaps deserved, seeing the war as the final, unarguable decision between the old gods and the new. Thus it is Christian accounts which depict the forces of the West as the last Roman army to march under the twin images of Jupiter with golden thunderbolts and his invincible son Hercules.

TRIUMPH AND DEATH

By rapid marches Theodosius' army reached and occupied the westernmost Alpine passes on the road to Aquileia by early September. From the vantage point of his camp he could overlook the plain below. There, with their rear to the river Frigidus, was Arbogast's army, drawn up in a strongly entrenched position with the standard of Jove overlooking their camp. Their lines extended to face across the mouth of the pass, and they had already occupied the critical high points so that Theodosius would have no room for flanking movements.[1]

On the afternoon of 5 September 394 Theodosius launched a frontal assault, with the Visigothic troops in the vanguard. Yet, after the fiercest fighting in which very great numbers were killed — including the general Bacurius — they failed to break Arbogast's lines; at nightfall they retreated, mauled, from the field. They left so many Gothic dead that it created a legacy of bitterness among the federate allies, who felt, not unreasonably, that their blood was more expendable than that of the Romans.[2]

Eugenius considered the battle all but won, and the mood spread among his troops. Arbogast detached a substantial force[3] to carry out a concealed movement across the passes to take Theodosius in the rear. In Theodosius' camp, we are told, the mood was one of near-despair, and the emperor spent much of the night in prayer to the God who seemed to have deserted him. Theodoret claims he was visited by two heavenly riders all in white, Saint John and Saint Philip, who bade him take courage.[4] More materially, the force sent to outflank the Eastern army instead signalled their readiness to desert Arbogast for a large financial consideration, which was naturally agreed instantly. Next day, the assault was renewed.

Despite Theodosius' new advantage the bitter fighting was indecisive, until the appearance of a quite unexpected natural phenomenon. In this region, there can arise an unusual pressure effect on the cold air coming from the mountains, which produces cyclonic winds of over 60 mph. Known as the 'Bora', this wind now blew across the battlefield directly against Arbogast's line, pressing against their shields, blowing dust into faces and deflecting missiles back against their own line; it forced their opponents on top of them, their formation was disrupted and finally they broke.

Their fortified camp was stormed, and Eugenius captured in person. As the broken army fled or hastily surrendered Arbogast escaped to the mountains. Eugenius pleaded for mercy but was quickly executed, and his head impaled on a spear for travelling exhibition. After some days of wandering in the mountains Arbogast realised the hopelessness of the situation, and slew himself in noble Roman fashion.[5] On learning the news Nicomachus Flavianus, faced with the devastating failure of all his gods and his cause, did the same.

Theodosius again entered Italy without opposition. Again — remarkably — he showed considerable clemency towards those who had quite openly been aligned against him. Nicomachus Flavianus the younger, former Prefect of the City, escaped serious retribution after the intercession of his father-in-law, Symmachus.[6] Others were forgiven but, it is suggested, on condition they became Christians.[7] Ambrose, who had returned to Milan almost as soon as Eugenius had departed for the war, recommended mercy to former enemies in letters to the emperor, and then travelled to welcome him at Aquileia in person (he also immediately defended his own actions in leaving Milan during the rule of Eugenius).[8] Theodosius for his part acknowledged the contribution of Ambrose's prayers to the victory and, instead of building a triumphal arch in pagan fashion, ordered a solemn service of thanksgiving by the clergy.

The moral impact of the Frigidus, with the miraculous intervention of the Divine Wind, was very damaging to paganism. Both sides had seen this battle as a contest between their respective gods, and the decision was unequivocal. Educated pagans, such as Claudian, acknowledged divine intervention on the Christian side, and Christian tradition naturally celebrated the great miracle thereafter.

Eugenius' policy — of religious toleration, but with a bias in favour of paganism — was cancelled, and all anti-pagan laws which had been promulgated were enforced in so far as this was possible in the West. However, despite the great blow to its prestige, paganism did not immediately collapse with a spate of mass conversions, as some of its opponents have claimed. Among the mass population of the countryside the church and state had a free hand to suppress (or re-christen) the local gods, ceremonies and temples; a process which took a generation or more. Under the influence of John Chrysostom the destruction of temples in the countryside was ordered in 399, although the more important public temples were often converted into churches or other, secular public buildings. Yet, as late as 435, we find emperors still reiterating the prohibition on sacrifice, and the instructions to destroy or convert pagan places of worship.

The Christianisation of the older Roman aristocracy was a very gradual, incomplete and civilised process, without overt imperial coercion. As always, the state made a clear distinction between the rustic or plebeian and the gentleman; between pagan worship and polite pagan opinion. The only hint of anything approaching the fierce medieval attitude is in a chilling letter of Ambrose to his friend, Pisidinius Romulus, in which he justifies the massacre in Exodus in barely coded terms, to suggest that the extermination of all pagans would likewise be justified; but his was never an acceptable political opinion, and Ambrose knew this very well.

There is a bogus story, related by both the Christian polemicist, Prudentius, and the pagan historian, Zosimus, that Theodosius, after his victory at the Frigidus, travelled to Rome and there convened a full meeting of the senate; at this meeting he put to the senators the question: should the worship of Christ or Jupiter be the state religion? According to Prudentius they voted decisively for Christ:

> The luminaries of the world, the ancient and revered assembly of Catos, eagerly cast off their pontiff's togas like the skin of the old serpent, and put on the white robe of baptismal innocence, humbling the consular fasces before the tombs of the martyrs.

Zosimus states, to the contrary, that:

> Not one obeyed his summons, nor chose to abandon those ancestral rites handed down since the foundation of the City.... By observing those rites they had possessed a City that was unconquered for nearly twelve hundred years, and they could not imagine what might befall it if they now changed their religion.

No such meeting took place. The propaganda of Prudentius, writing only a few years after the alleged event, seems to be an attempt to show that an official change in the state religion had been decided and endorsed with the utmost constitutional legality. It can only have been aimed at the politically unsophisticated. Apart from the ending of the state cults, the progress of Christianity among the senatorial nobility of Rome was not, and could not have been, the result of any legislation. It required gradual and subtle compromise between the spirit of Christianity and classical culture — in effect, the Gospels rendered into Virgilian hexameters. We see this compromise again and again in the monumental art of the aristocracy — the sarcophagus of Junius Bassus, or the mosaic art of Christ as a Helios figure in the Mausoleum of the Julii, or even the frescoes in the Via Latina where scenes from the Bible and from pagan mythology are mixed. Christianity was gradually accepted, provided that it was polite, polished and accommodating of the verities of Hellenic civilisation.[9]

Even so, the change took several generations. It was certainly helped by mixed marriages, which the church decided to tolerate, at least amongst the upper nobility. Two sons of the Caeionii, a leading pagan senatorial family, married devout Christian wives who passed their religion on faithfully to their daughters and granddaughters. In general, the traditional maxim that a wife should conform to the religion of her husband was abandoned, probably at the insistence of the church.

Male solidarity in paganism was matched by female solidarity in Christianity.[10] The son of Caeionius Rufius Albinus, Volusianus, remained a pagan until his deathbed in 437. Equally, the conversion to polite Christianity did not alter the secular prestige and traditions of the nobility, which continued well after the end of the Western empire. When the leading pagan Praetextatus died the court, although Christian, did not hesitate to erect public statues to him. A generation after the Frigidus the court even erected a statue to the pagan rebel Flavianus, commemorating his learning and public service.

Among the provincial aristocracies of Spain and Gaul Christianity was already well established, and at Constantinople and the Eastern capitals the upper officialdom and the upwardly-mobile secretaries and functionaries were largely of the new religion. Their Christianity had a more marked leaning to the ascetic, the miraculous, the monastic, the reverence for holy men and the desire to obtain grace and salvation thereby. Thus the unscrupulous Prefect, Rufinus, a pious Catholic, brought relics of Peter and Paul from Rome and installed them in a gorgeous martyrium at his own palace, to which he added a monastery and a community of monks imported from Egypt.[11] There was even a contest between the generals Victor and Saturninus, who both offered to build a monastic retreat for the holy hermit, Isaac.[12]

Theodosius' great victory was a glorious event for Christianity, but in other ways it had solved little. The Rhine frontier, which Arbogast had defended so ably, for the moment had no sufficient army or military leader to sustain that defence. The war itself had been much more costly in lives than the earlier campaign against Maximus, especially those of the Visigothic federates.[13] The urgent problem of securing effective rule in both halves of the empire was as pressing as ever. Theodosius was now, once again, unchallenged ruler of the whole empire in direct control of the reconstituted field armies of East and West. It was the greatest concentration of force available, or likely to be available for some time to come.

The court, army and its illustrious retinue of generals travelled again to Milan. In the winter Theodosius, who had been under severe strain, fell seriously ill with the vascular disease of hydropsy. Ever since his critical illness of 379–80 he had not enjoyed perfect health, and now his attendants and court were seriously alarmed. Urgent word was sent to Honorius at Constantinople to hasten to meet his father at Milan.[14]

Almost overnight the political atmosphere abruptly changed from the pride and relaxation of victory to the tense apprehension of an imminent change of monarch. If Theodosius died there was nobody of remotely comparable power and authority to replace him. Arcadius and Honorius, although both legally *Augusti*, were both too young and inexperienced to rule in their own right. The two most powerful figures in the background were, in the East, the Praetorian Prefect, Rufinus (who had shared the consulship with Arcadius — a singular honour); and in the West Flavius Stilicho, adoptive son-in-law of Theodosius, who by 393 had reached the top military rank of *Magister Utriusque Militiae*.[15]

In contrast to the East (where there were multiple holders of such offices, and the senior figure below the emperor was the civilian Praetorian Prefect), in the West there were only two commanders of such rank, and one was always, in practice, the senior figure. Stilicho's family links with Theodosius left no-one in any doubt that it was he, and not Timasius, his military colleague in command of the expedition against Eugenius and Arbogast, who was that figure.[16] Subordinate only to Theodosius himself in military matters, Stilicho was given command of all the remaining forces in the West after the Frigidus.[17] In effect, he was carefully being moved into the same position that Arbogast had occupied; something much more than merely a senior military commander. Like Arbogast (and unlike Maximus) he would not aspire to the purple himself, since his Vandal paternity made him *semibarbarus*. Additionally, he was bound to the Theodosian dynasty by marriage, and his legitimate ambitions depended on that.

The call to Honorius had indeed been prudent, for by the time Theodosius reached Milan he was critically ill. Stilicho wasted no time in coming to terms with that other key figure, the irrepressible bishop Ambrose. The meeting of Theodosius and Honorius was celebrated by the usual lavish public games, over which Theodosius managed to preside for some time, but by the afternoon his place had been taken by Honorius. The eternal roars of the crowd echoed on, while immediately behind the scenes was being enacted the most fateful transaction for centuries.

Theodosius died on 17 January 394, aged only forty-eight. But before he did, we are told, he appointed Stilicho guardian (*parens*) of both his imperial sons: Honorius in the West and Arcadius in the East. Unfortunately there were no witnesses to this deathbed scene. Ambrose, however, publicly avowed its enactment and authority, and most others concurred.[18] Stilicho's own propagandist, the court poet Claudian, later paraded Theodosius' solemn bequest in vivid tones at many places in his narratives and panegyrics, even suggesting — extraordinarily — that the dying Theodosius dismissed all of his attendants except Stilicho.[19]

There has been so much argument, both ancient and modern, over this canonical episode (especially amongst constitutionalists) that it would be idle for us to add to it. Theodosius' death was quite sudden, and no doubt many of the details of his intended settlement — especially concerning the East — were left unstated. What is undeniable is that he had deliberately advanced Stilicho to a special position beyond that of an ordinary military commander, even above that which Arbogast had enjoyed. Stilicho was *de facto* ruler of the West by virtue of his undisputed army command, and had a strong *de jure* presumption as son-in-law of the late emperor, with the consequent customary *parentela* status towards his two imperial sons.[20]

If Stilicho himself had to push the final keystone of his power into place then at least the structure had been prepared for him to do so. Roman family law provided for the position of a guardian, but there was no such office as 'regent' in the Roman constitution. However, the other generals and ministers at the court in Milan accepted the ill-defined position; except probably for Alaric. He was, by now, the leader of the Visigothic allies who had made such sacrifices at the Frigidus in the service of Theodosius, and whose treaty obligations had related to the person of the emperor and were now potentially void. Stilicho dismissed the federates in late January and they set off to return to their territory in Moesia, looting to supply themselves as they went.[21]

Ambrose sensibly recognised real power when he saw it, and was devoted to the house of Theodosius and its progeny. He therefore put all his influence as a churchman and politician into the scales in support of Stilicho. In return, he organised and managed Theodosius' lying in state at Milan with great panache, delivering his oration *De Obitu Theodosii* himself before Stilicho and Honorius. It differed radically from the form of Roman imperial funerals for the previous four centuries. It was, instead, an uncompromising Judeo-Christian apotheosis, delivered pointedly forty days after the emperor's death. Again Nathan the priest passed judgement on King David, to the greater glory of God.[22]

It was a masterly performance in buttressing the positions of the two imperial children, of Stilicho and, of course, the tutelage of God and his church personified in Ambrose. There is barely a mention of Theodosius' service in dealing with the Gothic menace, but a great deal about his suppression of heresy and paganism:

'Whoever in life celebrates fittingly the Passover of the Lord shall be in perpetual light. Who has celebrated it more abundantly than he who has banished sacrilegious errors, closed the temples and destroyed the idols?'

The victory of Eugenius is lauded repeatedly as proof that faith, not merely military prowess alone, brings victories. Like Elisha surrounded by the Syrian host Theodosius prayed, and God sent his wind to scatter his enemies:

'He is victorious who hopes for the Grace of God, not he who presumes on his own strength. Theodosius is now in heaven with the crown of saintliness, and he is now a true king in the company of Our Lord Jesus Christ.'

None of this prevented conventional inscriptions from elevating Theodosius to the ranks of the gods (*divus*), nor the poet Claudian later placing him among the stars.

Of the all-important bequest to Stilicho, Ambrose suggests (with great casuistry) that Theodosius had neither the time nor even the wish to make a testamentary will, since he had already bequeathed everything to his sons and all that was left was to provide them with a guardian:

'If the last wishes of private citizens have perpetual stability, even though testaments are lacking, how can the will of so great a prince be disregarded? Theodosius...did not attest by common law; for he had nothing to conceal from his sons, to whom he had given everything, unless it were to commend them to a father who was present.'

Any enemy could, of course, have torn holes in this kind of argument; but for the moment there were no enemies. Stilicho held — as it were — the boy king, the crown jewels, the barons, the castles and the Archbishop of Canterbury: this was enough.

The body of Theodosius was carried with great solemnity to the Church of the Apostles in Constantinople where he was laid to rest on 8 November 395, and where he lay in peace until the sack of the city in 1204. It is difficult to overestimate the significance of the transitions of 395, when a new and unprecedented set of conditions suddenly appeared. Never before in imperial history had both East and West found themselves ruled by such youths, and youths without any inkling of military experience. Indeed, they would probably not have benefited from it anyway. Compared with a youth like Gratian, who had been brought up by his warlike father to lead troops at the age of fifteen, both Honorius and Arcadius were unintelligent and pusillanimous. Theodosius had not been blessed in his male children. Tensions between the Eastern and Western courts came immediately to the surface.[23]

A just assessment of Theodosius can hardly be made at the point of his death. Not only did he die with much of his work unfinished, but his power and authority in the West passed not to a new emperor but to a new Arbogast figure, who protected Theodosius' progeny and continued his broad policies although operating under grave handicaps. A century earlier immature boy-emperors would have been snuffed out and replaced by the nearest ambitious general. It is a measure of the new dynastic authority that had carefully been built up since Constantine, and nurtured by Theodosius, that this did not now happen. Instead, power flowed into new, untried channels of indirect rule, and the fundamental loyalty that had always been assumed between the thrones of East and West crumbled away. (Indeed, popular history is prone to cite 395 as a formal separation of East and West, as if it were a constitutional divorce.)

These and other changes, foreshadowed during the reign of Theodosius, come into their own with the rule of his protégé, Stilicho.

PART IV
THE UNRAVELLING

'Woe to the land that's governed by a child!'

Shakespeare, *Richard III*, Act 2

'...the Goths, after the defeat of Valens, never abandoned the Roman territory...[this was] the principal and immediate cause of the fall of the Western empire of Rome.'

Gibbon, *Decline and Fall*, XXVI[1]

STILICHO: LAST GUARDIAN OF A
UNITED EMPIRE

There has been extensive argument about the actions, motives, and ultimate goals of Stilicho in the crucial years, 395–408. A full attempt to analyse all the political twists and turns in this period would be a separate book in itself.[1] But Stilicho, it is now generally agreed, continued the broad policies of his father-in-law Theodosius towards the barbarians — to conciliate them, manage them and use them, in what he saw were the long-term interests of the Roman Empire. If these policies ultimately failed (and that is still an open question), then the responsibility lies with Theodosius as well. For good or ill the ghost of Theodosius accompanies Stilicho, and that is our central concern.[2]

Stilicho had some cause to regret the untimely death of his patron, for his own ambitious plans were by no means complete by January 395. His loyalty to the dynasty of Theodosius did not prevent him from planning a far more binding web of marriage alliances between his own children and the imperial family, which would further underpin his own unique position (to be publicly confirmed by Theodosius) as Commander-in-Chief, 'regent', and protector of that family.[3] There is no reason to suppose that Stilicho himself aspired to the purple, but he may well have had this vicarious ambition for his own son Eucherius, whom Theodosius seems to have acknowledged as his grandson, born in the purple.[4]

But such plans were cut short. Stilicho had to improvise rapidly, so he probably took the wish for the deed and, in effect, sensibly siezed power with as much legitimacy as he could muster, and the broad consensus of his peers. He quickly filled the senior positions in the Western government with his own supporters, and his only military peer, the *Magister* Timasius, departed for the East early in 395.[5]

Even so, his position was by no means as strong as it looked. True, he had a secure monopoly of influence over Honorius, and could issue whatever orders and legislation he wished in the imperial name. But his wider claims over the Eastern throne were not recognised at all at Constantinople, where Arcadius was firmly under the influence of the Prefect Rufinus — who indeed, had as good a claim as Stilicho to be Arcadius' guardian.[6]

Stilicho commanded — for the present — the main armies of East and West; but it soon became clear that these two groups, who had so recently been slaughtering one another, were not going to cooperate harmoniously, and that large numbers of them were in such a poor state of discipline that their obedience might not be relied on in a new campaign.[7] Initially Stilicho hoped, on the basis of his guardianship and combined army command, to exercise authority over both halves of the empire just as Theodosius had done, and as he clearly believed was his legal and moral right. But from the outset it was obvious this was a very distant goal indeed.[8]

Claudian is one of our best sources for this early period, carefully composing events as Stilicho wished them to be presented, and he is every bit as significant in what he omits as what he says. He has been hailed as the last great poet in the classical Roman tradition, and he certainly played the old stops of that musical organ most faithfully to the senatorial aristocracy Stilicho needed to conciliate; but there is a sickening gulf between the bombastic, floriated, Olympian rhetoric, and what must actually have been going on. Instead of eternal Rome overthrowing the Mede and the towers of Semiramis, Stilicho was desperately scraping together armies of half-trained, half-reliable Germanic troops to counterbalance the Visigothic 'allies'; denuding frontier defences well below the danger level; and ignoring the fears and miseries of many provincial populations — from highest to lowest — who could barely depend on Roman government for basic security from outside invaders.[9]

The first challenge came almost immediately, from the Visigothic *foederati* who had only just been managed by Theodosius, but now sensed a power vacuum. They had returned promptly from the civil war, having been dismissed by Stilicho, to their allotted territories in the eastern Danube provinces, with great resentments. As they saw it, they had served loyally in the civil war and suffered great losses.[10] It was believed that Theodosius had deliberately placed them in the vanguard at the Frigidus so that Gothic blood could be sacrificed rather than Roman. It was also felt to be straining the alliance that they should twice be used in the emperor's internal quarrels against other Romans.[11] Most of all, their leader, Alaric, had wanted a top Roman command like Stilicho, Bauto, Arbogast, Gainas and other Germanic generals.[12] Theodosius had refused this, wisely: to combine the position of *Magister Militum* and the tribal chief of a settled barbarian federate nation in the same person would be a further and most significant shift in the Roman-Gothic balance, and was clearly contrary to the understanding of the alliance of 382.[13] For all these reasons Visigothic hostility and suspicion of the Roman Government were at their height when Theodosius suddenly died.

Given the speed with which the events of 395 unfolded it seems likely that the rebellion had been festering for some time, and it is possible that Alaric and his army looted their way back to join a revolt that had already broken out in Moesia. One further motivation for such an outbreak may have been Hunnic raiding across the Danube, and the Goths, along with all the other inhabitants of the Danubian provinces, must have felt extremely threatened. Whilst the greatest part of their fighting strength was being sacrificed for Roman aims in the West their own homelands were being threatened by the very people they had fled across the Danube to escape from almost twenty years earlier.[14]

Alaric was already pre-eminent among the Goths, as the senior figure of the dominant 'royal' line, the *Balthi*. Alaric still had to consult the representatives of the people before major decisions were made, as had Fritigern. However he was secure enough in his position to overrule opposition to his views, and after the decision was taken to leave their treaty-assigned lands Alaric's authority was not again challenged. The authority which he held amongst the Gothic leaders, due to his descent, was transformed by the forging of the various clans into one tribal army under his increasingly centralised authority.[15]

As king of the Visigothic army Alaric lost no time leading them out of their agreed territories against the Eastern Government, which was temporarily without its main field army. They marched on Constantinople, failed to take it, and then turned west again and plundered freely in Macedonia and Thessaly. It is likely that there was no real attempt on Constantinople: Alaric was making a demonstration, in pursuit of a new objective, a new and improved Treaty. Rufinus was certainly prepared to bargain with Alaric — he had no army and no choice — and the Gothic army may have moved west to new territories with his agreement.[16]

This was not just a revolt by a section of disgruntled Gothic warriors — which had happened before — but a national movement of major proportions.[17] Although its exact aims are unclear, Alaric wanted to put pressure on the Government to give him a top command, which would have enormously strengthened his position both within the Roman ruling strata and among his own followers. The mass of them may have cared little for Alaric's Roman ambitions, but wanted to be free of the treaty restrictions, or at least wanted larger, more secure lands and payments, whether as legitimate subsidy or just through plundering in their traditional manner.[18]

In the spring of 395 Stilicho marched from Italy with the combined field armies and confronted Alaric in Thessaly. As well as dealing with the Visigothic problem, he undoubtedly wanted to put pressure himself on the Eastern Government at Constantinople to further his claims of guardianship, whose main obstacle — he thought — was Rufinus. The Goths took up defensive positions and waited. Stilicho did not force a major conflict, but Alaric was penned in and unable to escape; a prolonged stand-off ensued.

According to Claudian, on the very eve of a decisive battle which would have crushed Alaric, orders came from the boy-emperor Arcadius (the senior Augustus) for Stilicho to return the Eastern portion of his army to Constantinople, and then withdraw himself and his Western army from the territory of the East. Claudian represents Stilicho himself as thunderstruck, and his soldiers beside themselves with frustration, robbed of certain victory.

But, loyally, Stilicho obeys, leaving Alaric to pillage the rest of Greece unopposed, including the cities of Megara, Corinth, Sparta and Argos; Athens bought off the Goths with huge payments.[19]

This account cannot be believed, and it is surprising that any modern historians at all have accepted it. If Stilicho had both the strength and the desire to crush Alaric's forces he would certainly have done it, and replied diplomatically and loyally to Arcadius' demands afterwards. There is reason to believe that Stilicho's numerically impressive army was far from being united and reliable. There had only been the minimal time since the costly battles of 394 to recover, regroup and organise the remaining troops into an effective force, all of which had been punctuated by the potential crisis of Theodosius' death and the effect it must have had in the armies. Stilicho could command and lead the uneasily combined force, but to commit it as a united whole to the hazard of a great battle he may well have baulked at. Not only was the Eastern component on bad terms with the Western, but it contained a substantial proportion of Goths, hastily recruited by Theodosius, who might be reluctant to fight their own kinsmen.[20]

Stilicho therefore seems to have made the best of a bad job, returned the more troublesome Eastern part of the army to Constantinople under the Gothic *Magister* Gainas, and retired to the West with a diminished field army. He spent much of the next year rebuilding this from whatever sources he could, in preparation for a fresh campaign against Alaric.[21]

It is implausible that Stilicho wanted to destroy Alaric's forces, any more than Theodosius had wanted to destroy Fritigern's in the 380s, and for the same reasons. They represented too valuable a resource. Even if a complete, annihilating victory could be achieved (which is doubtful anyway), it would be dangerously costly in both Visigothic and 'Roman' manpower. Like Theodosius, Stilicho wanted to chasten Alaric, defeat or replace him, but only if he could thereby get the mass of the Gothic warriors back to the earlier conditions of the treaty, or as close to it as possible.

Stilicho knew only too well that he was operating with the last substantial Roman army that was available in the West, and he was determined to husband it carefully,[22] but, as in the strategic doctrines of twentieth-century admirals, a 'force in being' imposes on itself severe limitations. It is too precious to be risked in an all-out battle, so has to be employed essentially as a threat, to wound, overawe and outmanoeuvre the enemy. But the enemy in turn will respond in the desired manner only as long as he fears and calculates that the threat will actually be cashed. This was what Stilicho was doing in his protracted and not unskilful conflicts with Alaric.

Gainas marched with the Eastern army to Constantinople, but before he arrived a careful plot had been woven, at the instigation or at least with the connivance of Stilicho. When Arcadius and Rufinus advanced out of the city to meet the advance guard on the parade field, at a signal the troops surrounded the Prefect and hacked him to pieces, along with his Hunnic bodyguard.[23] His body was gleefully mutilated by the mob only nineteen days after the burial in Constantinople of Theodosius.

But if Stilicho had hoped that Rufinus' removal would assist his own ambition in the East, he was quickly corrected. Gainas had his own fish to fry, but the place of Rufinus as protector of Arcadius was promptly filled by the adroit Master of Offices, the eunuch Eutropius.[24] He had no more intention than his predecessor of acknowledging Stilicho's Eastern claims, and he enjoyed an even closer relationship with Arcadius. For Rufinus too had sought a dynastic connection with the imperial house, hoping for a marriage between his own daughter and Arcadius. Eutropius thwarted this, by steering Arcadius' desires towards a rival, Eudoxia, the beautiful and spirited daughter of the late Frankish general Bauto.[25] They were married in April 395, demonstrating that the political infighting within the Eastern court had broken out immediately after Theodosius' death, if not before. Her role was to assist Eutropius in managing the young emperor, and for four years she did. By 404 she had been declared *Augusta*, much to the disgust of Western opinion which objected to such honours being given to a woman. Eutropius was a potential enemy of Stilicho, but at least his physical handicap excluded him from immediate dynastic ambitions himself.

For the present, relations between the two capitals stabilised sufficiently for Stilicho to secure from Eutropius an agreement which ceded to him the strategically important area of western Illyricum (Austria and Yugoslavia). In ten works between 396 and 404 Stilicho's spokesman, Claudian, makes no reference to the status of Illyricum — the division of his area between East and West was not an issue, and cannot be used to explain the conflict of Stilicho with the various leaders of the East.[26]

Outwardly, then, relations between the two thrones were cordial, but the fact that real power was now being wholly exercised by ministers and generals fatally undermined the kind of cooperation which had been normal and necessary when the emperors were independent monarchs with real authority. It had only been the prompt intervention, energy and foresight of Gratian which had prevented the irretrievable devastation and dismemberment of the East after Adrianople, and Theodosius in his turn had never forgotten his debt.[27] Now, alarmingly, these once automatic loyalties were eroding fast.

In many ways there was little unusual in the position in 395. There were two Augusti, but one of them was senior (Arcadius, by age and date of elevation) and might reasonably have been in control. He was young, but no younger than Gratian had been when he inherited the Western provinces from his father, Valentinian. The character of Arcadius (and to a lesser extent, Honorius), and the opportunistic ambitions of officials which it allowed, were the really significant factors.

As well as Stilicho's reasonable belief in his legitimate rights, and his mission to preserve the unity of the empire (under his own tutelage, of course), he had more immediate reasons for pressing his claims in the East. In established constitutional law and practice, Arcadius was the senior

Augustus, and could therefore — in theory — arrange the affairs and court of his junior colleague in the West. So long as Arcadius was being managed by an enemy of Stilicho, he could be used to subvert Honorius and undermine Stilicho's position. Of course, from the distant court in Constantinople these threats were titular only, so long as he retained the unchallenged command of the army. Yet Stilicho was very concerned about legitimacy and rectitude, as he clearly had need to be. Conservative senatorial circles in Italy could turn against a 'barbarian' military dictator (who could not aspire to legitimacy himself), and he could less afford to alienate them than could Theodosius. His persistent claim to guardianship of Arcadius as well as Honorius (from 395–400, when Arcadius was twenty-three), which he maintained despite the repeated and open rebuffs from Constantinople, was also a weapon for his own preservation.[28]

Stilicho's propaganda, through Claudian, frequently damns the ministers of Arcadius in the most splendidly lurid poetry of the age (the scalding invective against Eutropius, on the basis that he is a eunuch, provides two books). Arcadius himself, of course, is never criticised, although at one point there is a passing slight in the statement that Honorius did not choose his bride from a picture (as did Arcadius at Eutropius' instigation). There is some reason to credit Arcadius with a little more independence and initiative than his brother, if not much, and his antagonism may have been partly genuine, as a result of the claim to guardianship, rather a fabrication of his overbearing ministers.[29]

During 396 Stilicho went on a rapid tour of the Rhine frontier, and although his personal presence there was of short duration the settlement which was established held until 401. There was little fighting but, it seems, much diplomatic activity involving the frontier tribes. The aim was probably to raise much needed recruits to replenish the depleted army at his command, and to prevent any threat on the Rhine distracting him from unfinished business in the East. Treaties were no doubt concluded, with the Franks being likely allies as they had been at times since the third century.

The Pannonian federates, settled by Gratian, may have also become a more important element of the West's resources at this stage. A new law had been issued against deserters and anyone harbouring them, and Stilicho was clearly reaping the harvest of costly civil wars and the shift further in favour of available Germanic soldiers.[30] They represented an immediate resource, unlike the indigenous population. Both Theodosius and Stilicho had to accept this fact of life, and they were not unwilling to accept the taxes of the large landowners in gold, rather than recruits, provided that this bought them reliable soldiers. However, the terms of recruitment of these barbarians were becoming more and more *ad hoc*, which can hardly have added to Roman military prestige in their eyes. The treaties concluded by Stilicho at this stage almost certainly involved the ceding of further territory along the Rhine in return for recruits.[31]

Alaric and his followers spent much of 396 helping themselves to the wealth that they could extract from the Greek cities, plundering extensively in the Peloponnese with no opposition from the Eastern government or its army. The East was also beset by an invasion of Syria and Asia Minor by the Huns, and for the moment it was powerless to deal with Alaric.[32]

The following year (397) Stilicho was ready. Without consulting Arcadius or his ministers he landed with a new army at Corinth, intent on a showdown with Alaric. In the meantime Eutropius had not been idle: he may have already been angling for an agreement with Alaric (hence the lack of action against him), which he needed if he were not to suffer the fate of Rufinus. He must also have been in contact with Gildo, the *Magister et Comes* in Africa, who had exercised unusual power there with the acquiescence of Theodosius for a decade. Africa was not merely subject to Honorius, the Western emperor, but also provided the lifeline of grain to Italy. Even a short delay in the arrival of the ships at Ostia could lead to riots in Rome, and Gildo was later happy to support the East against the dangerously powerful Stilicho.[33]

In Greece, Stilicho engaged Alaric and blockaded his army, even diverting the water courses to force him into submission. The tactics were the same as always against the Goths since 378, and no less successful in their results and saving of lives for that. The outcome, however, was disappointing. For whatever reasons Stilicho withdrew, and Alaric moved north into Epirus. The simplest explanation may be the best: that Stilicho's newly raised army was just not reliable enough to force a decision in battle, and unhappy with the prolonged discipline of a siege with limited prospects for looting. It was also suggested (by Zosimus) that some of the army was bribed with the spoils of Greece.[34] At about this time, Eutropius and the East took the extreme step of declaring Stilicho a public enemy. If this happened during the campaign, it would have directly challenged Stilicho's authority in Greece.

The main outcome of 397 was the gravest public rift between the thrones of East and West, usually signalling the outbreak of civil war along with the overthrowing of imperial statues, but the two brothers Arcadius and Honorius were not going to fight. Their juvenile impotence could hardly be advertised more blatantly. Alaric, Gainas, Gildo and others of course knew of these rifts already, but such a message could not be lost on the wider mass of barbarian peoples, whether allies or not. Regardless of the sequence of events, the competition for the loyalty of Gildo, the declaration of public enemy status, demonstrate the depth of the breakdown in relations between East and West.

Stilicho withdrew from Greece, to find that Gildo had raised his revolt in Africa and cut off the grain shipments to Italy. Luckily, Stilicho was able to cope with the crisis quickly. A strangulation of the grain supply would soon have put him in the most precarious position politically, as it was clearly intended to. He rapidly and effectively organised alternative supplies from the Gallic provinces, buttressed his position by marrying his daughter

Maria to Honorius (although he was still only fourteen), and despatched an army to Africa under the convenient command of Gildo's brother and bitter enemy, Mascazel.[35]

Stilicho himself would have been unwise to leave Italy in such a crisis, and past experience showed that suppressing a revolt in Africa could be a prolonged affair.[36] Perhaps, too, Stilicho was not unwilling to have Mascazel shoulder the blame should the campaign go wrong. In the event Gildo was defeated very quickly, probably by his brother seducing the loyalty of his troops in time-honoured fashion. Stilicho's prestige rose with the reflected glory.

Soon after his return to Italy, while he and Stilicho were crossing a bridge with their retinues, Mascazel had an unfortunate accident: he fell into the river and was drowned. Stilicho must have shed few tears, and the suspicion of assassination lingered over the event. The success of Mascazel could have been embarrassing for Stilicho, who had no real military victories to his own name, and he took full credit for the African victory — just as any emperor would have done.[37]

Outwardly, Stilicho's propaganda still doggedly maintained the image of a united empire. Gildo and Eutropius are barely mentioned, and the plea of Claudian is that the two young Augusti should cement their unity by holding the consulship together. But Eutropius, Stilicho's equal in astuteness, took the logical but unpopular step of ridding the East of one major problem by finally giving Alaric what he had continually wanted: a full Roman command. He was officially appointed *Magister Militum* in eastern Illyricum, in theory responsible to Arcadius, but in practice to nobody. At the stroke of a stylus the barbarian plunderer of Greece was legitimised and promoted to be its supreme military commander and supposed defender.

The timing of this promotion is uncertain, but it seems plausible that Alaric broke out of Greece after the withdrawal of Stilicho and, in the absence of any restraint on the Goths, Eutropius had to come to terms with them. They were established in a new territory, in Macedonia, where their arbitrary depredations ceased and they began to be supplied quite legitimately with the produce of the Balkan provinces and the output of its arms factories. This was a good bargain for Alaric, which he exploited fully, and the new treaty held for four years.[38]

Although Alaric appears increasingly as a dangerous volatile force which will neither be satisfied nor controlled, at this stage his ambitions were at least rational.[39] A senior military command gave him the means to supply and settle his followers, to build up and re-arm his warriors, and to consolidate his position as king. Most importantly, it offered him a respected place in the decision-making circles of the empire, which might provide the secure political guarantees for the Visigothic nation within Roman territory which had eluded Fritigern and his successors; and which had allowed — as he saw it — betrayal and exploitation by perfidious Roman allies. From the Roman point of view, to the dismay of Stilicho, Alaric now had two horses to ride: he was both king of the Visigothic federates, and Roman military commander of one of the strategically pivotal areas of the empire. There is no doubt that this represented a crucial further step in the loss of Roman ascendancy and initiative — which is why Theodosius and Stilicho had opposed it so adamantly. Stilicho, who was secure enough in the West, was further than ever from realising his claims in the East, while Alaric was even stronger, able to play East off against West. His forces, despite some inevitable losses, had benefited from their habitual service with the Roman army, and were tactically a more formidable weapon than those commanded by Fritigern a generation earlier; they were also, of course, much better equipped and supplied.

There were thus three rival power centres: Stilicho, Alaric and Eutropius. Eutropius' deal with Alaric freed him from the short-term Gothic menace, and provided a useful counterweight to Stilicho. Several leading generals had been eliminated in a series of treason trials under Eutropius, establishing his authority over the military. His diplomatic policy had been successful, but war could not be avoided completely and it seems that Eutropius made his mistakes at the height of his success. Rather than give the supreme command of a campaign, against the Huns and other Caucasian peoples in 398, to any of Arcadius' generals, he decided to take it himself. The war was a success, and Eutropius the consulship for the following year. Claudian is scathing about the scale of the military success, and condemns the command of an army by a eunuch, no doubt in contrast to his own virile patron.[40] It may be that too much significance has been attached to Eutropius' victory simply because of the unusual nature of its general; however one of the results of the campaign was certainly weighty — a serious rebellion later broke out among federate troops in 399, which then threatened to embroil the whole of the East in civil war.[41]

Like Stilicho's suppression of Gildo, success was success, and Eutropius no doubt felt justified in his celebration of it, but this was a political mistake. For a eunuch to step into the consular dignity, whatever his merits and achievements, was too presumptuous.[42] It was as if a black ex-slave had run for President in 1880, or a British Catholic for Prime Minister in 1750. That the rewards of a campaign, in which experienced military leaders must have played a significant part, were to go to Eutropius, provoked those officers who had seen their military authority consistently eroded and unrewarded since 395. Stilicho was more sensitive to Roman aristocratic prejudices, and had not made this kind of mistake. Senatorial opinion was outraged, especially in Italy, and it gave Claudian a gratuitous propaganda weapon, which he instantly seized:

> All portents pale before our eunuch consul. O shame in heaven and earth! Our cities behold an old woman decked in a consul's robe, who gives a woman's name to the year.... Let the East be ruled by eunuchs...suffer not this thing of shame to cross the Alps.... Was it for this that Horatius kept the bridge, and Mucius braved the flames?

and so on for hundreds of lines. Victorian melodrama could not hold a candle to it.[43] As well as propaganda Stilicho may have tried to undermine Eutropius, as he had Rufinus, with the assistance of Gothic associates in the Eastern army, notably Gainas. Despite the removal of several rivals for high military office, and his great experience and seniority, Gainas had not been promoted as he might have reasonably expected.

Eutropius' blunder was compounded by the substantial unpopularity of the appointment of Alaric, which must have provoked even further the simmering anti-Gothic feeling in the East. That Alaric was now legitimate commander of the Greek cities of Illyricum was the latest in a series of affronts to civilised men, stretching back beyond Fritigern to the ravages of the third century. Even in an incompetent despotism a great surge of influential public feeling could make itself felt, and palace rivalries at Constantinople were compounded by a split into pro- and anti-Gothic factions, which erupted violently in 400. The empress Eudoxia, who had quarrelled with Eutropius, now struggled with him for control of Arcadius: as his wife, and the mother of his children, Eudoxia was in a strong position.[44]

For a year there was a complex political crisis, compounded by the revolt of Tribigild and his Greuthungian federates in Phrygia, demanding better, rewards for their participation in the campaign of 398. Gainas was sent to quell the revolt, but showed limited enthusiasm for the task, even after the Greuthungi had been heavily defeated by local militias. He was related to Tribigild, and must have sympathised with the reasons for the revolt: his own position after the conclusion of any conflict would not have been secure (he had seen other successful generals removed by Eutropius), and he soon halted action against Tribigild, to demand the removal of Eutropius. The army as a whole was behind Gainas, after the slights of the previous four years, and Eutropius was overthrown and exiled by his opponents at court, led by Aurelian.[45] Gainas then joined forces with Tribigild and forced Aurelian, suspected of being anti-military if not anti-Gothic, from office.

Gainas then received the full command of the field armies at Constantinople, which he had sought and believed he deserved: he was now theoretically as powerful as Stilicho, and more so than Alaric. Despite this position Gainas failed to master the politics of the situation: he lost the support of the army, Arcadius declared him an enemy and he was driven from Constantinople. After failing to establish himself in either Asia Minor or Thrace, he decided to seek power among the Goths beyond the Danube. Uldin, king of the Huns, did not welcome such a challenge to his authority and sent Gainas' head to Constantinople.[46]

The hostility to Gainas and 'his' Goths, in traditional Roman fashion, was exemplified by the orations of the philosopher, Synesius of Cyrene. It did not, however, reflect a general anti-barbarian policy in practice.

Against an idealised Hellenistic background, Synesius pronounces on the true nature of kingship. The emperor should not hide away in his palace, but should avoid the oppressive court ceremonial and palace intrigues and take the field with his army, as in the days of old. Above all, he should expel the treacherous German barbarians who cannot be trusted to defend the empire in the field or in the council chamber. Citizens alone should defend their country and win their own victories. Barbarians are born to slavery, and it is a disgrace that they should parade as army commanders. Let all fair-haired men be banished from positions of power. The policy of Theodosius was a mistake, made not out of weakness but his extreme clemency to a defeated foe (it would have been unwise to criticise Theodosius directly in front of his son!), but the barbarians do not understand clemency. They should never have been granted land — they should instead be forced to work the land for us, as the Spartans did with the Messenians.[47]

It is not recorded how such racist sentiments were received by the empress Eudoxia, or the loyal Gothic general Fravitta. They were, of course, the hopeless romantic fantasies of a literary mind, not practical politics. The aggressive Gothic elements such as Gainas and Tribigild were eclipsed for the present, but the East could not possibly do without the support of 'barbarian' forces. It was compelled to recruit Huns and Alans and establish treaty relations with Uldin. The attitudes of Synesius were widely echoed among the upper classes and the wider population, although those in power saw the realities of the situation more clearly. The Goths were barbarians, they were illiterate and untutored (although many soldiers would have learned some Latin), they were uncouth and wore strange or un-Roman dress, they were Arian heretics, they followed the traditions of their barbaric ancestors . . . they were an alien virus in the body of the empire. This attitude, untypically for the period, represents a surge of the kind of hostility to outsiders that we have witnessed in our own century. It was confirmed only a year later, in 401, when Alaric decided to invade Italy.

It was now, with the threat to Italy itself, that Stilicho began to face truly grave problems. His standing had been strengthened by the prompt suppression of the Gildonic revolt and the restoration of the grain supply to Italy, and he still controlled Honorius and enjoyed the undoubted support of the army. The senatorial aristocracy could never overlook his barbarian origins, but they generally acquiesced in his rule — that is, they did not lend comfort to his enemies — provided he protected the territory of the West and their own wealth. They only paid a fraction of the taxes which they owed from their great estates, and had opposed the raising of recruits for the African campaign, but they wished to keep the unity of the eternal empire — even if they imagined that this would happen as if by a law of nature.

The threat to Italy was twofold: there were threats from the north against the upper Danubian provinces and Italy, and against Gaul from across the Rhine; and Alaric was on the move from Illyricum. In 401 the Vandals and Alans had invaded Raetia and Noricum, forcing Stilicho to oppose them with the field army from Italy. Although the Franks held the lower Rhine as federates there was no such support elsewhere. Alaric marched from Illyricum, taking advantage of Stilicho's absence, and was in Italy by late 401 without encountering any real resistance. Some smaller cities were taken, but Aquileia held out under siege and early in 402 Alaric moved to threaten the imperial capital, Milan.[48]

Stilicho had been successful in both his campaigning and subsequent recruiting to the north, and he returned with the field army and various barbarian contingents (Vandals, Alans, and possibly Gothic federates from Pannonia) to force Alaric to retreat from Milan in March 402. After a series of strategic manoeuvres, in which Alaric sought to avoid being trapped by Stilicho's forces, the Goths were brought to battle at Pollentia on Easter Sunday. Alaric lost his camp and baggage to the Roman army under the leadership of the Alan general Saul (who proved his loyalty to the Roman cause by dying in battle for it!), and although the main part of their forces survived intact the Goths were driven to seek refuge in a fortified position in the mountains. Negotiations began again, and Stilicho held the upper hand: Alaric agreed to move out of Italy, and his forces marched north beyond the Po. Although Stilicho had successfully juggled the competing demands of frontier warfare and conflict within the empire, using his limited resources skilfully, Claudian felt a need to justify this diplomatic arrangement and referred to it as both a treaty (which it probably was not, in any formal sense) and as necessary due to the 'constraints of the circumstances'.[49]

For some reason Alaric halted his retreat near Verona, perhaps threatened by Stilicho searching for a more convincing victory. The battle of Verona was a major defeat for Alaric: his losses were high, his mobility lost to Stilicho's superior cavalry forces, and his prestige was in tatters. Many of his men deserted and joined Stilicho, including senior figures (Sarus, Ulfilas) with their retinues. Defeated and blockaded by Stilicho, Alaric had no choice: he left Italy and returned to eastern Illyricum, where he was limited to ravaging those provinces in an attempt to restore his strength. A letter referring to this period (403–4), from Honorius to his brother, laments the depredations in Eastern territory, and bemoans the lack of cooperation in dealing with it. Stilicho obviously still had his interests in the East, and must also have been concerned about the possibility of Alaric again representing a threat to Italy: certainly the East was making no move to deal with the situation.[50]

The relationship of forces within the empire was now dangerously unstable. Stilicho had been compelled to abandon, or at least postpone, his Eastern ambitions. He could certainly stand up to Alaric, although he may have been unable to destroy his power completely, and had demonstrated that he could successfully defend the heart of the empire and even the northern provinces. However, this was clearly dependent on only one crisis breaking at a time: when Alaric first invaded Italy Stilicho was on campaign in the north, and this must have concentrated his mind on achieving a more secure settlement of the Eastern Question. Italy had suffered in the invasions in 401–2. That the walls of Rome were repaired and the emperor, court and government and the capital itself moved from Milan to the remote, but more secure marsh-locked coastal city of Ravenna. In earlier centuries Milan had replaced Rome as the effective capital of the West, because it was closer to the frontiers and transit routes and offered a base from which major military efforts to defend the empire could be launched and controlled. Now, Ravenna was chosen because it was a refuge for the emperor from invaders who could not be kept firmly out of Italy — Honorius had even thought of fleeing to Gaul in the face of Alaric's invasion, and Ravenna must have seemed a reasonable compromise to Stilicho.

Stilicho had done all that he could in the circumstances, given the quality and numbers of troops which he had at his disposal and his great ambition to keep the empire united, without instigating a civil war. Conservative Italian senatorial opinion may not have seen it that way, after the threats to their heartland. He was concerned for the security of the central strategic territories of the empire — Italy, Africa, Illyricum and ultimately, of course, the East. To protect these he was prepared, and indeed forced, to sacrifice the integrity and security of some of the other, less essential areas of the empire. Much of the lower Rhine was now in the hands of the Frankish federates, and Pannonia, where Roman administration seems to have been tenuous, was increasingly important as a source of troops under the federates established there by Alatheus and Saphrax. Stilicho's regular forces were relatively small, and he had to rely increasingly on his barbarian federates and mercenaries.[51]

By 404 Honorius had fallen out with his brother: Arcadius had paraded statues of Eudoxia Augusta with his own through the empire, and the West was affronted by this Eastern constitutional innovation. Stilicho's concerns about the continuing threat of Alaric were compounded by the actions of the Eastern government, led by the *Comes* of the treasury, John, who had brought about the downfall of Fravitta, the Gothic general who had favoured imperial unity. It may be that John wanted to force the rampaging Goths of Alaric back into Western territory, as the East may have conspired to do in the first invasion of 401. In these circumstances lie the reasons that Stilicho now concluded an alliance with Alaric to annexe the eastern parts of Illyricum to the West, and to force a resolution to the conflict with the court in Constantinople.[52]

Before any action could be taken to follow this through, however, the plans of both Stilicho and Alaric were disrupted by a massive invasion of Goths under Radagaisus, a charismatic warleader who had attracted a huge following among the pagan Goths outside the empire (his forces were said to number 400,000!).[53] He crossed the Danube and ravaged northern Illyricum during the summer of 405, and towards the end of the year invaded Italy. Alaric remained out of the conflict, probably still weak from the losses of 402.

Stilicho took the field against Radagaisus with an army which he had hastily reinforced by rapid recruitment in Italy, and the recall of garrisons from the upper Rhine; large numbers of federate Alans, Goths, and a large contingent of Huns sent by their king, Uldin, also joined his forces. Radagaisus was decisively defeated in early 406 at Faesulae, and he was executed in August of that year. His huge forces were cut to pieces by the Huns as they fled, and many were taken as slaves by both Huns and Romans — the Roman slave markets are said to have collapsed under the flood of captives for sale.[54] Stilicho enrolled large numbers into his army (supposedly 12,000 *optimates* — suggesting that he only recruited the nobles and their warrior retainers, and celebrated his great victory with a triumph and the erection of an arch commemorating the achievement in Rome.[55]

From this time dates the employment of Huns as a significant addition to the forces of the West. Stilicho later had a Hunnic bodyguard. Uldin, of course, was keen to assist the empire against Radagaisus — he was trying to establish and maintain his authority over the subject peoples of the Huns north of the Danube, and he did not want any groups emerging to escape or challenge that authority.[56]

The cost of Stilicho's victory became clear as he was planning to resume his interrupted campaign with Alaric against the East. To defend Italy, and possibly also for his new campaign, he had stripped the Rhine defences to a dangerous level. On the last day of 406 several tribes crossed the Rhine in major invasions of Gaul, sacking Mainz, Trier and many other cities. The Franks had fought well to preserve Roman power, and their own preferential position within it, but they were defeated by the Vandals and Alans and the Rhine frontier collapsed. To make Stilicho's position worse, in early 407 the Roman commander in Britain, Constantine, declared himself Augustus and crossed into Gaul to fight the invaders. The campaign against the East was called off.

From this point on, despite the prestige of having saved Italy on more than one occasion, Stilicho was struggling against forces too many, too powerful and too complex for him to manage. He had stuck to his policy of seeking authority in the East, even resorting to using Alaric to help him secure it. His neglect of the Gallic provinces, although understandable and even necessary in the circumstances, alienated those provinces and the aristocracies who owned much of them. A barbarian general, it was murmured, was more concerned to do deals with other barbarian invaders for his own purposes than to defend Roman provinces against them. This was why he had spared Alaric time and again, when he should and could have crushed him as he had Radagaisus. We cannot trust barbarians in uniform. By now Stilicho's most useful propagandist, Claudian, was dead, as was his ally, bishop Ambrose. His only link to authority was his continuing control over Honorius, and the support of his increasingly motley and volatile army, part regular, part allies; part Roman, part Gothic, Alan and Hunnic.

Stilicho had to face the threat from the usurper Constantine or his hold on power would be lost: success against the East would not maintain his authority if a rival general was successful in the West, gained the respect of the army and provincials, and even threatened 'his' emperor, Honorius. The agreement with Alaric was broken, and in early 408 the Eastern Consul was recognised in the West: Alaric and his Goths were now unnecessary and probably an embarrassment.

Stilicho's commander, Sarus, had had limited success campaigning in Gaul against Constantine in 407, after Stilicho had Honorius declare him a public enemy. Now matters were complicated by Alaric, who marched on Italy and demanded a huge sum as payment for his — unused — services under the treaty of 405 with Stilicho. The situation was desperate: Stilicho could not campaign in the north-west with Alaric at his back, and he managed to force through, against strong senatorial opposition, agreement to the payment of subsidies to Alaric in return for his service against Constantine in Gaul. Although this must have made excellent military sense to Stilicho in the circumstances, it was hugely unpopular. Alaric was hated and feared in the West, and had done nothing but invade and plunder. Now he was to be given the senior military command under Stilicho, and a huge sum of money, to fight against the Roman, Constantine, who was at least trying to fight the barbarian invaders of the Western provinces. According to Zosimus one former supporter of Stilicho, Lampadius, spoke out for those opposed to the policy: 'This is not peace — it is a contract of slavery!' He then prudently sought sanctuary in a church.[58]

In this debate Stilicho first clearly quarrelled with Honorius, the last legal basis for his power. His daughter Maria, wife of Honorius, had died, and although he had promptly arranged for her sister Thermantia to marry the emperor the union proved as barren as the earlier had. Honorius was possibly sterile as well as feeble-minded, and the fecundity of Eudoxia in the East as a contrast must have made it more difficult for Stilicho to achieve any authority through his role as *parens* of the emperor and head of a potential dynasty.[59]

In May 408 Arcadius died in Constantinople, leaving the seven-year-old Theodosius II to succeed him. Stilicho, despite the obvious crisis unfolding about him must have seen this as one last opportunity to seize the initiative again, and proposed that he should go to Constantinople in person to establish his authority over the East (on behalf of Honorius, the senior emperor, of course). Honorius would remain in Italy, with Alaric to protect him and face Constantine in Gaul. Even his wife, Serena, tried to warn Stilicho, but to no avail.[60] He still held an unswerving belief in the unity of the empire, and this was the moment to reunite the leadership of all the empire against its enemies under a single emperor, Honorius, and a single general.

This expedition did not take place, possibly since Stilicho recognised the fragility of his position. However he found himself removed from the immediate presence of Honorius during the preparations for the war in

Gaul, and his enemies took the opportunity to stage what was a carefully planned coup. Stilicho was accused of wanting to place his own son, Eucherius, on the throne in Constantinople. His supporters were arrested and killed, and Honorius was placed at the head of this palace revolution. Stilicho hesitated to take the ultimate step of setting his largely barbarian loyal forces on the Romans who now surrounded the emperor, and in so doing he may have finally lost their respect and support.[61] Stilicho decided to reject the option of civil war and hurried to meet Honorius.

Imperial orders were then issued for his arrest, and it became clear that Honorius was under the control of Stilicho's opponents. He sought sanctuary in a church, faced with the ruin of all his ambitious, but largely unselfish hopes. Even at the end he remained loyal, and when he was assured that he was only to be arrested he gave himself up: even his Hunnic bodyguard was not to offer resistance. He was, of course, betrayed and he was executed on 22 August 408. His son was murdered, after briefly seeking refuge in Rome. His property was confiscated, his inscriptions erased, and his adherents arrested and tortured to secure evidence of his treasonable conspiracy. They died in silence.[62] The families of his loyal barbarian troops, including those recruited from Radagaisus' army, were massacred and most of Stilicho's surviving barbarian forces deserted *en masse* to their only hope of security: Alaric. He is said to have recruited 30,000 men from Stilicho's forces, and within two years he would sack Rome with them, while Honorius and his advisors who had overthrown Stilicho sheltered behind the marshes in Ravenna.[63]

This is not a work of drama. History, among other things, is about doing justice to the dead. Thanks to numerous historians Flavius Stilicho, who was accused of selling out the empire to the barbarians, now has the recognition denied him for so long.[64] He owed everything to Theodosius, and was completely loyal to his dynasty and his policies. He inherited a critical situation not of his making, and one which — as events proved — was impossible to manage. His errors, which caused his destruction, were not those of greed or personal ambition, but (and this can still be said of these politically squalid times) of idealism.

Stilicho, himself of barbarian origin and understanding barbarian aspirations, was best equipped to continue, as far as possible, the Theodosian strategy of conciliating and managing the more Romanised barbarians to defend a unified empire against other barbarians. He was in many senses, as Theodosius had been, the friend of the Goths, but also of the other tribes with whom he struggled to preserve the empire. Theodosius had had the advantage of doing so with the support of the whole empire, and of the Visigothic federates; Stilicho had no such imperial support, and had to fight Alaric as well as defend the frontiers. That he did so competently and loyally testifies that he was as dedicated to the empire as his imperial mentor.

THE INEVITABLE?

The large historical questions do not go away, but they easily relapse into vacuity, question begging or, at least, lack of focus. There is little point in rummaging yet again among the fifty-seven causes of the Fall of the Western Roman Empire until we have well-defined questions and as explicit as possible a frame of reference.

The dismemberment of the West was not a cataclysmic event. The sack of Rome in AD 410, to take the most hackneyed example, was quite avoidable, and was — in any case — of psychological rather than strategic importance. Nonetheless, if we take an arbitrary period of roughly half a century between the death of Valentinian I in 375 and the occupation of Africa by the Vandals in 429–30, we cannot possibly deny that profound and seemingly irreversible changes have occurred.

At the beginning of this period imperial power and authority are dominant within the traditionally defined frontiers, and are regularly projected beyond them into barbarian territory through successful campaigns. Its rule is in many ways predatory and oppressive, but nobody within or outside the empire doubts its reality. There are many Germanic newcomers settled in the provinces, but they are subordinate to Roman administration. Many of the soldiers, officers and generals of the Roman army are themselves of Germanic origin, but their command structures, ambitions and loyalties are firmly Roman. Pressing heavily along the frontiers are the external Germanic peoples who cannot be annihilated or dispersed, but can be managed by a diplomacy whose precondition is the mutual recognition of ultimate Roman military ascendancy. The barbarians may be victorious here or there for a time, but sooner or later the emperor will always assemble enough strength to defeat them, and they know this.

By the end of this period the state of things is quite different. The contingencies of frontier politics — threats, concessions, playing one tribal group off against another — are now being enacted *within* imperial territories. Emperors no longer lead armies, but are themselves managed by powerful generals, who are sometimes Germanic tribal leaders as well. No responsible Roman statesman is now so unrealistic as to suppose that Roman armies are any longer dominant. The provinces of the West have identity on paper only. Large Germanic nations in arms are established in Pannonia, Gaul, Spain, Africa, under nominal treaties of alliance, negotiated from a position of Roman weakness. Any serious military undertaking by the imperial government must be indirect, manoeuvring one barbarian people against another. This can still be achieved, but such diplomatic skills cannot compensate for the palpable lack of Roman strength. Imperial laws, symbols, titles and administrative offices continue, but they lack effective coercive power, unless they are vested in warlords who can command the loyalties of the Germanic or Hunnic armies.

We need an adequate understanding of the chain of events in this approximate period, and to distinguish contingent and fortuitous factors from those inherent in the conditions of the time. An immediate search for 'weaknesses' in the empire will not help much, simply because we find too many of them too easily. Weakness is only defined by the scale and likelihood of the task or threat. Every state and empire has many weaknesses, and what is a weakness in one circumstance may be strength in another (the separation of civil and military authority, for example). If a state is unable to survive the combination of every threat on every frontier, every economic disaster and every political crisis erupting simultaneously that is not *weakness*, but rare and senseless misfortune, like the disasters that engulfed Minoan Crete. This is not what happened to the Western Roman empire.

The Roman empire, while retaining a recognisable identity, had succeeded in both absorbing great changes and recovering with great resilience from defeats and disasters. Two large and crude contrasts arise: why was the empire able to resist and survive the great calamities and invasions that so nearly wrecked it in the third century, yet unable to resist similar onslaughts in the fourth and fifth; and why did the Eastern half of the empire ultimately survive, when the Western eventually went under?[2]

In the period in question we can see something of a ratchet effect of declining Roman authority, although it was not of course geographically uniform. At each stage, with each new treaty or bargain on whatever frontier, more concessions have to be made, more frontiers have to be ruthlessly prioritised, and the bargains are correspondingly difficult for the Roman side to enforce. It is not inevitable that the ratchet will move down to the next notch, but stabilisation at each stage becomes increasingly difficult. The margins for manoeuvre and mistake are narrowing. New precedents are already set and cannot be reversed. Once Visigothic *foederati* are established and recognised, for example, it is difficult for Theodosius to isolate this treaty settlement as a special and unrepeatable case. Once Alaric combines the office of Roman *Magister* and Gothic king others will aspire to that position if they are strong enough.

In this discussion we make some use of the word 'inevitable', but not in any interesting sense, There are no strict laws of history — perhaps there are no interesting laws at all. We mean, loosely, that certain kinds of outcome were to be fully expected, given the larger background constraints, irrespective of the fortunes and abilities of individual leaders. Thus, it was inevitable that the impact of Britain's industrial revolution abroad would lead some other nations, such as Germany and the United States, to repeat the process. It was certainly not inevitable that the European tensions and adjustments required by the very rapid growth of Germany should be resolved by war.

It was inevitable that the Roman empire as a whole should be in a virtually permanent emergency over military manpower, and that the armies had to use an ever-increasing proportion of barbarian troops. It was *probably* inevitable that certain kinds of political decision would be taken over the imperial succession, given the very strong nature of dynastic traditions that had been established since Constantine. It was not at all inevitable that Theodosius neglected to train his sons militarily, nor that they should have both turned out to be incapable, nor that Honorius should have lived so long — until 423 — under the constant management of military figures that by then the imperial prestige and authority was so disused and ignored that it did not recover.

Most importantly, it was not at all inevitable that the earlier policy of Germanic immigration and recruitment should later have been replaced by *foederati*, Germanic kingdoms and warlords. There is no inexorable continuity from one to another, as Gibbon supposed. It is ironic, perhaps, that until very late in the century the Germanic kings did not want to destroy the empire — in the sense of supplanting it with states of their own — they had no such states. What they wanted was settlement land, power and prestige within an imperial framework. Some, such as Athaulf and Wallia, were (in their good moods) decidedly pro-Roman. But, in the process we are describing, successful and enduring treaties and agreements depend less on the attitudes of the parties than on the coincidence of interests and the final constraints of coercive power.[3]

The Hun and Alan migrations into the Danube regions had disrupted the whole Roman military-diplomatic policy along much of that frontier. This was no longer a simple shift in the tribal power balances as before, which Roman defences and alliances had long been adapted to anticipate and manage. This was a new global situation: the Hun newcomers had rapidly conquered and assimilated parts of the Alan and Gothic nations, and driven the rest to flee from their homelands. These groups no longer had the options of war or peace with Rome, raiding or trade, ransoming prisoners, renting out warriors and all the other variations of the old chessgame. The Goths had either to acquire territory within the empire, by one means or another, or disappear as an independent people.

The only other option, pursued by Athanaric, was to acquire new territory outside the empire through conquest of neighbouring peoples. This was so unattractive, due to the hardships, uncertainties and loss of good quality agricultural lands in their former home, that the majority of the Goths chose to follow Alavivus and Fritigern into the empire, rather than their traditional and hereditary leader, Athanaric.

Valens was thus faced with two distinct peoples, Tervingi and Greuthungi (with an Alan component), who urgently needed settlement in the empire in large numbers. Valens probably had not the military strength to resist both simultaneously, even if he had wished to, so the Tervingi (Visigoths) were admitted.

The migration would have taxed the Roman capacity of absorption severely, even without the mismanagement that actually occurred, but the task was not impossible. Finally came the confrontation at Adrianople, which was lost — like so many battles — due to Valens' stupid mistakes and tactical misfortune, rather than any inherent Roman military incompetence. But the Roman losses were so great that, after this, the strategic balance was permanently changed. Theodosius' manpower shortage was now so critical that he could not realistically hope to regain the position before 376.[4]

Even more than Valens, Theodosius cast greedy eyes on the great reservoir of potential manpower that the Visigoths represented, and sought to harness it to the Roman standard whenever and however he could. Fritigern and his followers did not exploit their victory very intelligently in four years of wandering and warfare, and the combined campaigns of Theodosius and Gratian were able to split the Goths, cultivate a distinct pro-Roman faction among their nobles and pave the way for the treaty of 382.

The Goths were ready to deal, since they had nowhere else to go and would eventually have to reach an accommodation with Rome. The empire no longer had any control over the dispositions to the north of the Danube — these were rapidly becoming a Hunnic affair — and could only reach agreement with the Goths or seek to destroy them, which was not a realistic option by now.

This gave the Visigoths the core of what they wanted. After their victory at Adrianople, no secure Visigoth king or chieftain could again be satisfied with disarmed, subordinate *laeti* status, if there was any prospect of achieving something better. They thus became an allied nation on delineated Roman territory. The same kind of conditions had probably been granted, perforce, to the Greuthungi in Pannonia by Gratian. The legacy of hostility and mistrust was not to be wished away, however. The provincials in the East remembered the depredations of the Goths; the Goths remembered the many broken Roman promises, and the treacherous massacre of their kinsmen by Julianus shortly after Adrianople.

Still, Theodosius worked strenuously to overcome this mistrust, and certainly succeeded to a degree.[5] Despite some disorders and revolts, in which the name of Alaric first appears, filling the space left by Fritigern, the Visigothic *foederati* on the whole kept their part of the bargain, and supplied troops who helped to win both of Theodosius' civil wars. By about 390 the great historian Ammianus Marcellinus, looking back on Adrianople, can express confidence that the storm has been weathered and that, as with the disaster at Cannae six centuries earlier, Rome will emerge triumphant as always.

Theodosius perhaps hoped that, given time and superior Roman statecraft, the Visigothic settlement would insensibly come to resemble the conventional *laeti*, with the cultural absorption of the Goths into the Roman mosaic of nations. But this prospect was not helped by the fact that, though flattered and respected, the Goths were being treated militarily not as equal allies, but as tools: it was too obvious that barbarian blood, in preference to Roman, could be expended against other enemies. Theodosius could hardly conceal this from the Goths, however he might wish to, when his own internal propaganda to the conservative Greek and Roman nobility was making this very point (which was what they wanted to hear). Fritigern, Alaric and Athaulf might not have been classically educated, but they were anything but politically stupid. At all events, the time needed for stable assimilation was not available. Theodosius' untimely death in 395 immediately threw up a new world situation.

Three new conditions emerged in the period after 395, all of them gravely damaging to the power balance of Romans (including, it goes without saying, adopted Romans) against barbarians. The succession of two incompetent boy rulers gave imperial power into other hands — generals, ministers, empresses — an uncertain, indirect rule. However loyal and capable they might be this was no substitute for the concentration of imperial power in a single, strong, militarily respected emperor.

The powerful dynastic principle which had given unity, loyalty and cooperation between the thrones of East and West, and had saved the empire more than once, was now paralysed. Worse, it turned into the opposite. Instead of cooperating, the real governments of East and West — Rufinus, Eudoxia, Eutropius, Stilicho — conspired and intrigued against each other like separate states. Doubtless some of this was drastic necessity, such as the need of the East to deflect Alaric westwards away from undefended territory, and doubtless Stilicho's intrigues were in the larger interest of ultimate unity. But the split occurred, became publicly visible, and the gainers were the opportunist barbarians.

Alaric, who might have been held in check by a strong military successor to Theodosius, was quick to exploit the situation. Buying him off with a top Roman army command in combination with his Gothic kingship was a very distinct turn of the ratchet. As well as having control of the arms factories and supply lines, as well as having learnt Roman military skills from his service as an ally, he could now ride either or both horses, and did so most destructively. Alaric became a third power centre within the empire: the established barbarian warlord, whose loyalty and services were in no way committed but had to be bid for. Alaric's volatile temperament and the near-impossibility of holding him to any enduring treaty, were a potent cause of the disorder. That the two other forces, the courts of East and West, were trying to hold him to contradictory settlements did not help. To counterbalance and ultimately use Alaric (perhaps a hopeless policy, but the best one available) and to halt the Radagaisus invasion, Stilicho was forced largely to abandon the defence of Britain and even most of Gaul to protect his power base in Italy. The Vandals, Suevi, Alans and others burst across the Rhine in great numbers with very little opposition, and could never be dislodged again.[6]

There was a further development in the West, typified by Stilicho himself and copied and enlarged on by his successors. With immature, militarily and politically incompetent emperors, real power, including the civil administration, devolved on a supreme military commander (generalissimos, as O'Flynn calls them) who managed a puppet emperor. His position, though real and perceptible, was not legitimised since there was no legal office either of regent or protector. With Honorius imperial status became fatally divorced from any real political power: it shrank to a symbolic thing only, enacting a shadow show in the gaudy but cloistered palace of Ravenna.

From then on actual power in the West was wielded centrally by figures such as Stilicho, Constantius and Aetius, who were careful to base themselves in their largely federate armies rather than the purple, even if they could aspire to it. The new title of 'Patrician' came to denote this special position. Many were energetically devoted to defending, or holding together, the Western empire, or as much of it as they could. But it was no longer the same empire. The Djinn, which had first appeared in 382, became decidedly mischievous in 395 and crossed the Rhine in 407, would not go back into the bottle.

The usurper from Britain, Constantine, nominally ruled Gaul between 407–11, but control of much of it had passed to the newly arrived barbarian invaders. Some of these, especially Burgundians and Franks, were recruited by Constantine as federates. Honorius' government attempted to oppose him, but with no success, and was forced to recognise Constantine in 409. Through his son, Constans, and his general, Gerontius, Constantine took control of Spain, but could not prevent the Vandals, Suevi and Alans from crossing the Pyrenees and establishing themselves there in 409.

Eventually Honorius found a capable Roman general, Constantius, who was able to defeat the usurper in 411 and restore a minimal Roman order to the Gallic provinces, but not Spain. This, as usual, had to be an acceptance of the realities. The Burgundians were now settled as a federate kingdom (renowned in the Nibelungenlied) west of the Rhine, and with the Alans supported another usurper, Jovinus.

In 410, having sacked Rome and plundered throughout Italy, Alaric suddenly died and was succeeded by his brother-in-law, Athaulf; he proved to be a more rational ruler after initially continuing to ravage Italy, and eventually became pro-Roman through his marriage in January 414 to Theodosius' formidable daughter, Galla Placidia. Their son, who died early in 415, was named Theodosius. The Visigoths, under Athaulf, had moved to Gaul in 412 initially in support of Jovinus, but then put down the rebellion on behalf of Honorius. The agreement did not last, however, and Constantius drove the Visigoths into Spain where, starving under a Roman blockade, Athaulf was murdered, and his successor, Wallia, concluded a new treaty with the empire. After two years of suppressing the other barbarian invaders of Spain on behalf of Honorius the Visigoths were permanently settled in Aquitaine in 418. Roman landowners were compelled to relinquish large areas of land for the settlement. Although Gaul and Spain were now nominally back under imperial control this rested on a patchwork of barbarian settlements and treaties, increasingly dependent on playing the groups off against each other.

The redoubtable Galla Placidia worked valiantly to hold together whatever she could, and indeed, was the principal power behind the throne. She had already married Constantius on 1 January 417, and finally had him declared co-emperor in early 421, but this was not recognised by Constantinople. It is eloquent of the contempt in which the useless Honorius was generally held, that his half-sister could have her husband elevated to the purple as co-emperor while the legitimate emperor — aged only thirty-six — was still reigning. Constantius, who might have, at last, reunited imperial authority with real military power, died suddenly in late 421 after only eight months as emperor. Galla Placidia could not maintain her position at court and went into exile in the East. Honorius died only two years later.[7]

The dynastic heir to Honorius was the son of Constantius and Galla Placidia, Valentinian III. In a significant move Theodosius II decided to support his young relative against a usurper, and Eastern troops installed Valentinian as Western emperor. Galla Placidia acted as Regent in the West, but it was the authority and seniority of the East that had been clearly re-established after the lengthy divide which followed the death of Theodosius.

New generalissimos arose in their turn. Aetius, likewise a Roman, based his power on his unique association with the Huns and authority over them (he had spent some years as a hostage with them, and became close to the Hunnic royal family). He fought a series of battles and political struggles with rivals for the supreme military command in the West, and in 433 compelled Galla Placidia to recognise his authority as Patrician. He was, nonetheless, able to assemble a coalition of Romans, Burgundians, Franks and Visigoths that halted Attila's seemingly irresistible sweep across Europe in 451. But this cooperation did not survive the common danger.

Despite being the dominant figure in the West for over twenty years Aetius did not by now even bother to take the purple himself. His successor, Ricimer, grandson of the Visigothic king Wallia, defended Italy by similar coalitions and manipulations, but set up and demolished puppet emperors at Ravenna according to requirements. Increasingly, as he and other warlords needed a veneer of Roman legitimacy, they looked not to Ravenna but to Constantinople, where the emperors were still in command of a viable and more respected Eastern empire.

Stilicho's downfall after thirteen years leading the West did lead to somewhat improved relations between the courts of East and West: on several occasions Constantinople sent troops and fleets to help the Western government, although the effectiveness of these was extremely limited.

These were by now moves of national alliance, rather than the unquestioning loyalty by which strong, dynastically related military emperors had once bound themselves to support each other. Now, realistically, the Eastern government negotiated with the crippled West increasingly as if it were one more powerful foreign kingdom. Earlier civil conflicts within the empire had been a matter of contesting supremacy over the whole Roman world. Under Arcadius' weak rule and the struggle for survival of the competing factions at his court, the East had come to see the West as a rival state, to be resisted, feared and weakened if possible — a degree of self-interest unthinkable since the anarchy of the mid-third century.

Eventually nothing prevented a dubiously loyal barbarian general-king, such as an Alaric-style figure, from occupying the position of Generalissimo (Alaric had, in fact, set up a usurper, Attalus, when Honorius refused his demands). After Stilicho, and down to the death of Aetius, the principal military commands were mainly held by Romans, but as military-political power slipped irretrievably away from emperors the way was surely open for it to become united with that of the Germanic kings. Finally, when everyone — including Constantinople — quite understood the position, and the senatorial aristocracy of Italy was glad to have at last an effective protector, these kings found that they no longer needed even the ritual of a puppet emperor, and abolished him. The last incumbent was retired, and simply not replaced. Not a dog barked.

How was it that similar crises had been overcome a century earlier, but could not now be surmounted? Some possible answers have already been suggested. They have little to do with the vigour, patriotism or abilities of the leaders thrown up at this time, or the resourcefulness of the (greatly changed) Roman military machine. Aetius, for example, probably deployed his resources as skilfully and effectively as any leader could, but by then the whole polity had broken apart and he or anyone else could only hope to rescue and preserve fragments of it.

A century earlier, the restoration of a shattered empire in 268–330 was in the teeth of similar threats. It was achieved by soldier-emperors, continually fighting wars against each other as well as the foreign invaders, and each of them liable to be slain and replaced by their own officers in a moment of failure or lack of vigilance. This was all extremely destructive: it could have disrupted the empire for good and very nearly did. But at least the emperors had to be first-class fighting soldiers and generals, through the unforgiving process of selection. Aurelian, for example, unified the broken empire geographically through his ferocious military prowess: neither rebel nor barbarian wanted to fight *him* if they could avoid it.

Diocletian, through the hereditary accident of having no son, bolted together an artificial, adoptive dynastic system — the Tetrarchy — which proved remarkably effective in stabilising the empire (so long as he personally dominated it), by ensuring that there was a capable military emperor on every threatened frontier. The arrangement was so successful that he and his son-in-law Galerius were able to draw off a huge campaign army from the Danube which crushed the Persians, but without the Danube frontier itself being breached. The years 285 to 305 have rightly been seen as a restoration of the empire.

There were longer-term consequences. Diocletian's adoptive system broke down, and Constantine's dynasty replaced it. Both of them ransacked the available wealth of the empire as systematically and ruthlessly as possible to support the enlarged armies, hugely strengthened frontiers, and the new bureaucracy, without which the preconditions for any sort of survival would have been lacking.

The return to a dynastic succession under Constantine had been a stabilising process. The loyalty of the soldiery, Roman or Germanic, required this exact, unambiguous focus of kin and blood. By now, the rulers had also learnt the basic lesson of Diocletian's political experiment: that there must be at least two related emperors, in East and West, if the frontiers were to be adequately defended. Valentinian, elected by the armies at the end of the Constantinian line, naturally sought to perpetuate his own dynasty. His son, Gratian, declared Augustus at the age of eight, was trained vigorously as a soldier and commander almost as soon as he could mount a horse and swing a sword.

The new military-imperial command system bequeathed both a dynastic rule of succession, and a fiscal and governmental machine which was certainly efficient at the sharp end of military defence, but less successful in harnessing the loyalties, cooperation and confidence of the economy and society it was protecting. The costs of Diocletian and Constantine's changes took some time to work through, but they eventually did.

Some Marxist historians, such as Ste Croix and Anderson, have located much of the West's weaknesses in the increasing, glaring and destabilising polarisation of wealth: the swollen Italian-Gallic-Spanish senatorial families at the top, and the hopeless, enserfed peasantry at the bottom, with less and less in between. The period is punctuated by rural revolts, especially in the West. There is force in this observation, but not a simple revolutionary message, as indeed Ste Croix acknowledges. The reluctance of landowners to supply recruits and the reluctance of *coloni* to be recruited, would have been there in any case. Loyalty, patriotism and civic spirit could not be the kind of thing that they had been in a tightly knit aristocratic Roman republic, although they were not absent: Germanic and Roman parvenu rulers displayed them readily enough. Most crudely, when fighting soldiers were urgently needed in a given place they had to be bought, quickly and expensively. The Eastern government had the ready gold to do this — or if necessary to bribe the barbarians temporarily until it could buy the military force to confront them. The West did not.

Stilicho had the utmost difficulty raising either recruits or money from the Italian nobles. Alaric's demand for 4000 lb of gold was not much beyond the average annual income of one senator, but in the end these nobles were to barter a third or more of their ample lands to barbarian kings of Italy — Odoacer and Theoderic — in exchange for the security which they would not pay Stilicho to provide for them. As long as their remaining estates were secure, and they could continue their games, consulships, festivals and intermarriages, the empire was to them an irrelevance. After all, their families all went back to the republic, did they not? The Germanic kingdoms, wishing to be civilised, readily obliged in this charade and recruited Roman administrators to help them to create stable states and to draft codes of law.

There was, in both West and East, the proliferation of self-serving bureaucracies which led to a retarding of effective government — that is, coercive authority that might be resented, but was respected, feared and obeyed. What had been more or less designed as a meritocratic machine, in practice became one which could not be regulated. Both Julian and Valentinian tried to counteract the corruption, not without some success.[8] But when after 395 imperial authority devolved on children with neither military prowess nor any real understanding of political power, and when the courts of East and West, in desperation, intrigued against each other and tried to off-load their barbarian pressures on to one another, then the conditions for imperial control of the process were not promising.

All of these difficulties might still have been overcome — at enormous social costs, it goes without saying. Someone had to reimpose military imperial authority, justified alone by its success in defeating and managing the external forces. In the East this was eventually achieved; in the West it was not. The East, subject to the same historical accidents, fractiousness and intrigues, invaded by Visigoths and others, did hold its polity together. It had the advantages of greater realisable monetary wealth, more closely communicating, defensible frontiers and commercial cities in which the curial classes still had an economic, moral and political stake in the empire which they knew. The upper aristocracy and bureaucracy was indeed grasping (Rufinus was hardly the model of a Confucian public servant) but they did depend much more on imperial favour, not their own long-established family wealth. They knew where the source of power lay, and they never forgot it.

The East was able to stabilise its Euphrates frontier in a way that the West was unable to stabilise the Rhine. Persia took advantage of perceived Roman weaknesses twice, in 421 and again in 441: on both occasions Roman armies defeated them and, as is to be expected between sophisticated empires, they were held firmly to their peace treaties.

The separation of authority between Eastern civil and military officials, though cumbersome, gave a balance which could easily have fallen apart but which ultimately protected the imperial throne. Unlike the Generalissimos in the West, Eastern civilian ministers during a minority monarchy — such as Eutropius, Anthemius and others — could hire and bargain with barbarian army leaders, without delivering all power into their hands. Having, as they supposed, broken the power of the Goths, they of course had to recruit other barbarians, but one single block of barbarians did not dominate the political balance as the Visigoths had come to do.

The Huns were certainly rapacious, and a formidable military enemy, but unlike the Visigoths they were not forced to seek land for settlement; they dominated Europe outside of the empire. Their concern was to plunder and extort wealth from the empire on a large scale, and to hire out their superb cavalry forces as mercenaries. In the event of defeat or failure they could always move on. Attila attempted to transform them into something resembling an empire to challenge Rome, and the enterprise was terribly destructive for both East and West. However after his sudden death his empire quickly lost cohesion, and disintegrated with the rebellion of the subject peoples.

Against the Huns the Eastern government tried to balance military units of their tribal rivals and those elements seeking to break away from Hunnic domination. Most of the Eastern generals throughout the first half of the fifth century have Germanic or Alanic names, and *foederati* continued to be recruited, although in smaller groups than in the West. Recruitment among Eastern provincials seems also to have been strongly pursued, including the warlike Isaurians of Asia Minor. On the collapse of Attila's empire substantial groups of barbarians, including Huns, were settled in the East and recruited into the army.

This multiplicity of powers, combined with a wealthier economy, shorter communications and a ruling class that could not withdraw haughtily into its villas allowed the East eventually to reunite power and authority into one focal imperial centre. The emperors, thanks to a full treasury, were able to buy off Attila, and then to resist him; that is, to persuade him to try his fortunes westwards.

Theodosius has been widely blamed for the settlement of 382, which set the precedent for the *foederati*. In our view, this was not his major mistake, indeed not a mistake at all. In the circumstances he and Gratian did well to pen the Visigoths into such a settlement. Given time and diplomacy — which he believed he might have — this might well have worked to Roman advantage, especially if he had not then had to try the loyalties of the treaty through two civil wars.

His mistakes were elsewhere. Unlike Valentinian, he made no attempt to train his own sons in military and political leadership, in the same way that his father had trained him. He was so attached to his own progeny — a natural thing — that he did not see the steadily yawning power vacuum, and he did almost nothing to establish a collegiate rule of East and West, which was so badly needed. Both Maximus and Arbogast offered him this palpable lesson, but he did not heed it. Rather, when his own military resources were seriously depleted he fought two extremely costly civil wars, at least one of which was probably avoidable. Men fought and died as usual, but supplies, support, rewards, trained manpower were all being consumed at a faster rate than they could possibly be replaced. He must have known this. Stilicho knew this, and so did Alaric. All the great sacrifices were to put an incompetent, mentally backward child on the Western throne. Then Theodosius died suddenly, and the power vacuum was there for anyone to occupy.

Might it have been otherwise? The answer has to be yes. At a most primitive level, if Honorius had inherited half of the qualities that Galla Placidia possessed, if Stilicho had shelved his Eastern ambitions, if Honorius had been deposed or had died earlier then the stuffing might have been put back into the Western *imperium*. Contemporary historians, even the great Ammianus, still looked essentially backwards, as all their culture taught them to do: Rome survived Cannae, survived the destruction of Decius and his army by the Goths, and eventually recovered. Why should it not do so again?

The background conditions had changed radically. A comparison with the crises of the late second–early third centuries shows that very different forces were at work. The barbarian invasions of that period were, in the last resort, raiding and plundering on a grand scale, not migrations. The real danger then was not that the empire would be permanently swamped by new peoples, but that it would permanently fragment into separate *Roman* states, as it temporarily did. The Hun migrations created a genuinely new world problem, in which the skilful and previously successful strategy of assimilating Germanic and other peoples into the Roman polity was no longer given time and resources to work, and finally unravelled.

Certainly, states in adversity are often shrewder, more astute and vigorous than states lolling in unchallenged supremacy. But there are margins of allowable accident and incompetence, and by the death of Stilicho these were very thin. No longer was it Rome that was built to last and destined to survive, but the New Rome, Constantinople. The influx of Visigoths and Greuthungi had to be accommodated somehow. In prolonged global crisis, power centres closed in on themselves and held on, more or less intelligently, to what they had. The East helped the West sporadically, as well as it might another, fraternal state, but under pressure it exported its own European problems westwards. It did its deals with Goths, Huns, Alans and others, but also relocated and focused final authority at a central imperial point which everyone, barbarians included, understood.

The focal role of Constantinople can hardly be exaggerated. In the West, the function of political capital had shifted from Rome, the ancient and traditional City, to Milan, a working imperial capital close to the frontiers and main communications routes, and then Ravenna, a ceremonial refuge, perilously distant from the armies and the centres of real power. In the East, except for a brief period when Theodosius was forced to rule from Salonica, Constantinople was always the spiritual, imperial, administrative and strategic centre of power, with no rivals.[9] Its position on the straits, dominating the route to Asia Minor and the East, and its massive fortifications, greatly strengthened in the fifth century, made it impregnable until 1204. Whatever the temporary losses and setbacks of the Eastern empire, it was always a refuge, power centre and source of imperial authority.

Had the West been able to do likewise it might well have held the ring, and provided the emerging Gothic and Frankish kingdoms with a confident imperial Roman framework of law, statecraft, administration and religion within which they could have prospered, struggled and grown with a richer culture than they in fact inherited. Whether this would have been a Good Thing, in whatever sense, is of course a matter for argument. But look at the Papacy, and at Charlemagne: the successful followers of the Roman empire still wanted to be what they perceived Caesar Augustus to have once been.[10]

Theodosius has been called the Great, but principally in gratitude for his establishment of *Unam Sanctam Catholicam Apostolicam Ecclesiam*. We have been more concerned with the efforts of both he and his successor Stilicho to accommodate a new scale of barbarian challenge, in the most difficult of conditions, which few — if any — Roman rulers had faced before. Theodosius was not one of the greatest military emperors, such as Aurelian, Constantine or Valentinian, but his great diplomatic skills were badly needed in this crucial period. Perhaps no other emperor could have conciliated and managed the Goths as he did, and bought the empire a vitally needed breathing space to consolidate its resources. The adverse side of his warm, emotionally engaging nature emerged in several ways, which were both impolitic and damaging. He was too quick to anger and too quick to forgive. His devoted love for his family and dynasty led him to neglect the best interests of a united empire. It was his misfortune that he died early, that the breathing space for assimilation was cut short, and that the new barbarian pressures which his death released eventually proved too great for a united empire to accommodate in time.

From our Gibbonian armchairs we can only say that both Theodosius and Stilicho struggled with the problems manfully and heroically, but in vain.

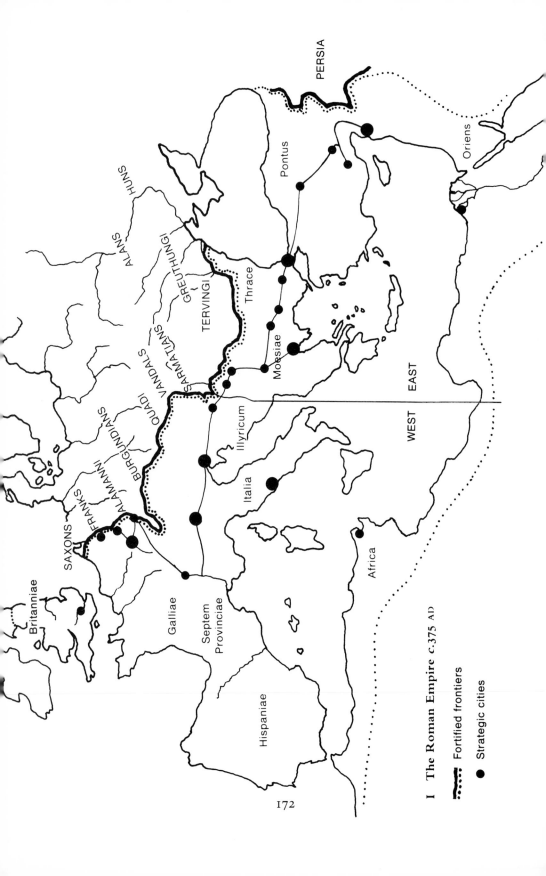

172

I **The Roman Empire** c.375 AD

······ Fortified frontiers
● Strategic cities

PERSIA

Oriens

Pontus

ALANS
HUNS

GREUTHUNGI

Thrace

TERVINGI
GREUTHUNGI

SARMATIANS

VANDALS

QUADI

Moesiae

Illyricum

EAST

WEST

Italia

BURGUNDIANS

ALAMANNI

FRANKS

SAXONS

Britanniae

Galliae

Septem
Provinciae

Hispaniae

Africa

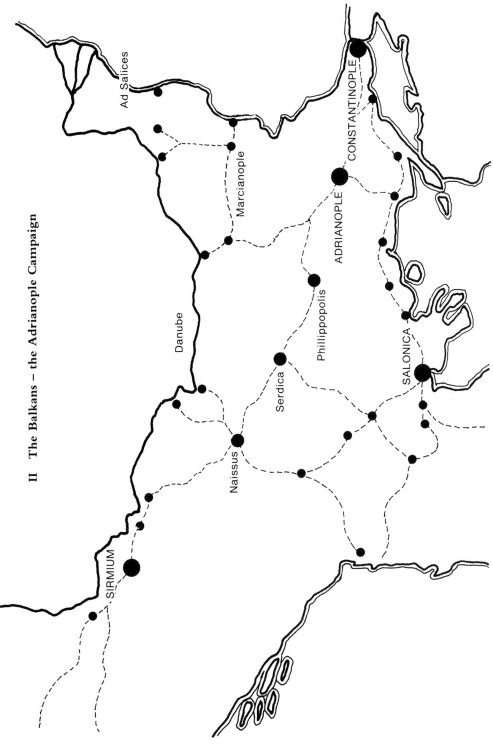

II   The Balkans – the Adrianople Campaign

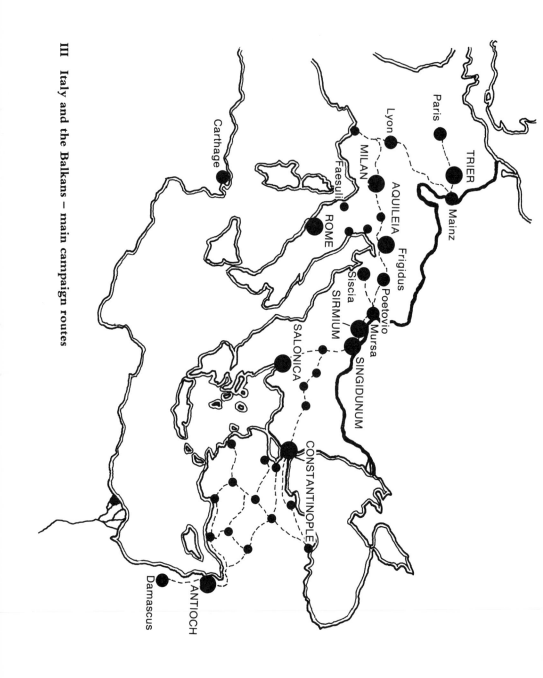

III Italy and the Balkans – main campaign routes

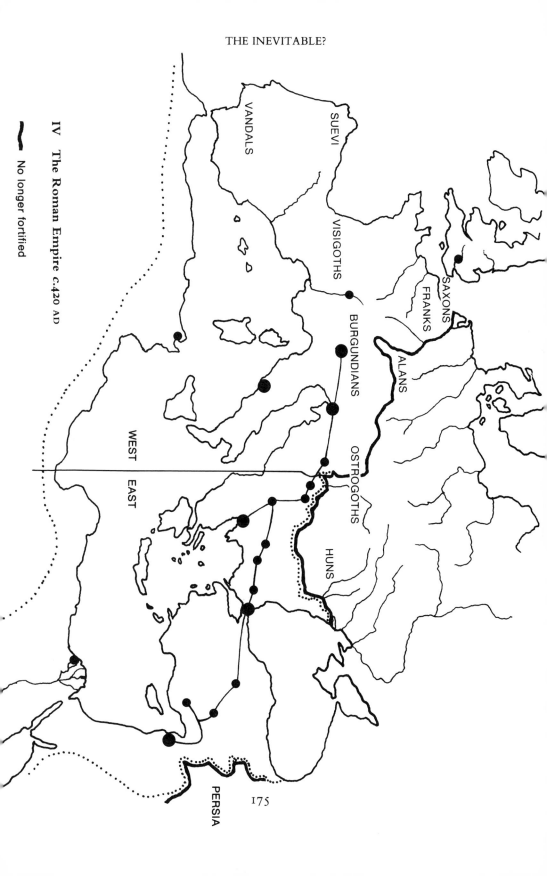

IV The Roman Empire c.420 AD

〰 No longer fortified

VANDALS

SUEVI

VISIGOTHS

SAXONS

FRANKS

BURGUNDIANS

ALANS

WEST

EAST

OSTROGOTHS

HUNS

PERSIA

APPENDIX I

The Battle of Adrianople —
its Military Significance

'The military importance of Adrianople was unmistakable; it was a victory of cavalry over infantry.'

In these words Sir Charles Oman[1] set out a view which, despite much recent work on the subject, still exercises a strong influence on studies of the period and its warfare.[2] The image of Gothic cavalry riding down the enfeebled infantry of the later empire was an attractive one to those who sought evidence of the decline of the army, and thus, symbolically, of the state.

In pursuing these issues almost all fail to appreciate the tactical dimension of the battle, and concentrate instead on details of army composition — especially that of the decisive charge of the barbarians which turned the flank of the Roman army and led to disaster. Ammianus compares the defeat to Cannae, where the Roman army was also outflanked, cut off from safe retreat and almost wiped out.[3] In terms of the scale of losses this is a fair comparison, and there is a further similarity in that cavalry played a decisive role in the manoeuvres which led to Roman defeat.

The similarity, however, extends solely to the tactical failures of the Roman armies involved. The army of the late fourth-century Roman empire was only vaguely similar to that of the middle republic which was destroyed at Cannae, and significantly it included a much stronger contingent of cavalry. It might even be said that it was the very success of this Roman cavalry which led to the downfall of the army at Adrianople.

Essentially, any warfare is determined by manoeuvre, and cavalry simply supply a degree of mobility with which to attempt to out-manoeuvre an enemy, tactically on the battlefield or strategically in a campaign.[4] There can be no doubt that, if it had been only Gothic infantry, rather than Gothic and Alan cavalry, which had surrounded the Roman army at Adrianople, the result would have been no different. Valens and his army failed tactically.

In chapter 6 we discussed the state of the Roman army of the later fourth century, and suggested that — certainly before the battle of Adrianople — it was a professional and competent force which achieved all that was asked of it (given adequate leadership). The descriptions of the army in action which Ammianus has given us, at Adrianople and elsewhere, reveal a competence and spirit which would not have been out of place in any of the conquering armies of the early empire. What, then, went wrong?

To answer this question we need to consider three aspects of the conflict: first, the size of the opposing forces; second, their composition, and last (but most importantly) their tactical deployment and leadership.

We have already briefly discussed the size of the army available to Valens (chapter 6, pp.80–81). The total number of *comitatenses* (the field army) in the East under Valens may have been in the region of 100,000 men at most, with a rather larger number (120,000) as static garrisons in the *limitanei*.[5] In any period it would have been a major effort to put one-third of any potential army into the field as a single force, and only in exceptional circumstances could such a proportion be exceeded, with all the attendant risks of denudation of some areas of defence in favour of others.[6] Valens had to conclude a hasty settlement of the Armenian question with the Persians to free his army for the Adrianople campaign, but he must have been compelled to leave a significant force behind on his eastern frontier.

The Gothic threat was obviously recognised to be significant, given the defeats which elements of the Roman army had suffered, and the assistance which Gratian was bringing to his colleague in the East. However, it should be considered that the Romans had also had their successes against the Goths since 376, some by the very commanders who were advising Valens in the Adrianople campaign. After their initial success against Lupicinus and the regional army of Thrace, the Visigoths had been penned into the Dobruja by numerically inferior Roman forces. The battle of Ad Salices which followed, had been a bloody conflict, but the heavily outnumbered Roman forces had at least held the Visigoths on the battlefield and maintained the blockade which was starving the enemy.[7]

The perception was clearly that a major effort was required to defeat the Goths, but not that a desperate situation demanded the stripping of frontiers and the resources of the whole empire being called on. The personal participation of the emperor, with the support of the principal field army of the East, was such a major effort and we have no need to query the absence of the total manpower resource of the empire in this campaign.

It is impossible to be precise about the strength of Valens' army, but we would suggest that a figure of 25–30,000 men cannot be far from the truth. The Roman army certainly outnumbered the Goths (see below, p.000 and chapter 6), but the higher figures which have been suggested, of up to 40,000 men, seem to be unrealistic given the strains of assembling such a force from throughout the East, and also the levels of force which had been put into other campaigns. Julian had assembled an army of 65,000 from the combined forces of East and West for a major and long-planned expedition, and the desperate exigencies of civil wars had only succeeded in drawing up combined armies on this sort of level under Constantius II.[8]

The numbers which the Goths could put into the field against Valens' army have also been discussed above (chapter 7, p.86). A Gothic army, in their homelands outside the empire, consisted of the tribal chiefs, their nobles and retainers and as such they constituted a warrior aristocracy rather than any general tribal levy. The descriptions of Gothic warriors supplied under treaty to serve in Roman campaigns, with their long mail shirts and comprehensive weaponry, suggest wealthy warrior elites and not any peasant force. The figure usually given for a tribal 'army' is 3000, and although there is an element of biblical orthodoxy in such repetitive figures there can be little doubt about the scale of resources involved in most warfare of that period. The destruction of the first greater Gothic kingdom by the Roman empire under Claudius and Aurelian, in the later third century, arose from the decisive defeat of Cannabas and his 5000 warriors.

What arose in the 370s was a greatly different situation, where the entire Tervingian association was on the move following the destruction of their security by the Huns. Although a part of the Tervingi remained outside the empire under the leadership of Athanaric, the bulk of them crossed the Danube with Alavivus and Fritigern, and the Romans faced a desperate people with every mature male fighting for the survival of the tribe. In such circumstances it would be no surprise to find 25 per cent of the population under arms, and a number of figures work towards an estimate of 100,000 for the total Tervingian immigration in 376.

Valens was encouraged by reports that the Tervingi numbered only 10,000 before Adrianople, and although this later proved to be a mistake it provides a broad order of magnitude which was expected. Theodosius later disposed of 20,000 Visigothic warriors in his campaign against Eugenius and Arbogast, and Alaric and Alatheus in their various negotiations with the Western Roman government asked for payment or supplies which suggest a similar total population and fighting force. Therefore we suggest that at Adrianople Valens faced a Gothic force which numbered roughly 20,000 men.

A further complication when considering the numbers of barbarians which Valens faced is the composition of the 'Gothic' army. We know that the Tervingi, both outside and within the empire, were foot soldiers. Their preferred mode of fighting, with a defensive base provided by their wagons (or even through the construction of field fortifications — such as Athanaric's attempts to hold off the Huns), demonstrate that they were not a mobile army. Outside the empire their cavalry was provided by the Taifali, who had also on occasion provided support for the Romans under treaty obligations, such as during Constantius II's campaign against the Limigantes. The immobility of the Tervingi in the face of organised Roman opposition in the years 376–8 emphasises their lack of cavalry, as does their rapid success in breaking out of the Balkans/Black Sea/Danube triangle after they had been joined by the Huns, Alans and Greuthungi.

There must, therefore, have been a significant addition to the numbers of the Tervingi through the arrival of the forces led by Alatheus and

Saphrax. The circumstances of their flight across the Danube, which was of a fragment of the Greuthungian people after their defeat by the Huns, must have led to a much smaller migration than that of their neighbours. However, the subsequent history of this group, especially their settlement in Pannonia by Gratian and their later significant contribution of cavalry to Stilicho's army, suggest that they crossed the Danube in numbers. Even so, it is unlikely that they rivalled Fritigern's people in numbers and, even allowing for their contribution, the total force opposing Valens must still have been in the region of 20–25,000 at most.

The significance of this mounted group lay in its contribution to the general mobility of the barbarians over a wide area and years of campaigning, or in their tactical surprise when they appeared as an unexpected element at Adrianople. However they did not, of themselves, constitute a particular threat: Roman armies had been dealing with mounted enemies very successfully for a long time, especially on the eastern frontiers where the principal threat to the empire — Parthia and Sassanid Persia — were based almost exclusively on cavalry forces. Similarly, on the Danube, Sarmatian forces had long been perceived to be dangerous in battle, but had never constituted a serious long-term threat. One of our best sources for Roman military manoeuvres, Arrian's Order of Battle against the Alans, recognised the potential threat of a cavalry opponent, but there is no indication that the Alans were ever seen to be beyond the capacity of a *well-organised* Roman infantry force to deal with.

In two incidents during the campaigns leading up to Adrianople we can see contrasting results in battle between Romans and mounted barbarians. In the first, Barzimanes — leading a mainly infantry force and heavily outnumbered — was surprised by the enemy, but organised a brave resistance and might have withdrawn with honours equal had he not been surrounded by cavalry and killed. Shortly afterwards, the *dux* Frigeridus met and comprehensively defeated the cavalry forces of the Taifali and Greuthungi under Farnobius: the survivors were settled in Italy, in the traditional manner.[9] The difference lay in the tactical circumstances.

This brings us to the final point of our discussion. The fatal flaw at Adrianople lay not in the size of the opposing forces nor the quality of the Roman army, nor in the composition of the two opposing forces. The Roman army was larger, and the main problem experienced by the Roman army (as on other occasions) was in storming the Gothic wagon laager defended by their infantry, rather than failing to stand up to Gothic cavalry (in fact the most effective cavalry available in the conflict — the Huns who rode with the Greuthungi and Alans of Alatheus and Saphrax — seem to have sat out the battle in true Hunnic style and waited to join the winning side!).[10]

Valens was indecisive, diplomatically and tactically. At one moment he wanted to attack, perhaps for vain motives, and at the next to negotiate a bloodless victory. Fritigern, too, probably wanted to avert an all-out conflict if he could, but had a cooler head and was in better control of the contingencies. Valens' army suffered a long, exhausting delay while the emperor vacillated, having already made the long march from their camp at Adrianople. The feeling of indecision and confusion, and perhaps even panic, at the top must have affected the generals and unit commanders, as well as the soldiers, every bit as much as the waiting and the heat.

Valens' intelligence reports were defective, and he seems to have veered rapidly between the conflicting advice given by his senior officers. All of this might have been recoverable, had not the tactical confusion caused by a lack of coherent and effective leadership resulted in battle being joined prematurely by the Roman cavalry (after the long stand-off such an 'accident' must have been increasingly likely). The Roman left wing, which had been deploying as the last element of the army, having been at the rear in the order of march, rushed ahead of the rest of the army and drove the Goths back to their wagons.

However this attack, initially successful or not, entailed the fatal mistake of leaving the left wing of the infantry centre of the army with no protection or reserves. The Roman cavalry broke in confusion, and the disorganised left wing was abandoned and swamped by the attacking barbarians. In this chaos the cavalry forces of Greuthungi and Alans attacked and achieved complete surprise: the Roman cavalry, and seemingly most of their infantry reserves, fled, leaving the rest of the army to face the Visigoths, who now pressed forward from their defences. Once the mobile Gothic forces had exploited the gap on the left wing and the failure of the Roman reserves there could be little doubt about the eventual outcome.

It is instructive to consider potentially similar situations, which developed under Julian, and against the Visigoths at Ad Salices. At the battle of Strasbourg the Roman cavalry on the right wing broke in disorder, to the encouragement of the Alamanni, and threatened to disrupt the infantry and expose them to envelopment and destruction. Since the Romans were outnumbered, the role of the cavalry in preventing such manoeuvres was all the more significant, but Julian, always present and in control on the battlefield, stemmed the rout by prompt and firm action at the critical moment. Having rallied his troops, he returned them to their place, and the battle was eventually won in the centre by the infantry.[11]

At Ad Salices, where the Romans were again outnumbered, the left wing was broken and ran. In this instance a strong reserve force deployed, rallied the left and the battle line held to enable the Romans to inflict serious losses on the Goths. Ammianus makes a particular point of the Roman discipline at the commencement of the battle, in strong contrast to the chaotic rush to destruction which we have seen above at Adrianople.[12]

When the Roman infantry, exhausted, surrounded and battered finally broke and ran at Adrianople, it is a clear sign of the confusion that the emperor was seen to be abandoned by his bodyguard and seeking refuge anywhere he could on the battlefield. His generals were still in positions to see the developing fray, and attempt to take action — Trajanus spotted the danger to the emperor, and Victor went in search of the reserves. However the reserves had already fled, and Victor, Richomer and Saturninus followed suit (Trajanus died on the field, perhaps in an attempt to save Valens).

The failures of coordination by Valens, his lack of leadership and the absence of any meaningful battle-plan to guard against surprise attack or deploy adequate reserves, stand out against the successes mentioned above by outnumbered Roman armies when they were well-led and organised. The army had not failed, its leadership had.

Whether that failure would inevitably turn into the longer-term consequences of Gothic settlement, and their role in the future survival of the empire, is a question which we have already discussed above (chapter 12). Wolfram states that 'Adrianople ... was certainly not a decisive battle' but only in the sense that Theodosius and his successors still had options to consider, and the outcome of the battle was the beginning of a process rather than a conclusion.[13]

APPENDIX II

The Roman Army in the Later Fourth Century —

Command Structures, Composition and Size

As the guarantor of the empire's security, and its greatest, dominant expense, the role of the army has been crucial in almost all of the aspects which have been discussed above (only in religion was its involvement peripheral rather than central). The developments which took place within the later Roman army had a profound influence on the shape and style of the empire, and to a large degree determined its fate. This section does not set out to be a major study of the army in this period (that work has yet to be written), but seeks to address those points which are directly relevant to the arguments which have been put forward in our main text, and to expand on some of the comments made therein.[1]

In chapter 6 we considered the condition of the army which had developed through the fourth century to be inherited by Theodosius, and briefly commented on the military resources which he (and Stilicho) had at their disposal. The size of those resources has always been a major point of contention, and we have made some assumptions and suggestions about the issue on which we will expand below. The theoretical total of Roman forces has relevance to the arguments about expense and allocation of financial resources, and the probable realistic figures for the availability of military forces will have determined the options open to the rulers of the empire.

The composition of those forces is also a material consideration, since much has traditionally been made of the 'barbarisation' of the army and of supposed declines in ability and organisation. Recent views on the 'demilitarisation' of the population of the empire have contributed to our understanding of the processes at work.[2]

The command structure of the army has been recognised as one of the more significant military developments of our period, contributing to the differences between East and West at a time when such variations may have had a decisive part in the ultimate survival of one and the decline of the other. In this we will argue that the East, as in other areas, proved the more adaptable and successful.[3]

We have referred (in chapter 6) to the general order of magnitude of the army throughout the fourth century, in both East and West. We have a number of documentary sources which can be made to provide figures for the size of the army at various points in its development, and many studies have attempted to analyse these in detail and produce 'accurate' figures for the military manpower of the empire at any one date. Our concern has been to consider the general level of resources available, and therefore this is not intended to be a detailed critique of these earlier studies, or an attempt to justify exact numbers for individual units or for the army as a whole.[4]

For the earlier empire, before the chaos of the third century, we have fairly reliable evidence for the theoretical size of the Roman army. This tends to be based on an accurate count of the numbers of legions, to which is added an equivalent number of auxiliaries. Such exercises suggest an early third-century army of some 330,000 men. There is, however, limited evidence for the real level of auxiliary numbers, but in the absence of any better figures this provides some sort of theoretical baseline for our comments. The real numbers involved in these early armies is another issue, with the general unspoken assumption made by modern commentators that numbers provided by early imperial (or even republican) sources are 'accurate', and those of the later empire 'inaccurate', or even hugely falsified.[5] The extent of the difference between 'real' and 'paper' numbers is still a major problem for army studies, and has probably received more attention in the later empire than other periods of Roman military history. We will however make some suggestions below.

That Diocletian and Constantine made great efforts to expand the army is not in doubt, even if the exact numbers are. We have made suggestions above (p.79–80) for this early fourth-century stage, and will only say here that, after the costly struggles of their successors and the obvious difficulties in recruitment that they faced, the army of the late fourth century must have been no larger — and probably significantly smaller. This is, of course, especially true after the losses at Adrianople.

The best guesses for this later army must be derived from the best available source — the *Notitia Dignitatum*. We have essentially taken the analysis proposed by Jones, and filtered it through a series of assumptions which we will now set out.[6] The army in the East in 395 was the result of the division of forces between the two parts of the empire, and the rebuilding of it after Adrianople by Theodosius. The theoretical figures produced by Jones indicate a total of 104,000 in the Eastern *comitatenses*, and we would accept that as a good general figure. However, he assumes that legions in the *limitanei* were three times the strength of those in the field army, and we cannot see any real justification for this: by changing that assumption (and using consistent theoretical unit strengths — of 1000 men in a legion — throughout) a figure of 190,000 is produced for the frontier troops — a total (theoretical) Eastern army of some 294,000 men.[7]

As MacMullen and others have made clear, however, the evidence points towards the theoretical figures produced by such arguments being far removed from the reality. To allow for this we have speculated that there was an overall factor by which all units were under nominal strength. Although this variation will have been unit specific (according to the honesty of its commander, for example), and there will have been differences between regions, frontiers, styles of units (horses were expensive to maintain), etc., we are — as we said above — concerned with general levels and not specifics. Therefore we have applied standard reductions to the theoretical figures mentioned above. We have also made the assumption that the *comitatenses* would have had better access to recruits, and be more likely to be nearer their complement than those units in the *limitanei*. Taking the field army to be at four-fifths strength, and the frontier garrisons at two-thirds, we arrive at figures of roughly 80,000 men in the former and 125,000 in the latter.

Using these numbers as starting points we have worked back (and forward) to suggest the forces available at a number of crucial points in our study. The losses likely to have been suffered in major campaigns have been considered, along with the potential for recruitment and the commentaries we have on the use of federate or other troops to make up for deficiencies in the regular army. We have also attempted to carry out a similar exercise for the Western army.

The lists in the *Notitia* for the West were amended until a much later date than those we possess for the East, reflecting the position in the early 420s after much of the Western army had been lost, and numbers made up from the promotion of many units of the *limitanei* to the *comitatenses* and the very extensive use of federate forces. We thus have rough figures which can be deduced from the *Notitia* for the end of the period in which we are interested, and will work towards these after tracing the development of the Eastern army.

Taking the figures suggested above for the Roman army in the East (80,000 and 125,000 in the *comitatenses* and the *limitanei* respectively) in 395, there were a number of occasions when significant changes to the size of the army may have taken place. Working back through time, the obvious points are the war against Eugenius and Arbogast (394), the campaign against Maximus (388), the Gothic wars of 378–82, and the Adrianople campaign (376–8) itself. These were not, of course, occasions of losses in isolation: there was continuous recruitment within the standard Roman conscriptive process, and there was also very substantial barbarian recruitment into regular Roman formations as well as the employment of federates. We suggest, however, that the regular Roman army declined throughout this period.

The campaign of 394 was expected to be a difficult one, and the position at the decisive battle of the Frigidus was not initially good for the Eastern forces of Theodosius. However, the very substantial losses in this frontal conflict seem to have been primarily among the Gothic federate forces, and there may have been limited losses among the regular forces of the East.[8] Similarly, against Maximus in 388, the East relied heavily on federates and achieved a rapid and relatively bloodless victory.

Apart from limited losses in these two campaigns, and others against the barbarian rebels in 391, neither field nor garrison forces of the East should have suffered more than the capability of the recruitment process to replace losses could bear in the period described. The chaotic period of fluctuating fortunes between Adrianople and the Treaty of 382 probably represented a time when Roman losses were just about matched by the strenuous recruiting efforts of Theodosius, especially among the Goths. The principal point of change for the army of the East in our period must therefore have been the loss suffered at Adrianople: having argued above (App. I and pp.79–81) that the total deployed by Valens was in the order of 25–30,000, and taking losses as two-thirds of the army, there must have been a loss of some 10–20,000 of the best troops in the East. The *comitatenses* in the East in 376–8 then probably numbered some 100,000 men; the only period of significant losses among the Eastern *limitanei* can have been in the preferential posting of recruits to the depleted field army, and in the limited losses of garrisons in the uncertainty after Adrianople, and so their total numbers are suggested to be in the region of 130–140,000 men.

We are also interested in the army which survived Theodosius, and make the following suggestions about the East after 395. There were obvious recruitment difficulties, compounded by the occupation of much of Illyricum by Alaric, and a general suspicion of the army by the civilian administrators who held sway in the East through this period (no doubt compounded by the removal, in one way or another, of both Rufinus and Eutropius by military means). The stability of the East and its wealth, despite occasional disruption, made the option of running down — or at least not vigorously maintaining — the army an attractive option, which was generally successful in facing or diverting the limited threats which arose. The overall size of the Eastern army, especially the field army which had relied so heavily on Gothic recruitment under Theodosius, must have declined under Arcadius.[9]

Despite not being involved at Adrianople, the army of the West faced a more destructive time in the late fourth and early fifth centuries. The vigorous and successful army bequeathed by Julian and Valentinian to Gratian was at least the equal of that of the East in 375, and enjoyed advantages in its recruiting grounds.[10] After Adrianople, this position must have been substantially emphasised, and Theodosius certainly inherited the weaker part of the army in 378. We need, therefore, to consider how this situation was reversed in the following three decades.

Gratian had to face a series of difficult campaigns to assist his colleague in the East after 378, and also to stabilise the position in his own territories against the other barbarian pressures from across the Rhine and upper Danube. In 383 the armies of the West faced each other in the civil conflict initiated by Maximus: but this was a war of politics and loyalties, and there can have been limited casualties. It may be significant, however, that Gratian was criticised for his favouring of Alanic soldiers, and that he was therefore taking advantage of his settlement reached with the peoples of Alatheus and Saphrax to substantially reinforce his army with federate contingents rather than recruiting regular forces.

Maximus did not create serious losses in the forces of the West in 383 against Gratian, or in 387 against Valentinian II. However the references to strong barbarian contingents in Western armies at this time suggest that the scope of the civil conflicts was already leading to greater reliance on federate forces. In 388 the victory of Theodosius, although rapidly achieved, must have resulted in considerable losses among the Western army. Apart from the ongoing difficulties of frontier warfare (we know that the Rhine demanded attention throughout these years) the next major conflict for the West was the revolt of Arbogast and Eugenius. The final battle of this war, at the Frigidus, caused heavy casualties on both sides; however the East took the blow with its Gothic federates in the front line, and the West did not have this resource. In the aftermath of victory, there can be little doubt that the more substantial and successful part of the army was sent back to the East by Stilicho.[11]

Under Stilicho, the West then suffered a debilitating series of conflicts, from the inconclusive campaigns against Alaric in Greece to the much more bloody struggles against him and other enemies in Italy itself and on the frontiers. Between 395 and his downfall in 408 Stilicho had increasing difficulties in mobilising large armies, and the use of barbarian contingents in *ad hoc* arrangements became a sign of these difficulties. The other interpretation of this development is that the focus of Stilicho's reign was the conflict with Alaric and the East, and that the ready availability of barbarian allied contingents must have been a welcome means to reinforce his regular forces and relieve distracting pressures on the frontiers. Despite these difficulties, Stilicho did manage to put significant armies into the field, and although he failed to hold all of the West together this must have been as much due to the combination of pressures as the deficiencies in his own resources.

After the fall of Stilicho the army of the West collapsed, and the regular Roman forces available to his successors became no more than counterweights to the dominant barbarian forces which had irrevocably taken possession of imperial territory after 407. Although the *Notitia* records a very substantial army apparently surviving in the 420s, much of the field army by that stage consisted of *limitanei* who had nominally been raised to the *comitatenses*. This was a paper exercise, and even if the garrisons had survived at any significant level through the turmoil of the late fourth and early fifth centuries they can have contributed little to the disposable strength available.[12]

The use of barbarian contingents, either Visigothic federates or others, has been extensively discussed above. The position in the East after Adrianople dictated Theodosius' military strategy, and the dire necessities of Stilicho's reign enforced the increasing reliance of the West on barbarian allies, recruited under much more vague terms than the original settlement of the Visigoths. Both Theodosius and Stilicho were responding to the demands of the situation, and while they were in command their successes justified the policies pursued out of necessity. When their strong personal authority was removed from the equation the balance swung irretrievably against the empire.

The position of Stilicho as supreme military (and effectively political) authority in the West, arose from the new command structure instituted by Constantine for his remodelled army. The most significant point is that there was least change in this structure in the West, with the exception of the role of the emperor as supreme commander. If there had been a strong imperial figure, with political and military credibility — such as Constantine himself — there would have been nothing unusual in the scope of Stilicho's official authority. The crucial change came with Theodosius, who provided that leadership in the East but created an effective power vacuum in the West, especially through his treatment of Valentinian.

The presence of Theodosius helped to maintain a broader spectrum of power among his civil and military officials in Constantinople, and after his death the struggles between them helped to prevent any domination of both spheres of government by a single figure. The broader power structure which emerged under Theodosius in the East was a significant factor in the different responses to crises in East and West under his sons, and although this was the unintentional outcome of his dynastic policies it was one of his most significant legacies.

The generalised power structure as illustrated below essentially held true for the West from Constantine to Stilicho, with the crucial change that — after Maximus — the emperor in the West was a nominal authority. The structure in the East which follows, is that bequeathed by Theodosius to Arcadius and his court.

Senior Military Hierarchy

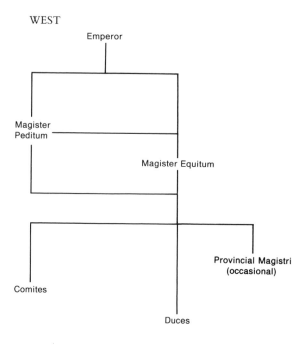

WEST

Emperor

Magister Peditum

Magister Equitum

Comites

Duces

Provincial Magistri (occasional)

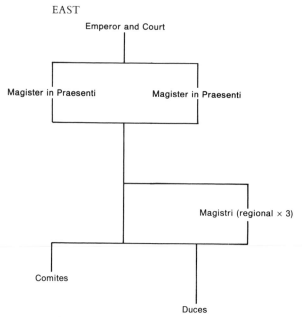

EAST

Emperor and Court

Magister in Praesenti

Magister in Praesenti

Magistri (regional × 3)

Comites

Duces

APPENDIX III

The Dynasties of Valentinian and Theodosius

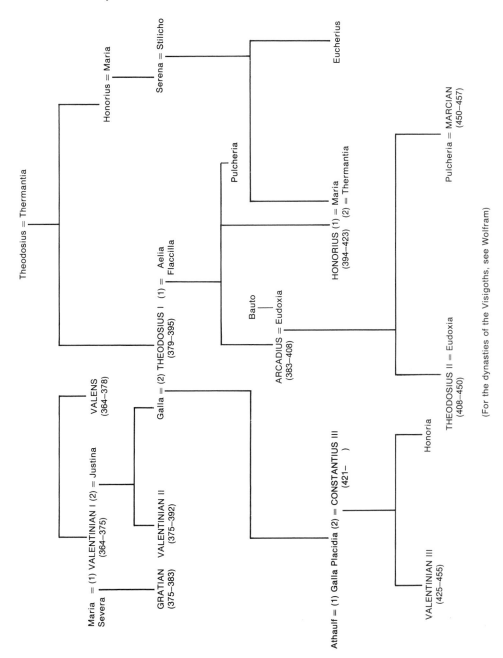

(For the dynasties of the Visigoths, see Wolfram)

APPENDIX IV

Barbarian Settlements

(Based on the comprehensive Appendix of Ste Croix, *Class Struggles in the Ancient Greek World*, 1981.)

AD 8. Tiberius settles 40,000 Suevi and Sugambri on the west of the Rhine.

AD ? Sextus Aelius Catus settles 50,000 Getae (Dacians) south of the Danube.

171 onwards? Marcus Aurelius settles Quadi and other peoples in Dacia, Pannonia, Moesia, Germania and Italy, but later removes them from Italy.

231–2 Gallienus (allegedly) cedes part of Pannonia to the Marcomannic king Attalus, but this is in extreme emergency.

268–270 After defeating the Goths, Claudius II settles many of them as *coloni*.

276–282 Probus settles many defeated barbarians: Burgundians, Vandals, Bastarnae, Gepids, Greuthungi, etc.

285–305 Under Diocletian's Tetrarchy, barbarians are settled in many provinces, and some frontiers (such as the Rhine estuary) are shortened, with client states occupying the previously Roman territories. Chamavi, Frisii and Franks are settled in Gaul; Carpi in eastern Pannonia, Bastarnae and Sarmatians in territories not clearly identified.

334? Constantine I settles over 300,000 Sarmatians in Thrace, Scythia, Macedonia and Italy.

337–361 Constantius II settles Visigoths in Moesia, and other (unnamed) barbarians in Thrace. Sarmatians also seem to be admitted, but the attempt by the Limigantes to gain a foothold in imperial territory is repulsed. The Caesar Julian concedes settlements to Salian Franks in Gaul.

370? Valentinian I settles captive Alamanni in northern Italy.

366 Valens distributes a number of captive Goths in the cities of the Danube, perhaps as *coloni*.

376 Valens allows the major Visigoth (Tervingi) immigration which leads to the Battle of Adrianople.

380 Gratian allows Ostrogoths (Greuthungi) to settle in Pannonia and Upper Moesia, but the treaty terms are not known. It was under pressure, and may have been a *foederati* settlement, anticipating 382.

382 Theodosius' treaty with the Visigoths, settling them as *foederati* in the diocese of Thrace.

386–7 Theodosius, after defeating an Ostrogoth invasion on the Danube, settles the survivors in Phrygia, presumably as *laeti*.

399 They revolt under Tribigild.

After 406–410, it becomes increasingly inaccurate to talk of 'controlled' barbarian settlements in the West, as distinct from adjustments to invasions.

APPENDIX V

Fourth-Century Barbarian Officers in the Roman Army

(Taken from Ramsay MacMullen, *Corruption and the Decline of Rome*.)

Key to Abbreviations

★ = not in Ammianus	a. = armaturarum
A = Alaman	c. = comes
F = Frank	m. = magister
G = Goth	ped. = peditum
p = pagan	eq. = equitum
	r.m. = rei militaris
	tr. = tribunus

pF Arbogastes (? son of Bauto? nephew of Richomer), c. r. m. 380; m. milit. 388–394 ('the emperor Valentinian II was almost reduced to the position of one of his subjects, and oversight of all military matters entrusted to his Frankish retinue...' [Greg. of Tours]); suicide 394.

A Agilo, tr. stabuli 354; tr. gentilium et scut. 354–360; m. ped. (E) 360–362; high general 365–66 (married dr. of Araxius PPO 365–66).

★G Alica, chief who led tribe in army of Licinius 324.
    Algildus, c. r. m. 361.

G Arintheus (Flavius), agens vice tr. 355; m. eq. 363; m. ped. 366–78; cos. 372.

★ Bacurius, king of the Iberi, tr. sagittariorum 378, dux Palaest. 378, c. domesticorum some time bet. 378 and 394; m. milit. 394.

pF Bauto, m. milit. (W) 380–85; cos. 385; his dr. Eudoxia married Arcadius.

F Bonitus, officer/general of Constantine 316–324.
    Bappo, praef. urbi Romae 372.

★ Buthericus, m. eq. (Illyr.) 390.

★F? Charobaudes, m. utriusque militiae (W) 408.

F Charietto, m. milit. (W) 408.

F Charietto, emigré German, freelance with Julian 355–58, c. per utramque Germaniam 365.
    Cretio, c. r. m. (Afr.) 349–61 (son is Masaucio).

★A Crocus, troop chief 306 (W).
    Dagalaifus, c. domesticorum (W) 361–63; m. ped. 364–66; cos. 366.

pG   Fravitta, serving Theodosius 380s, m. milit. per Or. 395–400, cos. 401.

      Frigeridus, dux (?Valeriae) pre-377 (pre-367?), c. r. m. 377 (Illyr.).

?F   Fullofaudes, dux (brit.) 367.

★G   Gainas, c. r. m. 395–99.

★   Gaiso, m. milit. 351?

      Gildo (Berber chief) serving 373, c. et m. utriusque militiae Afr. 386–98.

      Gomoarius, tr. scholae scutariorum 350, m. eq. 360–61, officer 365–66 (brother is Maurus).

★   Hellebichus, m. pedit. Or. 387.

      (H)ormisdas, Persian prince, immigré 324, cavalry officer 350s, c. 362–63.

      (H)ormisdas, son of the above, procos. Asiae 365–66, c. r. m. 380.

★   Aur. Ianuarius, dux Pannoniae 303.

★   Immo, c. r. m. 361.

A   Latinus, c. domesticorum 354.

F   Lutto, c. 355.

      Machamaeus (brother is Maurus), regimental commander 363.

      Magnentius (Flavius), tr. Iov. et Herculi, protector, then c. r. m. in 340s (W).

F   Malarichus, tr. gentilium 355, offered and declined to be m. eq. 363.

F   Mallobaudes, tr. scholae a. 354–55, rex Francorum et c. domesticorum 378.

★   Marcus (Flavius), natus in Dacia, serving in vex. Fesianesa under Constantius, protector later.

      Masaucio (son of Cretio), protector domesticus (W) 365.

F   Maudio, c. 355.

      Maurus (brother of Machamaeus), tr. 363, dux Phoenices post-363.

?F   Merobaudes, officer of 363, m. ped. (W) 375–88; cos. 377. II 383; III designate 388; suicide 387.

★F   Merobaudes, dux Aegypti 384.

G   Modares, m. eq. per Thracias, m. mil. 382.

G   Munderichus, Gothic chief emigré 376, dux limitis (Arab.) post-376.

      Nannienus, c. r. m. 370 (W), c. (utriusque Germaniae?) 378, m. mil. 387–88.

      Nectaridus, c. Brit. 367.

      Nevitta, emigré German, praepositus of cavalry (W) 358; m. eq. 361–64; cos. 362.

pF   Richomeres, c. domesticorum (W) 377–78, survived Adrianople; m. mil. (E) 383; cos. et m. utriusque militiae (E) 388–93.

?   Remigius (born Mainz), numerarius 355; m. offic. (W) 367–73; suicide ca. 374.

★   Rumoridus, m. mil. 384 (W).

★G   Sarus, rex Gothorum, m. utriusque militiae (Gaul) 407.

F   Silvanus, tr. scholae a. 351; m. ped. 352–55; c. et m. eq. et ped. 353.

★ Stilicho (Vandal), m. mil. 394–408 (W), cos. 400, II 405.
★ Subarmachius, c. domesticorum (a Colchian) 395/399.
   Theolaifus, c. r. m. 361.
A Vadomarius, rex Alamannorum by 354(–361); captured; dux Phoenices 361–66; commander 371.
★ Vallio, m. eq. per Gall. 383.
   Victor (Sarmatian), c. r. m. 362–63; m. eq. 363–79; cos. 369; survived Adrianople; married dr. of Arab queen Mavia.
   Vitalianus, protector domesticus 364; m. eq. per Illyr. 380.

TRIBUNES AND LOWER OFFICERS

   Abdigildus, tr. 359.
   Aliso, tr. (E) 365.
   Bainobaudes, tr. scut. 354.
   Bainobaudes, tr. cornutorum.
A Balchobaudes, tr. a. 366 (W).
F Bappo, tr. (W) 355.
   Barchalba, tr. (E) 366.
   Barzimeres, tr. scutarorum (E) 374–77.
   Bitheridus, tr. 372 (W).
★ Dagridus, tr. (W) late 4th.
?F Fraomarius, installed as rex Bucinobantium, then tr. numeri Alamannorum 372.
★ Gabso, protector domesticus (W) late 4th.
   Gaiolus (Flavius), tr. Quintanorum (Eg.) 398.
A Hariobaudes, tr. 359.
A Hortarius, emigré commander tr. 373 (W).
   Laipso, tr. cornutorum 357.
   Laniogaisus, tr. 355 (already serving in 350) (W).
   Marcaridus, tr. Iov. ca. 390.
   Memoridus, tr. 363 (E).
   Nemota, tr. (E) 363.
   Nestica, tr. scutariorum 358 (W).
A Scudilo, officer 351, tr. scutariorum 354.
   Seniauchus, tr. 355 (W).
   Sintula, tr. stabuli 360 (W).
F Teutomeres, protector domesticus 354 (E).
   nameless Vandal father of Stilicho, cavalry officer (E).

REFERENCES AND NOTES

These notes refer to authorities cited in the text, principal classical sources and major, readily available secondary authorities, most of which provide further, detailed references which we do not duplicate unnecessarily.

CHAPTER 1 (pp.13–22)

1   Wolfram, *History of the Goths*, 23–5; we broadly follow Wolfram's use of Gothic tribal names — Goths in the third century, Tervingi/Greuthungi in the fourth and on their admission into the empire, and Visigoths/Greuthungi on Roman territory. See Heather, *Goths and Romans*, pp.8–10.

2   Alavivus is mentioned by Ammianus as the joint leader of the Visigoths with Fritigern (see n.3) — Ammianus XXXI, 4, 1 and 7; see n.18, below, for his status. Also Jones, *PLRE*, I, 32.

3   Jones, *PLRE*, I, 374; and below, esp. nn.17 and 18. Fritigern was a major figure amongst the Tervingi outside the empire, and later became their sole leader within the empire. However, he may have been second in status to Alavivus at this time (immediately before and after the admission of the Tervingi to the empire).

4   Ammianus XXXI, 4, 1: the offer was of troops to be supplied as required by Rome; ibid. XXX, 2, 6: Valens calling for Gothic recruits for his Persian campaign. See Wolfram, pp.118–9

5   Ammianus XXXI, 2, 1–11, for contemporary perceptions of the Huns; Maenchen-Helfen, *The World of the Huns*, ch.1, examines the historic view of the Huns; ch.5 provides a detailed assessment of Hunnic military capabilities.

6   Ammianus XXXI, 2, 12; ibid. XXXI, 3, 1; Maenchen-Helfen, 18–9; for a general account of the Alans, see Bachrach, *A History of the Alans in the West*.

7   Ammianus XXXI, 3, 2–3; Wolfram, *History of the Goths*, 89.

8   Ammianus XXXI, 3, 3; Matthews, *The Roman Empire of Ammianus*, 320.

9   Ammianus XXXI, 3, 6–8; Ambrose *Expositio in Lucam* X, 10, summarises this sequence from the Roman viewpoint; Wolfram, *History of the Goths*, 70–3.

10   Ammianus XXVII, 5, 6: Athanaric is *iudex potentissimus*, a hereditary overlordship which is not monarchical. See Wolfram, *History of the Goths*, 94, for a discussion of the title and powers of Athanaric; also Matthews, *The Roman Empire of Ammianus*, 325 and n.32. Also Jones, *Prosopography*, I, 120–1. Also Heather, pp.97–107

11   Ammianus XXVII, 5 for Valens' three years of campaigning against the Tervingi (367–9). Wolfram, 66–7, suggests that Valens took the initiative in seeking this earlier Gothic war, but the terms of the treaty and the manner of its conclusion do not suggest that it was a complete Roman victory over Athanaric and the Tervingi (despite Valens' assumption of the title Gothicus); ibid. 68–9 for the terms of the treaty. Matthews, *The Roman Empire of Ammianus*, argues that the war, especially in its third year, was a considerable success (320, n.24). Certainly Valens undertook three years of campaigning in enemy territory without loss, and his

military ambition produced a treaty revised in favour of Rome: payments to the Tervingi were stopped, trade was more strictly regulated and Gothic hostages were given. This should be borne in mind later when the events of 376 are considered, and Valens' decision to attack at Adrianople without the Western reinforcements is analysed. Contra Heather, pp.115–20, payments were standard, even following a Roman victory.

12 Zosimus IV, 25, 1.

13 Ammianus XXXI, 3, 8 for the rejection of Athanaric; ibid. XXXI, 4, 1 for the leadership of Alavivus — Fritigern is not mentioned until XXXI, 4, 7 when the two leaders are received as part of the initial Roman transportation of their people. Wolfram, pp.69–70 for earlier divisions within the Tervingi (and between Athanaric and Fritigern); ibid. pp.71–2 for the breakaway of the majority of the Tervingi.

14 Ammianus XXXI, 4, 13; Wolfram, pp.72–3, nn.223–6. It may be that Athanaric maintained control over his own subtribe (?and others which owed it some loyalty) through a hereditary rulership which was specific to this group, rather than through the position as *iudex* which was lost with the collapse of the Tervingi under Hunnic pressure. It would also seem likely that this group was pagan (see Wolfram, pp.68–70, for the earlier persecution of Christian Goths by Athanaric — *c.*372–6), and this may have contributed to Athanaric's decision not to seek asylum within the empire.

15 Ammianus XXVII, 5, 9; XXXI, 4, 13. Wolfram, *History of the Goths*, 65 and n.164, suggests that the oath may relate to the position of the *iudex* as overlord *within* Tervingian territory, although there is an obvious connection with time that his father spent as a hostage at the court of Constantine in the 330s.

16 Ammianus XXXI, 4, 13.

17 Fritigern had opposed Athanaric in the Tervingian civil conflict of the early 370s — see Socrates, *Historia Ecclesiastica*, IV, 33, 1, 7 and Sozomen, *Historia Ecclesiastica*, VI, 37, 6f. and 12f., when Athanaric also led a persecution of Christian Goths; this conflict may have been due to a desire to limit the dominance of Athanaric on the part of a rival, rather than to any religious conviction held by Fritigern. In this conflict Fritigern seems to have adopted the Arian Christianity of Valens, possibly as part of an arrangement with Rome, which would no doubt have welcomed such internecine strife — see Wolfram, pp.68–72 and n.216. For the opposing view (that the adoption of Arian Christianity took place when the petition for admission to the empire was made in 376) see Heather, 'The Crossing of the Danube and the Gothic Conversion', *Greek, Roman and Byzantine Studies* 28:289ff. Chrysos states that the Tervingi under Alavivus and Fritigern were questioned about their Christianity prior to being admitted, and we suggest that Wolfram's view is more likely.

18 Wolfram, pp.72, nn.218–21; ibid. 424f. nn.8, 29: Fritigern was a prominent figure prior to entry into the empire, and may even have been the leader of the Christian Tervingi, possibly with links to Valens dating from the early 370s. However he was not the sole leader of those seeking entry into the empire: Alavivus may even have been of higher status, and only after his death (he disappears from our sources in 376 and Fritigern is mentioned alone thereafter) did Fritigern become the leader of the Visigoths inside the empire. Ammianus XXXI, 5, 5 for the last mention of Alavivus, whose name always precedes that of Fritigern in his narrative; Sozomen VI, 37, 6–8 for links between Fritigern and Valens; Jordanes, *Getica*,

mentions Fritigern as of equal standing with Alatheus and Saphrax, the Greuthungian leaders, who were explicitly not kings.

19   The status of a war leader, and his relationship to the tribal chiefs below him, is illustrated in the accounts of the campaign against Chnodomarius of the Alamanni — see ch. 6, esp. n.56. ch7, n.17

20   See notes 11 and 12, above.

21   Ammianus refers to these nobles as 'optimates' — XXXI, 3, 5; see n.18 above; also Wolfram, pp.100–105 for a discussion of this hierarchy. Also, pp.93–4

22   See ch.7, pp.91–2

23   As in the proposed admission of Sarmatians by Constantius II — Ammianus XIX, 11, 7.

24   Constantine settled a very large number of Sarmatians within the empire (probably mainly in northern Italy, southern Gaul and Illyricum) following his victories in the 330s; 300,000 is given as a figure. See App. V for some indication of the barbarian settlements under the *laeti* system. The Roman army had ceased to be 'Roman' early in the republican period: the trend throughout republic and empire was for army recruitment to concentrate on the newer, more remote and less civilised provinces, and the later imperial habit of recruitment from beyond the frontiers — whilst by no means a new phenomenon — was an extension of this process carried into a period where there were no newly-conquered provinces to be exploited for their wealth in goods and manpower. See Keppie, *The Making of the Roman Army*, esp. pp.180–1, for the very early realisation (under Augustus and Tiberius) that recruitment would in future be principally from the frontier provinces, and not from the older, more civilised areas of the empire.

25   Ammianus XXXI, 4, 2–3.

26   Wolfram, pp.97–8 gives some indication of the numbers involved; but the Romans were obviously not very well informed about the scale of the migration, and were overwhelmed by the numbers who crossed the Danube — Ammianus XXXI, 4, 6–8. See also App. I and p.86.

27   Ammianus XXXI, 14 for a commentary on the character of Valens; and Matthews, *Ammianus*, 189–91 for the appointment.

28   From Dagalaif, his *Magister Militum*, see n.80, and pp.21–2.

29   Jones, *LRE* for a general discussion and history of the institution of joint rule. Also Williams, *Diocletian*, for the beginnings of the structure.

30   Ammianus XXVII and XXVIII.

31   But see note 11, above.

32   Ammianus XXX, 6 for a graphic description of the event.

33   Jones, *LRE*, I, 333–41, for the role and composition of this advisory/administrative body.

34   Modestus had a long and distinguished career: Jones, *PLRE*, I, 605.

35   He was *Comes Rei Privatae* (see Jones, *LRE*, 412–17), Jones, *PLRE*, I, 369.

36   *Comes Sacrarum Largitionum* (see Jones, *LRE*, 369–70), Jones, *PLRE*, I, 876–7.

37   Ammianus XXXI, 4, 4.

38   Ammianus XXXI, 4, 6–8, records the Roman surprise and dismay at the numbers of the Tervingi who crossed the Danube. Our sources frequently mention the settlement of barbarians in tens of thousands, but this would be under controlled conditions and in a dispersed settlement pattern. However see n.24 for a very substantial barbarian settlement earlier in the fourth century, albeit under very different conditions.

39 See n.1, above. Ammianus XXXI, 4, 12.

40 See n.26. For the great invasions of the third century, see Wolfram, pp.43–57.

41 Ammianus XXX, 2. The peace concluded after Julian's failed campaign in 363 had generally held, but now there was the fear that the Persians might take advantage of any distraction in Thrace.

42 The treaty must have included a commitment by the Tervingi to disarm, as was expected by all supplicants. They were, after all, desperate to escape their plight north of the Danube after the Hunnic onslaught had destroyed their economy and supply base, and split their tribal confederation into rival groups: see Wolfram, p.118. Heather, pp.122–8

43 Sozomen VI, 37, 15ff. mentions this 'religious qualification', suggesting that the Tervingi under Alavivus and Fritigern were already Arian Christians by the time they arrived at the Danube — see n.17. It is possible, however, that the acceptance of Arian Christianity was a condition of entry to the empire.

44 Ammianus XXXI, 4, 6.

45 He was *Comes rei militaris* (see App.II) for Thrace. Lupicinus had enjoyed a distinguished military career to date, serving in the *Schola Gentilium*, an elite cavalry corps, in 368: Ammianus XXVII, 10, 12. Jones, *PLRE*, I, 519 for his career. This makes his subsequent failures difficult to understand.

46 He was *Dux* (see App.II) of Moesia or Scythia; Jones, *PLRE*, I, 585.

47 See n.1 for terminology. Ammianus XXXI, 4, 10–11 and 5, 1 for the wretched condition of the Visigoths.

48 This is the standard assessment of Fritigern's motives, but it may be unduly influenced by hindsight, especially that of our classical sources. Bearing in mind that Fritigern had strong Roman connections from earlier times (see nn.17 and 18), he may have still been seeking a genuine accommodation with Rome. Against this, our main source for these events, Ammianus, probably had a Tervingian source and may have had a real insight into Fritigern's motives — see Matthews, *Ammianus*, 379.

49 Ammianus XXXI, 4, 12–13.

50 Jones, *PLRE*, I, 32.

51 Jones, *PLRE*, I, 802; Zosimus IV, 34, 2; Jordanes, *Getica*, 134, 140. There has been debate as to the ethnic origin of these leaders, and we would agree with Wolfram that they represent the Greuthungian and Alanic elements of the tribal grouping respectively, 115 and 252–5. Heather, pp.144–5.

52 Ammianus indicates in his account of the battle of Adrianople that the two Gothic groups were linked — XXXI, 12, 12 — but in XXXI, 5, 3 the crossing of the Danube by Alatheus and Saphrax takes place well away from the Tervingi, and there may have been no real intention of cooperation at this stage.

53 Ammianus XXXI, 5, 7. Alavivus disappears at this point. There is no evidence of his death at Lupicinus' hands, but Fritigern may have been glad to leave him behind.

54 See n.1, above.

55 Ammianus XXXI, 7, 1–3.

56 Wolfram, 121–5.

57 Ammianus XXXI, 11, 1.

58 Ammianus XXXI, 10.

59 Sebastianus had a long and very successful military career, and had served with

distinction under Valentinian as *Comes Rei Militaris*. He was either asked for by Valens (Ammianus XXXI, 11, 1), or left the West (perhaps being dismissed after the death of his mentor, Valentinian) to go to Constantinople (Zosimus IV, 22, 4). Eunapius, fr. 47, praises his military skills. See Jones, *PLRE*, I, 812 for his career. This military experience and ability should be considered when the conflicting advice received by Valens before the battle of Adrianople is considered below.

60 See n.11, above, for Valens' own earlier successes against this same enemy.

61 Ammianus XXXI, 12, 12.

62 The very large army which he had assembled could not have been accommodated within the city.

63 He was a Frank, and *Comes Domesticorum* to Gratian when sent to aid Valens. This was his second such journey, having taken part in the campaigns against the Goths in 379. See Jones, *PLRE*, I, 765 for his career.

64 He was a Sarmatian by origin, and was a zealous Nicene, having criticised Valens for his persecution of the opponents of Arian Christianity. See Jones, *PLRE*, I, 957–8 for his lengthy career.

65 See nn.11 and 59, above.

66 Wolfram, pp.72 and n.221 for the status of Fritigern and his authority to negotiate binding treaties with Rome.

67 Ammianus, XXXI, 12–13, see App. I for a more extensive discussion of the battle.

68 Matthews, *Ammianus*.

69 See App. I.

70 Ammianus XXXI, 16.

71 This had been his temporary base on his march to the east.

72 Ammianus XXXI, 5, 11–17. The view that Rome had lost many battles but never a war comes from the early 390s, when the Visigoths had become useful allies.

73 Ammianus XXXI, 15 and 16.

74 From 371–8. See Jones, *PLRE*, I, 481 for his career.

75 Ammianus XXXI, 16, 8. Heather suggests these were the Gothic hostages of 376. But why then the two-year interval?

76 Emperor 306–37; Jones, *PLRE*, I, 223–4.

77 Emperor 337–61; Jones, *PLRE*, I, 226.

78 Caesar 351–4; Jones, *PLRE*, I, 224–5.

79 Emperor 360–3; Jones, *PLRE*, I, 477–8.

80 Ammianus describes the demand of the army that Valentinian elect a colleague — XXVI, 2, 3–4.

81 See Ammianus XXIX, 1 and 2 for the purge.

82 Jones, *LRE*, 578–82.

83 Ammianus XXVI, 1–2.

84 See Ammianus XXX, 10 for the posting of Sebastianus out of the way when Valentinian died.

85 Jones, *PLRE*, I, 239.

86 Ammianus XXX, 10, 4–6 for his elevation on the death of Valentinian.

87 Ammianus XXIX 6, 15–16.

88 The title of Count, by which he is often distinguished from his son, refers to his service as *Comes Rei Militaris* in 368–9. He was later *Magister Equitum*, 369–375; Jones, *PLRE*, I, 902–3.

89   Orosius VII, 33, 7, and ch.2.
90   Pan. Lat XII, 9, 1.

CHAPTER 2 (pp.23–35)

1   Sozomen VII, 2, 1; Theodoret, *Hist. Eccles.* V, 5; Pan.Lat. XII, 5, 31.
2   Pacianus of Barcelona, see Matthews, *Western Aristocracies*, 111 and n.7.
3   The earliest reference to him is in the British campagin.
4   Ammianus XXVII, 8, 6–10; XXVIII, 3, 1–9; XXVIII, 5, 15; XXIX, 4, 5 and Pan. Lat XII, 5, 2 for his campaigns.
5   Ammianus XXVII, 8, 1–5.
6   See App. II.
7   See App. II. He held this office 369–75.
8   Pan. Lat. XII, 8, 3; Zosimus IV, 24, 4 and 35, 3.
9   Ammianus XXIX, 6, 14–16; Zosimus IV, 16, 6.
10   Jones, *PLRE*, I, 340; for the campaign see Ammianus XXIX, 5, 2–55.
11   Jones, *PLRE*, I, 768; Ammianus XXVII, 6, 26.
12   Orosius VII, 33.
13   Ammianus XXVIII, 1, 5 for his career.
14   This regional factionalism is well illustrated later, when Theodosius I filled many of the places at court with his Spanish associates — see Matthews, *Western Aristocracies*, 108–112.
15   Ammianus XXX, 6, 3–6 and ch.1, p.14.
16   Valentinian II was at Sirmium with his mother, Justina. The four year old was proclaimed by the ministers of Valentinian and the *Magister Militum*, Merobaudes, probably as a focus for the loyalty of the Illyrian army since Gratian was far away at Trier: Ammianus XXX, 10 and Zosimus IV, 19.
17   See ch.1, n.59 for Sebastianus' career; for his transfer, Ammianus XXX, 10, 3.
18   Gratian had been made a full colleague in the empire, Augustus, by his father eight years earlier (367) — Ammianus XXVII, 6. He was now sixteen.
19   Jones, *PLRE*, I, 898; he was a pagan.
20   Jones, *PLRE*, I, 52 — Bishop of Milan, 374–97.
21   See ch.1, n.90.
22   Matthews, *Western Aristocracies*, 94–5.
23   Matthews, *Western Aristocracies*, 94, nn.5 and 6.
24   Against this should be noted the long careers of professional soldiers and high officials, e.g. Sebastianus and Victor.
25   Courteousness, cheerfulness, affability.
26   See Tacitus and Suetonius for the handicap of lacking social graces. For the genuine personal nature of Theodosius' qualities, exhibited to the full during his visit to Rome in 389, see Matthews, *Western Aristocracies*, 228.
27   For Aelia Flaccilla, see Jones, *PLRE*, I, 341–42 and Holum, *Theodosian Empresses*, 22–4; Pulcheria died c.385.
28   Pacatus, *Pan.* 10–11, for the summons and Theodosius' reaction. See Matthews, *Western Aristocracies*, 91–2.
29   For a detailed account of these campaigns, see ch.5; also Matthews, *Western Aristocracies*, 91–2 and nn.91 iii and iv, 92 i and ii. Maenchen-Helfen, *World of the Huns*, 30–36 outlines the threats to Pannonia in 378 and early 379, and suggests

Hunnic involvement along with Sarmatians and Alans invading Valeria. Theodosius' victory in December 378 as *Magister* would seem to have been against those Sarmatians displaced by Athanaric's Goths as they fled from the Huns, but the struggle was continued by Gratian against the above groups until June of 379. For the elevation, *Cons. Const* 379. *Chron. Min* I, 243 and II, 60. For the Macedonian provinces, see Mazzarino, *Stilicone*, 1–59.

30   This title had formerly been restricted to the senatorial order.

31   Wolfram, pp.7–9 for the attractions of joining the Goths for many classes.

32   Ammianus XXXI, 6, 4.

33   Libanius, *On Avenging Julian*. These orations were not read publicly to the emperor, but intended for his ears.

34   Indicating the success of both imperial colleagues — and there had been victories in late 378 and 379 to celebrate, such as Theodosius against the Sarmatians, and later Gratian against the Greuthungi/Alans/Huns of Alatheus and Saphrax.

35   Matthews, *Western Aristocracies*, 98 for the political activity trying to secure the position. *C.Th.*VI 30,1.

36   See n.35, above.

37   Ammianus XXVII, 8.

38   Jones, *LRE*, app.2 lists units probably raised by Theodosius at this time.

39   Liebeschuetz, *Barbarians and Bishops*, ch.3 for the rebuilding of the army under Theodosius.

40   See Matthews, Maenchen-Helfen, Wolfram for Gratian and the West's role in these years. Heather, pp.153–5.

41   Maenchen-Helfen, 36–7.

42   Wolfram, pp.131.

43   It is quite possible, and indeed probable, that this was a reflection of a lack of change in perspective amongst the barbarians despite the victory at Adrianople. Apart from the initial flush of enthusiasm, and the aspirations of their leaders, it may be that there was no appreciation of their changed status among the Goths. It would only be with the Treaty of 382 (see below) and its aftermath that the perception emerged among the barbarians that their position vis-a-vis the empire had changed fundamentally. Therefore the entry into the Roman army of prominent individuals, their followers and common recruits is to be expected rather than a matter of surprise.

44   See ch.4 for his baptism and its significance.

45   Wolfram, pp.131–2 and Liebeschuetz, ch.3.

46   Wolfram, p.132. Heather, p.153 and App. B, argues against such a settlement, but the sources are inconclusive.

47   Heather, pp.153–4, on a possible meeting at Sirmium; Zosimus IV, 33, for Theodosius' celebrations.

48   Ammianus XXXI, 4, 13.

49   Wolfram p.132.

50   Wolfram, pp.73–4

51   See n.53 below for the campaign and eventual Treaty.

52   Wolfram, 133 and esp. n.99.

53   For the likely Treaty provisions and the conclusion of it, see Wolfram, 133–4.

54   See Liebeschuetz, ch.3 for the response to the Treaty in particular and the recruitment of barbarians in general.

CHAPTER 3 (pp.36–46)

1 Matthews, *Western Aristocracies*, 95–6, 175, and Jones, *PLRE* I, 588. Maximus was a Spaniard, had served with Theodosius' father, and was probably an early supporter of his cause in 378–9.

2 Commander of the mobile field army element of the British garrison — see App. II.

3 It seems certain that this step must have been prepared in advance, given the speed and ease with which the move was accomplished.

4 This was another in a lengthy series of campaigns against the Alamanni: Gratian had been delayed in his move to assist Valens in 378 by an urgent campaign to counter this threat, and it had taken five years for their strength to revive and become a threat again.

5 A rapid march given the basic mobility of an army on the march, of *c*.16 miles a day.

6 The term *Mauri* (Moors) was applied to some units of Roman cavalry from at least the second century; this does not necessarily mean that they were ethnically of African origin, since many such titles were indicative of unit history rather than recent recruitment. Units were recruited locally, rather than from areas of first establishment, so that within a fairly short time the ethnic composition of a unit reflected its station and not necessarily any title it might bear.

7 A Frank by origin, he had served with distinction. See Matthews, *Western Aristocracies*, 173 for his standing.

8 This may have been his bodyguard of Alans: his reliance on these troops and favouring of them, even to the extent of wearing their style of dress, was one of the complaints levelled against Gratian as justification for army disaffection: Zosimus, IV, 35.

9 The forces stationed in northern Italy, and the defensibility of the Alpine passes, would have given Gratian hope of holding off Maximus — who later was to wait for four years before he moved against Valentinian II.

10 Matthews, *Western Aristocracies*, 173, n.3.

11 Ammianus XXXI, 10, 18–19.

12 One potential criticism of Gratian, in the eyes of the Western provinces and their commanders, was that his energies had been almost entirely devoted to the defence of the Illyrian and Alpine provinces, and of Italy itself. Valentinian had ruled from Trier, and the lack of an imperial presence and field army based there may have contributed to a sense of abandonment which could have been exploited by Maximus.

13 Matthews, *Western Aristocracies and Imperial Court*, 174 and nn.2–5.

14 Matthews, *Western Aristocracies*, 154–160, for background on Martin.

15 For this embassy, Matthews, op cit.

16 Zosimus IV, 37

17 In the 260s.

18 Under Diocletian.

19 Who challenged Constantius II for supreme power.

20 Matthews, *Western Aristocracies*, 174–5 and nn.1 and 2; *CIL* II, 4911 for Maximus' elevation of the province of Tarraconensis to consular status, indicating a particular favouring of it.

21 Ammianus XXXI, 10, 18–19.

22 See chs.6 and 7.

23 See above, n.12. Gratian had, of course, devoted much of his time and military resources to 'Eastern' problems, and this may have given Maximus an opening to accuse him of neglecting the West.

24 See Matthews, *Western Aristocracies*, 109–13.

25 The appointment to Britain was not a demotion, but could not have been seen as a reward for support. Maximus may well have felt slighted by this lack of recognition, and, importantly, so may his colleagues and supporters in the Western provinces.

26 Ammianus XXXI, 10.

27 Ammianus, *passim*; Johnson, *Late Roman Fortifications*.

28 See pp.32 for this settlement. It must be borne in mind that Gratian, like Theodosius, was operating under extreme pressures after the Gothic victory at Adrianople, and this accommodation with the Greuthungi and Alans was part of a plan to relieve pressure on Theodosius' forces facing the Visigoths further east.

29 See Matthews, *Western Aristocracies*, ch.7 for the relations between the rival courts.

30 It is unlikely that Maximus sought such a rapid move. To invade Italy would have provoked Theodosius into an unavoidable all-out war, and Maximus needed time to make his acquisition of the Western provinces secure: thus we find him placing his appointees in positions of power and removing (through retirement, rather than violently) those loyal to Gratian — see Matthews, *Western Aristocracies*, 174.

31 The rather half-hearted nature of this 'campaign' has been taken as a sign that Theodosius was not intent on removing Maximus, or avenging Gratian. However, having indicated above pp.38–9 the difficulties of mounting a major expedition at this time, the political impact may have been more important than any failure to pursue a military option — Maximus did not invade Italy for another four years: see Matthews, *Western Aristocracies*, 178 and nn.1–3.

32 Role of Alans and Huns, esp. as mercenaries — is relevant (Ambrose, *Ep.* 24,8). These troops may well have been recruited from among the Pannonian federates settled by Gratian.

33 Matthews, *Western Aristocracies*, 177 and nn.2–4.

34 From Ambrose, *Ep.* 24,7 it seems that both Maximus and Valentinian were attempting to reach an accommodation with neither, perhaps, feeling secure in their position at this stage.

35 Matthews, *Western Aristocracies*, 180–1.

36 Ambrose *Ep* 20 for the affair. Again, as for n.32, these Goths were probably recruited from among the Pannonian federates, that is Greuthungi.

37 Matthews, *Western Aristocracies*, 181.

38 Matthews, *Western Aristocracies*, 165.

39 King, p.51.

40 Ambrose, *Ep.* 24, 4.

41 See n.10, above.

42 Ammianus XXV, 7, 9–14.

43 Jones, *PLRE*, I, 854. Claudian *De Cons. Stil.* I, 51, f, for the embassy.

44 Matthews, *Western Aristocracies*, 179.

45 Claudian, *De Bell. Gild.*

46 See p.23, above.

47 See below, ch. 11 for further discussion of this constitutional position.

48   Matthews, *Western Aristocracies*, 185–8 for the development of Ambrose as a leading civil, and then religious figure.

49   Milan had been the principal seat of the emperor in the West since Gallienus in the mid-third century, and had the legitimacy of being Valentinian II's capital. Although the other imperial cities such as Trier had high status, this was mainly as the residence of the court: without that imperial government presence they began to slide in relative importance.

50   pp.29–31, which included calling on the goodwill of the new Visigoth allies.

51   *C.Th.* II, 33, 2; III, 4, 1; and others which bear his consulship.

52   Zosimus IV 37, 3; this was tantamount to formal recognition of Maximus.

53   Ambrose, *Ep.*, 24; Matthews, *Western Aristocracies*, 180.

54   Wolfram, pp.134–5.

55   Zosimus IV 38–40 for the conflict.

56   Ibid. The survivors of these Greuthungi were settled in Phrygia, well away from any of the other Gothic settlements.

57   Ammianus XXXI, 2, 1.

58   Jones, *Later Roman Empire*, 871–2; also Zosimus, and Libanius for the riots and the tax.

CHAPTER 4 (pp.47–60)

1   Represented later by the Council of Nicea. Constantine's conversion seems to have been genuine at a personal level: there was little political gain in what was still a minority faith, and his bequests and granting of privileges to the church began almost immediately after his victory over Maxentius, probably in gratitude for that 'divinely-granted' success — see Jones, *LRE*, 80–1.

2   For the persecutions, see Jones, *LRE*, 71–6; for the immediate outbreak of factionalism within the church, ibid. 81–2; also Williams, *Diocletian*, chs. 13–14.

3   Constantine's on-off attempts to resolve the Donatist schism in Africa after 313 demonstrate the importance he attached to the problem, but his failure to grasp the difficulty of its resolution.

4   Among many sources for this major cult, perhaps the best is Ferguson, *Religions of the Roman Empire*.

5   Gregory of Nyssa, *Oratio de deitate Filii et Spiritus Sancti*.

6   For the controversy, see any account of early church history such as Jones, Chadwick, Cambridge Ancient History — see bibliography.

7   In Leibniz' famous principle, if two things are identical, then all non-modal, non-intensional properties of one will be properties of the other. If x = x expresses an axiom of identity, then in an extensional logic there is a second axiom: Not-[(x = y) and (Fx but not-Fy)], which allows of a proof procedure for quantification and identity. In lay language, if two particular things are identical then anything true of one will be true of the other: identity is that unique relation a thing has with itself and no other thing. Difficulties arise because, for example, things can be identical without us knowing they are: the Morning Star is identical to the Evening Star, but we did not always know this. The awkward, differential properties are intensional, that is (roughly), they belong to our naming and describing of these things, not the things themselves. If there were no intelligent beings in the universe, then the problem of identity could not arise. But then, nor would any other. On personal identity, see for example Strawson, *Individuals;* Parfit, *Reasons and*

Persons; Kripke, *Naming and Necessity*; Wiggins, *Sameness and Substance*; Bernard Williams, *passim*; also the very accessible and useful debate between Shoemaker and Swinburne (1984), in the Blackwell 'Great Debates' series.

8 But see n.1, above, for the sincerity of his conversion. His lack of orthodox rigour is demonstrated by his suggestion to the warring factions of the Eastern church that they simply agree to differ: Eusebius, *V. Const.*, II, 64–72.

9 Jones, *LRE*, 80, n.5, for the immediate granting of privileges by Constantine after his victory in 312, including the exemption of clergy from curial duty.

10 See any standard Church history for the Council of Nicaea in detail; the official creeds of the present Roman Catholic, Anglican and Orthodox Churches are derived, with significant alterations, from the resolutions of the Council.

11 Jones, *LRE*, 87. It was Constantine, possibly briefed by Hosius, who proposed the formula accepted by the Council.

12 Chadwick, 139–40 and *passim*.

13 Chadwick, *passim*.

14 Athanasius, *Historia Athanorum*, 4.

15 Constantine did issue an edict following the Council of Nicaea which banned a number of heresies, confiscating their churches and forbidding private meetings: Eusebius, *V.Const.*, III, 64–5. He had also demolished a number of famous temples, partly due to the ritual prostitution practised in some, and he seems to have prohibited sacrifice: Jones, *LRE*, 92 and nn.32 and 33. For his policy of toleration, see Eusebius, *V.Const.*, II, 48–60; also Jones, *LRE*, 93 and n.37; *ILS* 705.

16 Ambrose, *De Obitu Theodosii*, 12.

17 *C.Th.* 16, 1, 2.

18 See ch.2, above; the correct sequence for this episode was established by Ensslin, *Religionspolitik*, 17.

19 Liebeschuetz, *Barbarians and Bishops*, 157–8; Matthews, *Western Aristocracies*, 121–3. For the purge, Soc. 5, 7; Philost. 9, 19; Soz. 7, 5; Ambrose, *Ep.* 12; Gregory, *Vita*, 1305–95. There are numerous modern accounts of Theodosius' religious settlement: cf. Seeck, Ensslin, Piganiol, Palanque, Holmes Dudden, etc. The most recent accounts include King (1961) and Lippold (1968).

20 For this conflict over the see of Antioch: Liebeschuetz, *Barbarians and Bishops*, 160–1 and n.37.

21 *C.Th.*116, 5, 6 — of January 381.

22 For heresies in general at this period, see Jones, *LRE*, 950–6; for Manicheans in particular, ibid. 951–2. Also Soc. 5, 20; Soz. 7, 17; Philost. 10, 6. Also, of course, Augustine's *Confessions*.

23 Soc. 5; Soz. 7; Theoderet 5; cf. King, ch. 2; and Chadwick, 150–1 and *passim*.

24 The technicality was his translation to Constantinople from the see of Sasima. On his resignation, one tradition is that Theodosius promised to grant him a request before knowing what it was, and could not then oppose him. Gregory, *Vita*, 1796ff.; King, ch.2. A most unlikely tale.

25 *PLRE*. I, 621.

26 Liebeschuetz, *Barbarians and Bishops*, 160–2 and 171.

27 *C.Th.* 16, 1, 3. The *Optimus* of Antioch named in the law refers to Antioch in Pisidia, not the great city of Syria.

28 The *Quamlibet*, probably midsummer 381; cf. King, ch.2.

29 Damasus' views as expressed to Paulinus: Theodoret 5, 10. Alexandria owed its second place to the fact that Mark was Peter's disciple, and Antioch third because

Peter had his seat there, and that allegedly it was where the name 'Christian' was first used. Clearly, any number of combinations is possible in this competition of holy symbols.

30   *C.Th.* 16, 1, 4.

31   Gaudentius, *Praef. et Benevolum*, 5; Ambrose, *Ep.*, 20. There may be a link between this 'Arian' episode at Milan and the 'recognition' of Maximus by Theodosius in the same year.

32   See King, part 1 and appendices for detailed references.

33   *PLRE* I, 235–6.

34   For a useful discussion of this see King, appendix D.

35   Eusebius, *V Const* II, 60 and see n.15, above.

36   Zosimus, a zealous pagan, relates that he suppressed pagan worship from the beginning (4,33). But he seems to contradict himself (at 4,29). His chronology is notoriously faulty, and he is clearly referring to the legislation after 391.

37   For discussions of these issues, see Palanque, Piganiol, Jones, Ensslin, Lippold, King and, especially, Matthews.

38   Ambrose, *Ep.*, 17.

39   For these laws, *C.Th.*, chs. 9, 10, 16.

40   At the temple referred to, the *vota* was ordered to be observed in January. This involved vows for the safety of the empire and the associated *convivia* and *ludi*: *C.Th.* 16, 10, 8.

41   Libanius, *Orat.*, 30, prob. in 388. For Themistius, see *PRLE* I, 889–94. For Libanius, ibid. 505–7.

42   Libanius, *op. cit.*, 44; Theodoret 5,21.

43   *PLRE* I, 246.

44   Libanius, *Orat.* 33,46.

45   See below, ch. 5, for the clash over the demolition of a synagogue.

46   Horace, *Carmina*, 3, 6.

47   Following Zosimus, 4, 36 it was traditionally and wrongly assumed that the repudiation of the title occurred at Gratian's accession. This was rejected by Palanque, 1933 and Alfoldy, 1937. See esp. Cameron, 'Gratian's Repudiation of the Pontifical Robe', in *JRS* 1968. The date is probably 383.

48   Symmachus, *Relationes*, 3.

49   Ambrose, *Ep.*, 17 and 18.

CHAPTER 5 (pp.61–72)

1   Zosimus IV 42, 6f.

2   Zosimus IV 45–7, and Pacatus *Pan.* 44, 2f. for the fate of Victor.

3   Holum, *Theodosian Empresses*, 45–6.

4   Zosimus, IV, 43; and Holum, n.10, above.

5   Theodosius' first wife, Flaccilla, had died early in 387 and his dynastic ambition may have been a motive for re-marriage; the creation of a sound motive for war against Maximus (who had only recently — in 386 — been officially recognised by Theodosius) through this alliance with the house of Valentinian may have also been a factor.

6   Matthews, *Western Aristocracies*, 224, n.3.

7   *PLRE* Proculus 6; Matthews 224 n.4.

8   Wolfram, p.136 for the suggestion that this group may have included Moesian

federate Visigoths; they remained a problem for some years to come.

9   It was in Egypt that imperial portraits of Maximus had been displayed in 386 — Egypt had strong links, especially religious, with the West.

10   See Zosimus, IV, 42–7 for the campaign.

11   See ch.3, n.10.

12   Maenchen-Helfen, argues that the speed of Theodosius' advance and his sudden victory at Siscia were due to Hunnic (and Alan) contingents in his army.

13   Pacatus, *Pan* 35

14   For Theodosius' attitude, see Pacatus, *Paneg.* 44, 2f. and Zosimus, IV, 47, 1. For Andragathius, see Zosimus, IV, 46, 1f. Theodosius was, however, merciful to the rest of Maximus' family: Ambrose, *Ep.*, 40, 32.

15   Salway, *Roman Britain*, 405.

16   Matthews, *Western Aristocracies*, 223, n.4. The Panegyric is lost.

17   This has been seen as possible evidence for kinship.

18   Matthews, *Western Aristocracies*, 226.

19   Ambrose, *Ep* 40–41. The law is *CTh* XVI, 8, 9. Matthews, *Western Aristocracies*, 232–3 for the episode.

20   Matthews, *Western Aristocracies*, 237.

21   Matthews, *Western Aristocracies*, 228.

22   *PLRE* I, Flavianus 15

23   *CTh* XVI, 5, 18; *CIL* VI, 31, 413

24   *ILS* 4154

25   Pacatus *Pan.* 24–5.

26   Matthews, *Western Aristocracies*, 228–9.

27   For the status and practice of the imperial cult since the conversion of Constantine, see Jones, *LRE, passim*; the legislation against sacrifice was very carefully framed to satisfy Christian sensibilities, whilst preserving the unifying focus of the emperor as the divinely-sanctioned guide of the fortunes of Rome.

28   The Latinised *basileus* was adopted from the Greek to avoid theoretical Roman sensibilities about kingship (*rex*).

29   Frontispiece, and Plate 1.

30   Theodoret, V, 18.

31   For which, see above pp.44–6.

32   *C.Th.* IV 40, 13.

33   For the whole affair of the massacre at Thessalonica and its aftermath, see Sozomen VII, 25, 3.

34   Ambrose, *Ep.* 51.

35   See p.52, above.

36   Matthews, *Western Aristocracies*, 236–7.

37   Holum, *Theodosian Empresses*.

38   Contrast this with Gratian, who had been emperor in his own right at sixteen; it seems unquestionable that Theodosius was keeping the way open for his own sons, Arcadius having already been created Augustus at Constantinople in 383 (Honorius became Augustus in 393).

39   *Chron. Min.* I, 244 for Arcadius as Augustus. Honorius presented at Rome: Claudian *De Vi Cons. Hon*, 53f.

40   For Valentinian's campaigns and fortifications, see Ammianus, *passim*, and pp.14 above.

41   But see pp.62, for the defection of barbarian troops in 388–91.

42   See above, pp.43–4.

CHAPTER 6 (pp.75–90)

1   Gibbon, *Decline and Fall*, XVII, 3: the reforms of Constantine are viewed as divisive and weakening the army and the frontiers.

2   See Jones, *LRE*, XVII and XXV for an overall account of army development and causes of 'decline'. Grant, *The Fall of the Roman Empire — A Reappraisal*, usefully summarises the contesting views.

3   Matthews, for a full account of his career and history.

4   Ammianus XVII 5, 14: quoted from a letter of Constantius II to Sapor, the Persian king, in 358. Although MacMullen, *Corruption and the Decline of Rome*, 175, views Ammianus as presenting a very negative picture of the late Roman army, he places too much emphasis on the commonplace greed and laxity of soldiery of any age. Similar accusations were levelled at the Roman army throughout its history, and not just in the later fourth century.

5   Josephus, *Jewish War*, III.

6   Richmond, *Trajan's Army on Trajan's Column* (1982 reprint).

7   Connolly, *Greece and Rome at War*, 229–33 for a brief description. Bishop and Coulston, *Roman Military Equipment*.

8   Webster, *The Roman Imperial Army*, 29 for the *gladius*; ibid. ch.1, for a general indication of the adaptability of the Roman army.

9   Richmond, *Adamklissi*, in *Trajan's Army on Trajan's Column*.

10   Ammianus XXXI, 13, 19: 'the Romans more than once... yielded for a time to ill-success in their wars', emphasising that even after the disaster of Adrianople victory was only delayed.

11   See Tomlin, *The Mobile Army*, in Connolly, *Greece and Rome at War*, for a general summary of army development AD200–450. Jones, *LRE*, XVII, gives a detailed analysis of the army which is still essentially valid.

12   Johnson, *Late Roman Fortifications*; von Petrikovits, *JRS* 61 (1971).

13   For a general study of earlier forts, see Johnson, *Roman Forts of the 1st and 2nd centuries AD in Britain and the German Provinces*.

14   The building (or rebuilding) of city walls in this style began earlier, under Aurelian (Rome) and Probus (northern Gaul), but was continued and extended under Diocletian and his successors — see Johnson, *Late Roman Fortifications*.

15   Another major function of these new strongpoint fortifications was to secure the supplies which would be needed by the Roman army to campaign against invaders, and to deny them to the enemy.

16   The name first appears in 325: *C.Th.* VII, XX, 4.

17   Jones, *LRE*, 54–6.

18   The earliest references to *magistri* and their status show several holding the consulship, sometimes alongside the Prefect, in the 340s — Jones, *LRE* 97, n.42. Although the titles imply a split in control of infantry and cavalry this can never have been a practical division, and in practice one officer — the *Magister Peditum* — must always have been the senior colleague (in later developments there were often additional subordinate *Magistri Equitum*, but not the reverse). Ammianus does add that, as late as 361, all military and civil officials regarded the Praetorian Prefects as the highest authority below the emperor — XXI, 16, 2.

19   Under Diocletian the only distinction was between the legions and cavalry

vexillations, who made up the more privileged class, and the cohorts and *alae* —
the auxiliaries of the early empire — with lesser status. It is with Constantine that
status is determined by the distinction between field army and frontier garrisons,
rather than between types of unit. The *ripenses* ('river' troops) are mentioned along
with the field army in 325, with the term *limitanei* appearing in 365 — Jones,
LRE, 97.

20 Jones, *LRE*, 54–5 and n.34.

21 Moorish cavalry (*Mauri*) were no doubt originally raised from the African
provinces, and became a highly-regarded element of the army from the third
century onwards.

22 Jones, *LRE*, 609–10.

23 Jones, *LRE*, 55.

24 See p.19, above.

25 Jones, *LRE*, 680, n.168 for these figures.

26 Jones, *LRE*, 683–4: the real significance of the figure is that the economic
drain on the empire's resources was for 645,000 men, whether they were fraudulent
inventions of their unit commanders or not.

27 See MacMullen, *Corruption and the Decline of Rome*, 173–7.

28 These calculations are based on an analysis of Jones' study of the *Notitia
Dignitatum* — see App.II.

29 Ammianus XXVIII, 5, 7 comments on the great losses in the mid-fourth-
century civil wars, and the danger this brought of a Persian invasion taking
advantage of Roman weakness.

30 See n.33, below.

31 Both situations are reflected under Julian, when initially units of the Gaulish
army refuse to leave their homes, which they are happy to fight to defend, and
travel beyond the Alps at the behest of Constantius; and later, when he leads such
men initially to challenge the throne, and later into his Persian war — Ammianus
XX, 4, 2–16 and XX, 8, 8 and 15; XXI, 5 and XXIII, 5, 24–5.

32 We consider the likely numbers to be about 20,000 Goths facing at most
30,000 in the Roman army — see App. I for a more detailed discussion of this.

33 See Jones, *LRE*, ch.17 for a general description of the army command structure
in the fourth century.

34 Ammianus XX, 5, 7–8. For the professional structure of civil and military
commands see Ammianus, XXI, 16, 1–3.

35 Jones, *LRE*, 639.

36 *Tribunus* seems to have been most commonly used as a general title for officer.
Many of these served as staff officers, either between commands or as part of their
general training progress, when they were known as *vacantes*. Ammianus often
mentions them amongst Roman losses in battle, emphasising their importance
within the command structure.

37 Such as Modares, the noble Goth recruited by Theodosius in 379, who became
Magister Militum and a successful Roman general in the difficult campaigns against
his own people following Adrianople (he may have opposed Fritigern due to his
own kinship with Athanaric — Wolfram, 131.

38 See above, p.23–4.

39 Severus had initiated such a division at the end of the second century when
he appointed a second prefect with especial responsibility for legal matters.

40 Ammianus XV, 4, 1 and 8, 17 for his career.

41   Ammianus records Julian's offer to supply Germanic recruits for Constantius' *scholae* as a peace offering — XX, 8, 13.

42   Ammianus XVI, 12, 1–63.

43   See Matthews, *Western Aristocracies*, 129–30 for the extent of his assimilation.

44   In the sense that barbarians did not expect any quarter from their ethnic counterparts serving in the army.

45   Ammianus XIV, 10, 7–8 mentions that suspicion fell on Germanic officers when information seemed to have been betrayed to the Alamanni. However he hints that such suspicions were unfounded (and possibly malicious, by his comments), and the individuals concerned certainly kept their posts and suffered no penalties. This should be contrasted with the frequent and extremely damaging defections of Roman officers (not of barbarian background) to the Persians — e.g. Ammianus XVIII, 6, 16.

46   The *Gentiles* were one of the *scholae*, the elite imperial bodyguard units, mainly recruited from Germans, though many Romans also served.

47   Ammianus XV, 5, 1–35.

48   Jordanes and Cassiodorus to provide insights, although writing for particular audiences at later dates. See Wolfram, Introduction for a commentary on Gothic history.

49   Wolfram, 164–7.

50   Wolfram, 42–57.

51   The first use of the term occurs in 296, when it is clearly a well-established system — Jones, *LRE*, 60.

52   Wolfram, 6–7 argues that population pressures as such were not responsible for barbarian raiding, rather that the social imperatives and expectations of Germanic society drove young males to seek their status and fortune in this way. The constant taking of captives, who could later gain their freedom and membership of the tribes, suggests that there was no absolute population pressure in barbarian lands, and that there may even have been a shortage of warriors which had to be redressed in this way after the losses in combat with Rome or tribal rivals.

53   Ammianus XVII, 12, 15–20 for the appointment of Zizias as king of the Sarmatians by Constantius II.

54   Wolfram, 59–64.

55   Wallace Hadrill, Germanic Kingship, *passim*. Wolfram, *History of the Goths*, 61–2.

56   Matthews, *Ammianus*, 314–7 for Chnodomar, and ch. XIV for a general survey of the development of the main barbarian opponents facing the empire.

57   See ch.7 for an extended discussion of Gothic kingship.

58   This accords well with figures based on the *foederati* who fought for Theodosius (20,000), the Vandal nation which crossed to Africa in 429 (80,000) and the amounts demanded by Alaric and, later, Walia to supply their followers (again in the region of 15–20,000 warriors out of a total Visigothic population of about 100,000). See Wolfram, 7, 97–8, 226–7; Jones, *LRE*, 194–6.

59   Salway, *Roman Britain*, 542ff. provides a good summary of the question of the population of the empire. See also Jones, *Later Roman Empire*, 1040–45.

60   See above, pp.79–81.

61   See App. II.

62   MacMullen, *Corruption*, 171–7. See ch. 8.

63   See Matthews, *Ammianus*, for an assessment.

64   Although there is the example of Cerealis, a *dux*, who even sold the horses of a unit of mounted archers. Jones, *LRE*, 644–6 for examples.

65   See Liebeschuetz, *Barbarians and Bishops*, ch. 3.

66   Boak, *Manpower Shortage and the Fall of the Roman Empire in the West*, see ch. 8 for a discussion of these issues.

67   Ammianus XVIII, 5, 7. Zonaras gives figures suggesting 54,000 casualties and is clearly excessive, but even accepting this criticism it indicates that this conflict was notably bloody.

68   See App.II and p.88 above.

69   Given recent reductions in the physical standards of recruitment to the Metropolitan Police force in Greater London, we should be wary of seeing an impoverished and enfeebled population in these changes in Roman patterns.

70   See ch. 3.

71   See ch. 10.

CHAPTER 7 (pp.91–102)

1   Machiavelli, *The Prince*, ch. 5.

2   Livy, Polybius, Josephus.

3   Thucydides, *Peloponnesian War*, and see n.5 below.

4   Keppie, *The Making of the Roman Army*, 68–70.

5   Tacitus, *Annals*, XI, 22–4.

6   Appendix V lists major barbarian settlements within the empire. Suetonius, Augustus 21 and Tiberius 9 for the settlement of Germans in Gaul under Augustus.

7   These motives were given as early as the speech of Claudius to the senate in AD 48 which justified the admission of Gauls to that body — see n.5 above.

8   Jones, *LRE*, 85.

9   Wolfram, 44: this seems to have been part of a treaty arising from the Gothic war of 238, in which Rome agreed to pay annual subsidies to the Goths.

10   Ambrose, *Ep* 24, 4, referring to Maximus.

11   MacMullen, *Corruption*, 52–5, esp. 53; the reluctance of Romans to serve in the army was not a recent problem — Suetonius, Tiberius 8, describes men preferring to serve in the Italian slave barracks than be drafted, and ibid., Augustus 24, describes an equestrian cutting off his sons' thumbs to avoid their military service: this very problem was legislated against by Theodosius in the years after Adrianople (ch.2, pp.29–30). Liebeschuetz, *Barbarians and Bishops*, ch.2 describes this process as the demilitarisation of the empire, resulting in an essentially mercenary army: this does not imply any lack of commitment to the cause which the army served, but it did make the replacement of losses harder since general levies of recruits were no longer available as they had been in the republican and earlier imperial national armies. This view ignores the very large numbers of Roman provincials (such as the Gauls mentioned by Ammianus who made good soldiers) who did serve, but it does highlight why Theodosius and Stilicho had such need of barbarian recruits after the losses at Adrianople and elsewhere.

12   Tacitus, *Germania*, 33 describes how 60,000 of the Bructeri were killed in battle with their German neighbours, to the great satisfaction of the watching Romans. See Wolfram, under *foedus* for references to all the possible Roman-Gothic agreements.

13   Wolfram, 73–4 for Athanaric's reception at Constantinople.

211

14 Ammianus XXVII, 5, 7, referring to the Tervingi in AD 369, who sued for peace 'since commerce was cut off, [they] were so distressed by extreme scarcity of the necessities of life that they often sent suppliant deputations to beg for pardon and peace'. Tacitus, *Germania* 41, describes a unique privilege, that of trading freely with the empire, granted to the Hermunduri because of their loyalty. See Matthews, *Ammianus*, ch.14 for a general description of the Alamanni and of the Goths. The picture of settled agricultural peoples seems to have held true for the main Germanic groups facing the empire (Franks, Iuthungi, Burgundians, etc.).

15 Matthews, *Ammianus*, 310 gives the example of a reused and extended villa in the Main valley, associated with a high-status Alamannic burial.

16 See Matthews, op.cit. 309–12 for examples.

17 Although occasionally exceptional leadership did result in more competent and organised barbarian forces, such as under Maroboduus in the early first century when the Marcomanni were seen to be a threat — Millar, *The Roman Empire and its Neighbours*, 297.

18 See Ammianus XVII, 12–13 and XIX, 11 for descriptions of Constantius II campaigning against them and their territories.

19 Ammianus XVII, 13.

20 For this version of the development of Gothic institutions, see Wolfram, ch.2.

21 See Wolfram, 94–6; also pp.32–3 for the suggestion that Athanaric, his grandfather and father who preceded him as leaders of the Tervingi (Ariaric and Aoric), Alavivus and Alaric were all related and representatives of this royal clan, the *Balthi* (Heather, pp.10–12, 28–32 for an opposing view).

22 Manifestations of this are still to be seen in the dispute over Alaric's actions in 395, when he established his full authority over the other leaders of the Goths — see p.144.

23 This does not mean that every treaty was preceded by a Roman military victory: there were many occasions when strategic decisions required a (usually economic) concession from Rome to achieve its ends. In such circumstances the empire was still the dominant partner, however, since it could afford to obtain a result without military risk, and often benefited through the recruitment of soldiers as well as the relieving of frontier pressures.

24 Constantine's treaty with the Goths was certainly the most significant (and well-respected by them) prior to the settlement of 382 with Theodosius: see Wolfram, 60–63 for these diplomatic arrangements. Ammianus XVII, 12, 15 describes the Sarmatians as 'permanent clients of the Romans'.

25 Wolfram, 63–4.

26 Wolfram, 56–7.

27 See Liebeschuetz, *Barbarians and Bishops*, ch.2 for a general discussion.

28 See Liebeschuetz, *Barbarians and Bishops*, 11–15 for a review of the varying kinds of barbarian settlement; also Jones, *LRE*, 620. The first mention of *laeti* is in 296, but the system seems to have been well established by then, and may date to the beginning of Roman recovery in the middle of the third century when substantial settlements of barbarians (and Roman provincials) were made, especially in the 270s and 280s.

29 The law was never re-issued, unlike most others which were frequently restated, but it survived to become part of the law codes of the Gothic successor kingdoms in Italy and Gaul. Liebeschuetz, *Barbarians and Bishops*, 13–14.

30 The only treaties which were concluded after Roman defeats, such as against

the Goths in 251 or the Persians on other occasions, were with groups who were not seeking territory within the empire, but economic and political concessions from it while remaining in their own lands. Similarly the Huns did not seek to exploit their military superiority over the empire by demanding settlement — what would they have wanted when they already controlled all the lands beyond the Danube and Black Sea? — but by demanding tribute.

31   Wolfram, 131–3 and 250ff.

32   One of the most significant outcomes of the process was the re-emergence, in the person of Alaric, of the higher Gothic kingship and the forging of the Visigoths into a single national army. In many ways he was the model (rather than Stilicho) for the generalissimos of the fifth century, after he combined the office of Roman *Magister Militum* with the leadership of a federate army.

CHAPTER 8 (pp.103–115)

1   Jones, *LRE*, 67–8 and nn.56 and 57, 468–9: the exactions of every period of the empire were seen to be intolerable by contemporaries. Although Diocletian was criticised for increasing the tax burden, Aurelius Victor later complained that it had doubled in the intervening period. It is significant that Valentinian III only complained of the inability to meet costs from taxation after the loss of Africa, Spain and most of Gaul. MacMullen, *Corruption*, 41–4 suggests that it was really the effect on the *curiales* which was significant, rather than late Roman taxation in general being unsupportable. See MacMullen, 'Tax Pressure in the Roman Empire', *Latomus* 46 (1987), 733–49.

2   For *agri deserti* (deserted land) see Jones, *LRE*, 812–23 and 1039–40; for depopulation, ibid. 1040–5; also Boak, *Manpower Shortage*, for a traditional view of serious population decline.

3   Williams, *Diocletian*; Jones, *LRE*, esp. ch.2.

4   Jones, *LRE*, chs. 2 and 3 for general commentary on the tax reforms of Diocletian and Constantine, and chs. 20 and 21 for the structuring of society. Also, Jones, *The Roman Economy, passim*.

5   See ch.6 and App.II.

6   The only real exception to this position was the continual game of manoeuvre with Persia, which tilted in both directions at different times without either side completely dominating the other.

7   See Jones, *LRE*, chs. 11 and 12 for an indication of this proliferation and complexity.

8   MacMullen, *Corruption*, 122–170 summarises the whole process and its effects.

9   Constantine had initiated this series of exemptions for the church, developed and enlarged by his successors: see Jones, *LRE*, 89–90.

10   Williams, *Diocletian*. Jones, *The Roman Economy*, ch. 9.

11   Although there does not seem to have been a significant influx to the cities, and movements were frequently from a more to a less oppressive landlord: see n.2. The food dole to the population was limited to Rome and Constantinople, although other large cities, such as Alexandria, subsidised food prices — Jones, *LRE*, 695–705 and 735.

12   The frequent outbreaks of mass, organised brigandage which took place in the fifth century were more occasional and geographically limited in the fourth. The principal problems were caused by the Isaurians of Asia Minor, who continued to

be a threat to imperial security into the sixth century, and the occasional serious outbreaks in Gaul, such as those suppressed by Maximian in 285 and those which endangered the Alpine passes between Italy and Gaul in the early fifth century. Another problem lay with the significant numbers of disaffected poor who joined the barbarians, and became Goths, Huns or whatever (this process was one of acculturation and group identity, not restricted by ethnic origins): see Wolfram, 7–9.

13   Jones, *LRE*, 774–5.

14   For labour shortages and the flight and harbouring of deserters or runaways, see Jones, *LRE*, 1042; for military recruitment of peasants, see the opinions portrayed by Ammianus, XIX, 11, 7.

15   Jones, *LRE*, 712–3, 724–57.

16   Jones, *LRE*, 69 and n.60; Williams, *Diocletian*, ch.10.

17   Ammianus XXVII, 6, 7.

18   For *principales*, Jones, *LRE*, 731; for *honorati* and other ranks, and the expansion of the senatorial order, ibid. ch.15.

19   Jones, *LRE*, 554–7 for the wealth of the senatorial order; also MacMullen, *Corruption*, *passim* for their financial power *vis-a-vis* the state.

20   Williams, *Diocletian*, for his origins.

21   Matthews, *Western Aristocracies*, ch.10 for the maintenance, and enhancement of the power and influence of the Western aristocracy in the later fourth century.

22   MacMullen, *Corruption*; also the difficulties faced by Stilicho when trying to raise an army to defend Italy and secure the African grain supply — see ch.11.

23   Cameron, A., *The Mediterranean World in Late Antiquity*, ch.4.

24   Matthews, *Western Aristocracies*, 253ff.; Jones, *LRE*, chs. XV and XVI.

25   See MacMullen, *Corruption*, 15–35 for a brief regional survey.

26   MacMullen, *Corruption*, 44ff.

27   Percival, *The Roman Villa*; Salway, *Roman Britain*; Wacher, *The Towns of Roman Britain*. MacMullen, *Corruption*, 19–35 provides a good general survey of the economic condition of the provinces. Also see Liebeschuetz, *Barbarians and Bishops*, 18–19, 228–32.

28   Jones, *LRE*, 796, 799.

29   Ammianus, *passim*, for reforms under Julian.

30   Liebeschuetz, *Barbarians and Bishops*, 231–2, 247; Jones, *Later Roman Empire*, 1061; Wolfram, mentions a number of occasions when local militias were raised to face the Goths, beginning in the third century. MacMullen, *Corruption*, 20 on fortified villas in the Danubian area, and see n.27 above.

31   See MacMullen, op. cit.

32   Julian's recovery of Rhineland cities indicates the decay of these regions — see ch. 7 for the frequent settlement of barbarians, indicating that there were obviously neglected areas with the capacity to absorb them.

33   Liebeschuetz, *Barbarians and Bishops*, 18–19.

34   See MacMullen's regional survey, n.25 above.

35   MacMullen, *Corruption*, 32–3.

36   Ibid.

37   MacMullen, *Corruption*, 149–50 for the extent of the abuse, especially by the official government agents, the *agentes in rebus*.

38   Ammianus XXVII for the Romanus case.

39   See Ammianus XV, 2 for the story of Ursicinus and his rivals at court, and

passim for many similar incidents. The rebellion of Silvanus is another prime example of a competent officer lost through court politics — Ammianus XV, 4.

40   See n.37, above.

41   See p.50, above.

42   Although many of the barbarians who threatened the empire were Christian by the late fourth century this did not provide any common identity of religious purpose which contributed to good relations. They were usually Arians facing a Catholic state (under Theodosius), and the strongest support for the Roman state seems usually to have come from pagan barbarians, such as Fravitta and Sarus. Although Ambrose and others were major political players, they were not *within* the state system and often were in conflict with it.

43   The empire could withstand the temporary loss of Danubian and Illyrian provinces, and after 395 the East, in particular, did not concern itself about the links to the West. This was, after all, the direction from which the perceived threat from Stilicho's ambitions came.

44   Jones, *LRE*, 162–3.

CHAPTER 9 (pp.119–133)

1   Theodosius had not appointed any senior colleague to share the rule of the empire with him, and was obviously intent on a dynastic solution to this question. Although he had spent three years in Italy, he had never visited the Western provincial areas of Gaul or the German frontier. He did make provision for the security of the West (see below), but his main concerns were obviously political and religious, and could be dealt with from Italy.

2   Arbogast had originally been sent by Theodosius to Gaul to dispose of Victor, the son of Maximus. Valentinian was despatched to Gaul in early 389 at the latest, as attested by *C.Th.* IV 22.3 given at Trier on 14 June 389, under the care of Arbogast and other loyal appointees of Theodosius — Constantianus and Neoterius, successively Prefects of Gaul in 389 and 390 — *PRLE* I, 222 and 623.

3   Contrast this with the treatment of his own sons, who were being quite obviously prepared — through the holding of appropriate titles rather than through any military training, for which they were still too young — for the succession. Valentinian's elder brother, Gratian, had become emperor in his own right at sixteen. While Valentinian was removed to Trier rapidly after the defeat of Maximus, Honorius was presented at Rome during his father's visit. Theodosius arrived in Rome on 13 June 389 — *Chron.Min.* I, 245;298.

4   *PLRE* I, 347–8.

5   Theodosius' first rescript, from Thessalonica in 379, had been to protect the sacred cypress grove of the shrine of Daphne, near Antioch — *C.Th.* X 1.12. For the new law, see below n.11.

6   See Jones, *Later Roman Empire*, 168 and n.78 for the extent of the repression, esp. in *C.Th.* XVI, 10, 12.

7   Cf. King, ch.5; Matthews, 236ff.

8   This seems implausible. The earlier *modus vivendi* with paganism does not seem to have been politically calculated.

9   Libanius is almost the only possible support for this unlikely view. If Valentinian II could defy the old gods, then surely so could Theodosius.

10   *PLRE* I 778–81; he was appointed in 388 and accompanied Theodosius to

Rome in 389.

11   C.Th. XVI, 10, 10, of 24 February 391, from Milan to Albinus, Prefect of Rome.

12   Concordia lies at the head of the Adriatic, on the main route to Aquileia and the East to which Theodosius was returning; C.Th. XVI, 7, 4–5.

13   King, Ch.5.

14   This was, however, an exceptional case. Priscillian was condemned, justly or otherwise, not as an 'ordinary' heretic Christian, but as a crypto-Manichean. Manicheism had carried the death penalty, at least for the lower orders, since Diocletian's law of 302.

15   PLRE I 140–1 and 736–40.

16   C.Th. XVI, 10, 11 from Aquileia, to Evagrius, Prefect, and Romanus, Count of Egypt.

17   Ammianus XXII, 15, 3–13 for the contemporary view of the importance of the Nile floods.

18   Libanius, Or. 30, 18.

19   See Alföldi, Die Kontorniaten, Budapest 1943.

20   C.Th. XVI, 10, 16–17 prohibiting festivals. The frequency of legislation against pagan practice suggests that observance was not universal!

21   PLRE I 722–4.

22   PLRE I 38.

23   PLRE I 311.

24   E.g. ILS 4154, dating to 390.

25   See Ammianus XXII, 16, 12. The date of its destruction is discussed by Jones, LRE, 431–2 and n.77. Also King, op. cit. app.C. It obviously post-dates Libanius' oration 30. Sozomen 7, 15–20 indicates a date in 391, supported by Jerome and the Gallic Chronicle, and Matthews, Western Aristocracies, 236–7 accepts this view. For various accounts, Eunapius Vita Antonius; Rufinus 11, 22–30; Sozomen 7, 15–20; Theodoret 5, 22.

26   Rufinus, 11, 22. It is not extant in any official source (Rufinus is not, of course, to be confused with the Prefect of the same name).

27   Vita Antonius.

28   Libanius, De Templis.

29   Zosimus IV 37; Chron.Min. I, 244; Theodoret 5,2; Sozomen 7,15.

30   Flavianus in the West, and Tatianus (PRLE I 867–8) in the East.

31   C.Th. XVI, 10, 12 from Constantinople, to Rufinus, Prefect of the East.

32   Ambrose, De Obitu.

33   Gibbon, Decline and Fall, Ch.28. Ferguson, passim.

34   Libanius, Or. 30.

35   Jullian, Histoire de la Gaule, 1926.

36   Men such as Flavianus, Nestorius and Albinus (Prefects), Messianus and Aurelianus, Court Ministers.

37   Theodosius' dynastic ambitions were clear from an early stage — he had Arcadius declared Augustus early in 383, which may have added to Maximus' sense of injustice. His treatment of Valentinian suggests a compromise between the loyalist protecting a legitimate colleague, and a dynast ensuring that no-one stood in the way of his own family succession to complete power. This ambivalence may have also played a part in the reaction to Maximus in 383.

38   Probably in 388 — see Soz. 7, 14; Ruf. 2, 17. But Zosimus IV 47 still has her

guiding Valentinian II to reclaim his throne in Italy later.

39   *PLRE* I 95–7. For his ascendancy, see Zosimus IV 53; Paulinus *VSA 30;* Gregory of Tours *Hist. Franc. 2, 9.*

40   *The only others recorded for the West in this period are Rumoridus, in Italy in 384, and Gildo, in Africa from 386 — see PRLE.*

41   Paulinus *VSA* 30; Gregory of Tours, *Hist. Franc.* 2, 9; *ILS* 790 (Cologne). The campaign was probably in 393, after the elevation of Eugenius.

42   Zosimus IV 53; Philost. 11, 1 says that Valentinian even tried to stab Arbogast with his sword. John of Antioch, frag. 187, *FHG* 4, has Arbogast slaying one of Valentinian's friends, Harmonius, when he sought the ultimate protection of the emperor's robe. A classic scene.

43   Gibbon, ch. 27. There are different versions of the death: Zosimus IV, 54; Philost. 11,1; Soc. 5,11; Oros. 7,35; John Ant. 187, have Arbogast murdering Valentinian, either in person or through agents, either by strangling, suffocation or stabbing, either in or outside the palace. Murder became the official (Theodosian) version — Claudian *De IV Cons. Hon.* But Rufinus 2,31 and Soz. 7,22 are non-committal. Most importantly, Ambrose *De Obit. Val.* 33 first talks of it as sudden death ('*de celeritate mortis non de genere loquor*'), and then most significantly in 395, *De Obit. Theod.* 39–40, he omits any mention of the murder and avenging of Valentinian alongside that of Gratian. The suggestion that Ambrose later ruled out murder is supported by Paulinus, *VSA* 26, who merely says that 'Valentinian, of sacred memory, had ended his life in the city of Vienne'. The evidence is collected by Rauchen, *Jahrbucher der Christlichen*, 361, and Croke, 'Arbogast and the Death of Valentinian II', *Historia* 1976. As is evident from the main text, we incline to the suicide view, with Matthews, Croke and others. But an alternative scenario might be this: after the damaging public showdown, news of which soon reaches Constantinople, Arbogast realises that he must neutralise Valentinian. His agents then do a clumsy job of murdering him. Arbogast, still hoping to placate Theodosius if possible, puts the best face on it. But to suppose a premeditated plot before the breach becomes public — as Gibbon does — deprives Arbogast of any credible motive.

44   Gibbon, ch. 27.

45   RIC 9, 1951, 32–4. Pearce, *Numis. Chron.* 17, 1937.

46   Ambrose, *De Obit. Val.* 33 — see n.43 above.

47   Zosimus IV 55.

48   *PLRE* I 750–1.

49   On this story, Theodoret *HE* 5,18. This accusation levelled against Rufinus may have much to do with the desire of contemporary and later commentators to exonerate the Most Christian Emperor Theodosius — see Matthews, Liebeschuetz. Certainly, if it was widely believed at the time it would have undermined Rufinus' position.

50   Zosimus, *passim.*

51   *PLRE* I 293. For a detailed discussion of this 'revolt', Straub, 1966; Szidet, *Historia,* 1979.

52   *PLRE* I 765–6.

53   Abundantius was *Magister Militum* in the East — *PLRE* I, 4–5.

54   Ambrose *Ep.* 57.

55   For the pagan revival of 393–4: Gregory of Tours *Hist. Franc.* 11,9; *Carmen Contra Paganos* (anon.); Boissier, *La Fin du paganisme*, Paris 1891; Cumont, *Les*

religions orientales, Paris 1929; Bloch, 'The Pagan Revival in the West' in Momigliano (ed.), *The Conflict of Paganism and Christianity*, Oxford 1963; Forte *et al.* 'A New Document of the Last Pagan Revival in the West', *Harvard Theol. Review* 1945; King, op. cit.; Matthews, *Western Aristocracies*, ch.9.

56 Matthews, *Western Aristocracies*, ch.9.

57 Ambrose *Ep.* 57.

58 *PRLE* I 380, 809, 144.

59 *PRLE* II 43–9; but the numbers suggested by Seeck *et al.* (1913) are surely exaggerations.

60 Ruf. 11,32; Palladius *HL* 35; Augustine *Civ.Dei* 5,26.

61 King, ch.6.

62 Paulinus *VSA* 32.

CHAPTER 10 (pp.134–140)

1 See Vieth and Seeck, *Klio* XIII (1913), 451–67 for a detailed account of the battle.

2 It was, of course, standard Roman practice to minimise losses of regular troops through the use of allies and auxiliaries; this must have been especially important to Theodosius who had inherited the devastated army after Adrianople. These losses may also have further influenced the attitude of Alaric, who already felt slighted in not receiving the command of the federate forces: Wolfram, *History of the Goths*, 138 and n.129.

3 Matthews, *Western Aristocracies*, 246.

4 Rufinus XI 32 mentions that Theodosius had sought blessing from the hermit, John, before setting out, and the religious motif of the campaign is continued by this story.

5 Although the reference by Claudian to two swords bearing Arbogast's blood may suggest that his suicide was assisted by an attendant — Claudian, *De III Con. Hons.*, 102f.

6 He was required to repay the salary which he had received as Prefect of the City under Eugenius. This obligation was later cancelled under Honorius and Stilicho — Matthews, *Western Aristocracies*, 266. Symmachus had maintained formal and social links with Eugenius' regime, but had avoided any display of support and implication with the rebellion, no doubt mindful of his difficult position following the fall of Maximus — Matthews, ibid., 243–5.

7 Although there can have been little time for Theodosius to enforce any major initiatives before his death early in 395.

8 Matthews, *Western Aristocracies*, 247 and nn.4–6.

9 For the two accounts of the Senate's debate, see Prudentius, *Symmach*, 530ff. Zosimus IV. This pagan/Christian synthesis had been ongoing for a long time, and there are numerous examples of Christ identified with classical mythological figures — such as Orpheus.

10 See Holum, *Theodosian Empresses, passim*, for the piety of the imperial court and its women in particular. K. Cooper, *JRS*, 1992.

11 Jones, *LRE*, 929–33 for the development of monasticism, especially in Egypt.

12 Matthews, *Western Aristocracies*, 120–1.

13 As many as 10,000 are suggested to have been casualties at the Frigidus. Even if this is a highly exaggerated figure (possibly including wounded with the dead?)

it is still indicative of the scale of the conflict and its impact on manpower.

14   Claudian *De VI Cons. Hon.* 88f.

15   See Appendix 2.

16   Gildo had been, exceptionally, appointed to the office of *Comes et Magister Utriusque Militiae* in 393 to secure Africa against Eugenius and Arbogast, but he was no rival to Stilicho (at this stage) and his power and influence were limited to his native African territories.

17   See ch. 11.

18   See ch. 11 below for the presentation of Stilicho's legitimacy by Ambrose.

19   See Mazzarino, and ch. 11 below.

20   There can be no real doubt that Theodosius intended Stilicho to be regent in the West, and that if Theodosius had lived to return to Constantinople Rufinus would have continued to be the senior civilian figure beneath the emperor — and nothing more.

21   Wolfram, 138–9.

22   For this analogy earlier, see ch. 9. For the oration and audience: Ambrose, *De Obitu Theodosii*; Claudian, *De VI Cons. Hon.*, 88f. See Matthews, *Western Aristocracies*, 248–9 for refs.

23   For the nature and character of Arcadius and Honorius, see Jones, *LRE*, 173.

CHAPTER 11 (pp.142–158)

1   The fullest account is still Mazzarino, *Stilicone*.

2   Claudian, the chosen propagandist of Stilicho, emphasised the continuity of policy from Theodosius to Stilicho: *De bell. Gild.* 305–6.

3   O'Flynn, *Generalissimos*, argues cogently that Stilicho's formal titles were vague and unilluminating, simply because his actual position was a genuinely new one for which there was as yet no name: that of a supreme military commander ruling through a puppet emperor. Successor figures used the new title of 'Patrician' (*Patricius*). See Matthews, *Western Aristocracies*, 265, n.7, for a range of titles used by Symmachus to address Stilicho after 395 (*potissimus magistratus*, etc.). It does seem, however, that Theodosius had appointed Stilicho to the supreme Western military command in late 394 before his illness — his intention was always to rule from Constantinople, and there was the Hunnic threat to Thrace which required his return to the East: Cameron, *Claudian*, and Zosimus IV, 58, 1f. for Stilicho's military command over Gaul, Spain, Italy, Africa. See also *ILS* 797, 1277.

4   Claudian, *De consulatu Stilichonis*, III, 176. cf. Cameron, *Claudian*, 47. Eucherius appears on the obelisk at Constantinople along with Arcadius and Honorius, and Claudian later hints at a marriage for him to Galla Placidia.

5   Matthews, *Western Aristocracies*, 258–64: many of these supporters had links with earlier court circles, especially in the West, and there is thus a strong element of continuity which was no doubt intended to reinforce Stilicho's authority.

6   Rufinus had been left in control of the East, nominally under the authority of Arcadius, when Theodosius set out to the West against Arbogast and Eugenius. He had been advanced rapidly by Theodosius, and was clearly a favoured official. For his position, see Zosimus IV, 57; John Ant. fr. 188, 190; Eunapius fr. 62–3; Orosius VII, 37. That Theodosius left Rufinus as *de facto* guardian of Arcadius does not, of course, directly contradict Stilicho's claim: Theodosius did not expect to die so abruptly, and his final wishes may — possibly — have overridden any earlier,

temporary arrangement.

7 Cameron, *Claudian*, ch.7.

8 We need to consider why Stilicho had no power base in the East, despite his unrivalled military position and obvious favoured relationship with the imperial family: the answer must be that his legitimate authority, granted by Theodosius before any 'deathbed bequest' in 395, lay in his appointment to supreme military command in the West as a successor figure to the role played earlier by Arbogast.

9 This position took several years to reach, and was only really true after Alaric's invasions of Italy. However Stilicho had a manpower problem as soon as he returned the Eastern troops to Arcadius in 395. See Liebeschuetz, *Barbarians and Bishops*, 41–2.

10 Orosius, VII, 35. It was claimed that 10,000 Visigoths died in the vanguard of Theodosius' army out of a total force of 20,000. It was certainly a bloody head-on conflict, and a 50 per cent casualty rate (including the injured) is not implausible.

11 Against this, it should be remembered that the focus of the treaty was loyalty to the emperor in person — Valens had gone to war against the Tervingi in the 360s because they had supported the usurper Procopius, claiming that such service was due to their treaty with Constantine, whose descendant Procopius claimed to be: Wolfram, 65–6.

12 Zosimus, V, 5; Heather, 199ff. Such a post would have reinforced his authority against the other Gothic princes who might have felt equally well qualified to rule their people.

13 The other Germanic generals within the Roman army had no tribal base — they were Roman officers within the standard Roman command structure. It would, however, have been a major insult to Alaric as senior representative of the emerging Visigothic royal line, the *Balthi*, to serve under Gainas who had risen from humble origins to a high Roman command — Wolfram, 138. But see Heather on this question.

14 Wolfram, 139; Maenchen-Helfen, 49ff, suggests that, rather than Hunnic invasion, the Goths were threatened by federate groups of Huns settled in Thrace and loyal to Rufinus. They had fought for Theodosius against Eugenius. Rufinus certainly favoured the Huns, and may have wished to use them to counterbalance the Goths and their loyalty to Stilicho (that is, the Goths in the Roman army and not the federates, who were now loyal only to themselves). In either case, the Goths were not content with the lands which they had held since the treaty of 382 and their wanderings over the next few years under Alaric may be partly explained as a search for a safe (and wealthy) homeland, away from the rapidly consolidating Hunnic dominion north of the Danube.

15 Wolfram, 143–6, 211. He suggests that Alaric was born outside the empire, possibly in the lower Danube area, and that — based on his 'royal' descent and name — he may have been related to (the son of?) Alavivus. See ch. 7. Liebeschuetz, *Barbarians and Bishops*, 65–7 suggests that many (most?) of the Moesian Goths did not leave their treaty-assigned lands and follow Alaric.

16 Wolfram, 140–1. Claudian, *In Rufinum II*, 70–85, suggests that Rufinus concluded a treaty with the Goths and presents this as a heinous betrayal; however Cameron and Heather suggest that no formal agreement was concluded and Alaric simply led his people away from impregnable Constantinople towards rich settlement lands. There is the possibility that, since the focus of the original *foedus* — Theodosius — had died, Alaric and the Goths sought, and received, confirmation

of a new treaty from Arcadius (in the person of Rufinus), who was the senior Augustus. Claudian carefully avoided any direct criticism of Arcadius, and may have therefore pinned the blame on Rufinus. The ritual demonstration of a Gothic federate army before the gates of a Roman (provincial) capital was a standard feature of the attempts of the Visigoths in Gaul to improve their terms of service — Wolfram, 175.

17 Such as the minor outbreak in 391, when Gothic federates from Moesia and barbarians who had deserted from Theodosius' army in 388 caused serious trouble in Macedonia and defeated the emperor himself. This is the first occasion Alaric appears in our sources, as the leader of these rebellious Goths, and also the first time that Alaric is 'defeated' by Stilicho, but is then let go on the orders of Theodosius himself — Wolfram, 136–7.

18 See Thompson, *Visigoths*, on the divisions between leaders and followers in Gothic society.

19 Claudian represents the whole episode as further treachery by Rufinus, who was afraid of Stilicho. However it is still a radical suggestion that the East would behave like a separate, independent state, and that the senior Augustus would see the army and empire being divided in this way — in this we see the clear signs of conflict between rival courts and officials whose legitimacy is territorially based: *In Rufinem II*, 145–220.

20 Claudian's emphasis on the unity and loyalty of the combined army is suspicious, and may attempt to cover this very weakness. In addition, Stilicho managed to defeat Alaric on later occasions without the help of Eastern forces, suggesting that any doubts in 395 relate to the reliability of his army and not its numbers. For the recent, most important discussions of this episode, see O'Flynn, *Generalissimos*, 28ff. and Cameron, *Claudian*, chs. 4 and 7: they argue that Stilicho was having trouble with his army, especially the Eastern elements who must have wanted to return home. Among those who accept the Claudian version are Mommsen, Bury, Seeck, Stein, Mazzarino, Demouget and Jones. Cameron was the first to dismiss the whole thing as 'a tissue of tendentious falsehoods' (op. cit. 89), but he does not give due weight to the point that a fight to the finish, even if victorious, was not the optimum outcome for Stilicho. O'Flynn recognises that a reinstatement of the *foedus* was a more realistic and desirable aim. Cameron has also doubted the existence of any such order from Arcadius (read Rufinus), suggesting Stilicho voluntarily returned his unwieldy Eastern forces; but it is inevitable that the East would want and need its field army, especially in view of the Hunnic invasion of the Eastern provinces in 395 — Maenchen-Helfen, 51–9. The main successes of Valens, Theodosius and his generals against the Goths in the 370s and 380s were achieved through the very denial of mobility and plunder which Stilicho managed to enforce without a set-piece battle.

21 Stilicho had inherited a field army which had lost two civil wars in six years, and which did not have the resource of the Goths for recruitment.

22 His Western army had lost both of Theodosius' civil wars, and the Eastern army had been strengthened at its expense.

23 It can be no coincidence that the — substantially Gothic — Eastern army is portrayed by Claudian as reluctant to return to a court dominated by Rufinus, since he will make them subject to Huns and Alans: *In Rufinum II*, 270–1. For the Hunnic associations of Rufinus, see Maenchen-Helfen, *World of the Huns*, 50–1. Cameron has suggested that Eutropius, who was to succeed to Rufinus' power,

was responsible for the assassination since he was on the spot and stood to gain most; Matthews proposes collusion between Stilicho and Eutropius, who initially improved relations between East and West. Most importantly, however, Stilicho claimed the credit through his propagandist, Claudian: *In Rufinum II*, 400–404.

24 *PLRE* II, 440.

25 *PLRE* II, 410; Holum, *Theodosian Empresses*, 52–80.

26 Cameron, *Claudian*, for this question; also Mazzarino, *Stilicone* and Grumel, in *Rev. Etud. Byz.* ix, 1952, 5f. Although it is possible that Illyricum was split by Theodosius after his victory over Eugenius, when he clearly designated Stilicho as his commander in the West, it seems unlikely that this was a priority in the short time before his death. Regardless of the timing — 395 following the death of Rufinus seems most likely — we do not consider that the possession of Illyricum was contested, and so we can fortunately leave this over-debated question.

27 Although this did not prevent him promoting his own dynastic ambitions rather than those of Valentinian.

28 Claudian mentions the issue of guardianship for the last time in 400 (Arcadius was already father of two children of his own by this time!); it does not appear in 402, and in 404 only Honorius is mentioned. It would seem that Stilicho, perhaps secure enough in the West and his command of the now adult Honorius, dropped what was obviously a dead issue.

29 See the collection of contemporary opinions of Arcadius collected by Holum, *Theodosian Empresses*, 50, where he is compared to an ox and has a foggy mind! His lack of any military training or interests is also attacked by Synesius, who comments that he (Arcadius) cannot engage in the art of war if he does not make the acquaintance of the tools of his trade, his soldiers — *De Regno*, 14.

30 *C Th.* 7, 18.

31 Claudian, *De IV Cons. Hon.* 445ff.

32 Maenchen-Helfen, 51–9. Liebeschuetz, *Barbarians and Bishops*, 93–7 for the civilian, diplomatic basis of Eastern policy at this time, rather than the military resolution sought by Stilicho. It might also have been the case that the East could not trust its army in battle against Alaric, due to mistrust of the Germanic generals and soldiers at the civilian court, just as has been suggested for Stilicho's army.

33 Claudian suggests, as he would, that Theodosius was about to deal with Gildo when he died. *PRLE* I, 395 for Gildo. The fact that Stilicho marched against Alaric, rather than on Constantinople, confirms his legitimist stance — he wanted power and recognition, but not civil war. Matthews, *Western Aristocracies*, 272 has suggested that Gildo was constitutionally correct to obey the senior Augustus, but the real issue is of the intriguing of one court against the other when they both had many real enemies to confront. Liebeschuetz, *Barbarians and Bishops*, 97–9: he argues that the actions of Eutropius and the Eastern government fit into a general diplomatic offensive, which avoided giving real power to any of its generals.

34 Wolfram, 142 for the 397 campaign. The absence of the Eastern army throughout this episode can only mean that Eutropius was waiting to see the outcome: he would not support Stilicho despite the depredations of the Goths.

35 This sort of fratricidal conflict seems to have been endemic in Africa.

36 See ch.2 for the campaign of Theodosius the Elder in Africa.

37 Zosimus 5, 11 accuses Stilicho of murder; Claudian just fails to mention Mascazel entirely.

38 Wolfram, *History of the Goths*, 142–3. Liebeschuetz, *Barbarians and Bishops*,

59–60 for the conditions of the Gothic settlement: he suggests that Alaric's forces remained in being, as an army billeted in and around the cities of his new territory rather than on the land. Although his general thesis — that the Alaric Goths were a conglomeration of federate troops, Roman provincials and others, and not the nation of the Tervingi who had been settled in Moesia and Thrace in 382 — is not accepted by us, it does seem that Alaric led an army which sought regular army maintenance and not land for settlement: see ibid. 51–2, 56–7, 59–60.

39 Liebeschuetz, *Barbarians and Bishops*, 57–9 for some discussion of his motives.

40 *In Eutrop.* I, 244–86.

41 Maenchen-Helfen, certainly dismisses any idea of a serious campaign against the Huns at this time, and suggests this is another character slight linking Eutropius and Huns as he had done with Rufinus earlier. There must have been some fighting, however, or else there is little justification for the slight felt by the leaders of the revolt and their followers. See Wolfram, 148–50 for the revolt; also Liebeschuetz, *Barbarians and Bishops*, 100–103.

42 Eunuchs were seen, especially by the West, as a detestable Oriental corruption of Roman values.

43 Claudian, *In Eutropium*, I and II.

44 Eutropius had also alienated the civil establishment at Constantinople, since he controlled all access to the emperor — senators, and even Eudoxia, had to pay court to him to obtain an audience with Arcadius.

45 *PLRE* I, Aurelian 3. See Liebeschuetz, *Barbarians and Bishops*, 133 for his career.

46 Liebeschuetz, *Barbarians and Bishops*, 111–125 for a summary of the Gainas affair, and the significant differences between East and West in Gothic policy.

47 Synesius, *De Regno*.

48 See Wolfram, *History of the Goths*, 150–153 for this campaign.

49 Claudian, *De VI Cons. Hon.* refers to Alaric breaking his bond, and violating a treaty after Pollentia (vv.204, 210), and to force of circumstance or political considerations requiring Alaric's life being spared (128).

50 *CSEL* xxxv, 85, dating to 405, but referring to earlier events in 403–4.

51 See ch.6 and App.II for a discussion of the army's decline.

52 Liebeschuetz, *Barbarians and Bishops*, 65–6. Stilicho did not recognise the Eastern consuls for 404 or 405, although Claudian, writing in early 404 on the sixth consulship of Honorius does not display any open hostility to the East, or raise the question of control of Illyricum. It seems that resentments and hostility were accumulating during the course of 404, and that open conflict broke out later, perhaps over the winter or early in 405. Certainly Honorius appointed his own Prefect for Illyricum, and possibly also gave Alaric the rank of *Magister Militum*, in 405 — this amounted to a declaration of civil war.

53 *PRLE* II, 934; Wolfram, 168–70.

54 Orosius VII 37, 16; Zosimus V 26, 4.

55 Zosimus V 26,5; see Wolfram for references to Stilicho's success — p.444, n.338.

56 A further significant development from this event may have been the emergence of the Amali as nominated kings of the subject Goths under the Huns, to units and control them — Wolfram, 170 and n.334.

57 Maenchen-Helfen, 71–2.

58 Zosimus V 29; Matthews, *Western Aristocracies*, 275–6, 278–80.

59 Holum, *passim*, on the importance of producing children in the Theodosian dynastic regime.

60 Zosimus V 30.

61 Some of their commanders, such as Sarus, must have been hostile to the accommodation reached with Alaric and his appointment over their heads. Some of them had left Alaric to serve with Stilicho after his victory at Verona in 402.

62 Zosimus V 30–34.

63 Matthews, *Western Aristocracies*, 279–83; Liebeschuetz, *Barbarians and Bishops*, 67–8; Wolfram, 154.

64 Orosius and Rutilius took the official line and damned Stilicho as a fifth columnist who sold the empire to the barbarians. Among modern writers, Bury and Seeck have accepted this almost uncritically. Mazzarino is far more balanced, but still suspects that Stilicho and Alaric were in league from early on. Gibbon is an exception, and although he takes the classical attitude towards the barbarisation of the armies, he cannot conceal his admiration for 'the great Stilicho', and dismisses the charges as fabrications by his enemies. Finally, Cameron's critical analysis of Claudian, supported by O'Flynn's thesis on the generalissimos, have rehabilitated Stilicho.

CHAPTER 12 (pp.159–171)

1 Vol. III, p.66, n.1.

2 Jones, *LRE*, ch.XXV for a general analysis of this contrast between East and West.

3 See Wolfram, *History of the Goths*, ch.3 *passim*.

4 See ch.6 and App.II for the military 'manpower shortage'.

5 He is described by Jordanes as 'the friend of peace and the Gothic people', *Getica*, 146.

6 See ch.6 and App.II for Stilicho's military weakness.

7 See Wolfram, 161–4; Matthews, *Western Aristocracies*, 307–19.

8 Ammianus XXVII, 3, 1–6 for Julian's success in reforming the government of Gaul as Caesar.

9 This was confirmed by the establishment of Constantinople as the most senior episcopal see in the east, second only to Rome.

10 For the more prominent views on the dismemberment of the West and the survival of the East, see: Gibbon, *Decline and Fall*; Seeck, *Geschichte der untergangs der Antiken Welt*; Bury, *History of the Later Roman Empire*; Walbank, *The Decline of the Roman Empire in the West*; Boak, *Manpower Shortage and the Fall of the Roman Empire in the West*; Piganiol, *L'Empire chrétien*; Demouget, *La formation de l'Europe et les invasions barbares*; Vogt, *The Decline of Rome*; Ste. Croix, *The Class Struggle in the Ancient World*; MacMullen, *Corruption and the Decline of Rome*; Tainter, *The Collapse of Complex Societies*.

APPENDIX I (pp.176–181)

1   Oman, *A History of the Art of War in the Middle Ages*, I, 13.

2   Burns, 'The Battle of Adrianople: A Reconsideration', *Historia*, 22 (1973), 336–45, describes it as an infantry battle, but others still persist in the myth of Gothic cavalry ushering in the Middle Ages and the dominance of heavy cavalry — see Pavan (1979). Bury accepted the 'obvious' success of east Germanic cavalry without question — *LRE*, 41–2. Wolfram, gives a more reasoned view: 'Above all, it is not true that Gothic horsemen were from this time invincible, and it is equally inaccurate to infer from the disaster of Adrianople a fundamental superiority of cavalry over infantry' (p.127).

3   Ammianus XXXI, 13, 19.

4   As the Tervingi managed to break out from the Danube–Black Sea–Balkans area, where they had been penned in by a Roman blockade, by recruiting Alan and Hun allies who outflanked the Roman garrisons and forced their withdrawal — Ammianus XXXI, 8, 4–5; Maenchen–Helfen, 27–8.

5   See Luttwak, *Grand Strategy of the Roman Empire*, Table 3.1 for a review of figures for the proportion of *limitanei* to *comitatenses*. We suggest 40:60, given the likelihood that the units of the *limitanei* are more likely to have been seriously under strength than those of the field army — see Appendix II.

6   For his Dacian wars Trajan, with the resources of the whole empire at his disposal, may have assembled campaign armies of some 100,000 men out of a total military force of roughly 300,000. Such high figures became increasingly difficult to assemble, given the multiplication of threats faced by the empire simultaneously from the latter second century onwards.

7   Ammianus XXXI, 7, 16.

8   See MacMullen, *Corruption*, 173–4 for a discussion of these numbers.

9   Ammianus XXXI, 8, 9; XXXI, 9.

10   Maenchen-Helfen, *World of the Huns*, 29. The security provided by the Gothic laager of wagons is a feature of the campaigns of 377–82, and again when they faced Stilicho.

11   Ammianus XVI, 12, 37–41.

12   XXXI, 7, 10–16.

13   Wolfram, 130.

APPENDIX II (pp182)

1   Of the available studies of the later Roman army, the following are the most comprehensive and helpful to an understanding of the changes taking place in our period: Jones, *LRE*, chs. 1–6 *passim*, and esp. chs. 17 and 25; Hoffman, *Die spatromische Bewegungsheer und die Notitia Dignitatum.*

2   Liebeschuetz; see Ch. 6, *passim*, and esp. ch. 7.

3   O'Flynn, *Generalissimos*; diagrams below; ch. 11 for Stilicho generally.

4   See Luttwak for a general picture of the emergence of the later Roman army; also Tomlin, R. in Connolly, *Greece and Rome at War.*

5   See MacMullen, *Corruption*, 171–7 for this kind of assumption.

6   See Jones, *LRE*, app. II for the baseline figures used in this analysis.

7   Jones, app. II, table 15, taking all legions — *comitatenses* and *limitanei* — as nominally 1000 strong and all other units as 500 strong.

8   See ch. 10.

9   Liebeschuetz, *Barbarians and Bishops*, arguing for a decline in the recruitment potential and the favour of the army in the civilian-run East after 395 — ch. 3.

10   Ammianus, on Julian, Constantius, etc.

11   See ch. 11.

12   Jones' analysis demonstrates the extent of the West's losses after 395.

SELECT BIBLIOGRAPHY

This is not intended to be a comprehensive or exhaustive listing of relevant sources, but a guide to the principal authorities referred to in the text. Many of these contain extensive bibliographies which we will not duplicate here.

Standard abbreviations

BAR   *British Archaeological Reports*
CAH   *Cambridge Ancient History*
CIL   *Corpus Inscriptionum Latinarum*
CJ   *Codex Iustinianus*
CSEL *Corpus Scriptorum Ecclesiastiorum Latinarum*
CTh   *Codex Theodosianus*
IGRR *Inscriptiones Graecae ad Res Romanas Pertinentes*
ILS   *Inscriptiones Latinae Selectae*
JHS   *Journal of Hellenic Studies*
JRS   *Journal of Roman Studies*
PLRE *Prosopography of the Later Roman Empire*
PWRE *Pauly-Wissowa Real Encyclopaedie*

Principal classical sources

Ambrose of Milan *De Obitu Theodosii; De Obitu Valentiniani Iunioris; Epistulae; Expositio in Lucam*
Ammianus Marcellinus *Rerum Gestarum*
Cassiodorus *Chronica; Historia Ecclesiastica*
Claudian *Carmina*
Codex Iustinianus
Codex Theodosianus
Eunapius *Historiarum fragmenta*
Eutropius *Breviarum ab urbe condita*
Gregory of Nazianzus *Orationes; Epistulae*
Jerome *Chronicon*
Jordanes *Getica*
Libanius *Orationes*
Notitia Dignitatum
Olympiodorus of Thebes *Historiarum fragmenta*
Orosius *Historiarum adversum paganos*
Pacatus *Panegyrici*

Paulinus of Milan *Vita S. Ambrosii*
Philostorgius *Historia Ecclesiastica*
Rufinus *Historia Ecclesiastica*
Salvian *De gubernatione Dei*
Socrates *Historia Ecclesiastica*
Sozomenus *Historia Ecclesiastica*
Symmachus *Epistulae*
Synesius of Cyrene *Epistulae; De regno*
Themistius *Orationes*
Theodoret *Historia Ecclesiastica*
Zonaras *Epitome Historiarum*
Zosimus *Historia Nova*

Secondary sources

Albert, G. 'Stilicho und der Hunefeldzug des Eutropius', *Chiron* 9, 1979, 621–645

Alföldi, A. *A Conflict of Ideas in the Late Roman Empire: The Clash between the Senate and Valentinian I*, Oxford 1952 tr. Mattingley, H.

Alföldi, A. and Straub, J. 'Transformation et Conflits au IVe siècle ap. J.C.', *Antiquitas* 29, 1978

Alföldy, G. *Noricum*, London, 1974 tr. Birley, A.R.

'Barbareneinfalle und Religiöse Krisen in Italien', *Antiquitas* 3, 1–19, 1966

Altheim, F. *Der Krise der alten Welt*, Berlin 1943

Anderson, P. *Passages from Antiquity to Feudalism*, London 1974

Andersson, T.M. 'Cassiodorus and the Gothic Legend of Ermanaric', *Eurphorion* 57, 28–43, 1963

Aricescu, A. *The Army in Roman Dobrudja*, Oxford 1980

Arnold, C.J. *Roman Britain to Saxon England*, London 1984

Austin, N.J.E. *Ammianus on Warfare*, Brussels 1979.

Bachrach, B.S. *A History of the Alans in the West*, Minneapolis 1973

Barkoczi, L. *History of Pannonia*, Lexington, Ky. 1980

Bartholomew, P. 'Fourth-Century Saxons', *Britannia* 15, 169–85, 1984

Bayless, W.N. 'The Visigothic Invasion of Italy in 401', *Classical Journal* 72, 65–67, 1976

Bell, H.I. et al. *The Abinnaeus Archive: Papers of a Roman Army Officer in the Reign of Constantius II*, Oxford 1962

Bichir, G. *Archaeology and the History of the Carpi from the Second to the Fourth Century A.D.*, Oxford 1976 (BAR 16)

Boak, A.E.R. *Manpower Shortage and the Fall of the Roman Empire in the West*, Ann Arbor 1955

Bonanni, S. 'Ammiano Marcellino e i Barbari', *Rivista di Cultura Classica e Medioevale* 23, 125–42, 1981

Breeze, D.J. *The Northern Frontiers of Roman Britain*, London 1982

Bregman, J. *Synesius of Cyrene*, 1982

Brisson, J-P. (ed). *Problème de la Guerre à Rome*, Paris 1969

Brown, P. *Religion and Society in the Age of St Augustine*, 1972

The Cult of the Saints: its rise and function in Latin Christianity, 1981

'Aspects of the Christianisation of the Roman Aristocracy'. *JRS* 51, 1961

Browning, R. 'The Riot of AD 387 in Antioch', *JRS* 19, 1952

Burns, T.S. *A History of the Ostrogoths*, Bloomington 1984

Burns, T.S. 'The Battle of Adrianople: A Reconsideration', *Historia* 22, 336–45, 1973

'Calculating Ostrogothic Population', *Acta Antiqua* 26, 457–63, 1978

The Ostrogoths: Kingship and Society, Wiesbaden 1980

Bury, J.B. *History of the Later Roman Empire*, New York 1957, 2 vols (reprint)

The Invasion of Europe by the Barbarians, New York 1967

Cameron, A. *Claudian, Poetry and Propaganda at the Court of Honorius*, Oxford 1970

Cameron, A.D.E. 'Theodosius the Great and the Regency of Stilicho', *Harvard Studies in Classical Philology* 73, 247–80, 1969

Cameron, Averil, *The Mediterranean World in Late Antiquity*, 1992.

Cesa, M. and Sivan, H. 'Alarico in Italia: Pollenza e Verona', *Historia* 39, 361–74, 1990

Chastagnol, A. *La Fin du Monde Antique*, Paris 1976

Cheesman, G.L. *The Auxilia of the Roman Imperial Army*, Chicago 1975

Chrysos, E.K. 'Gothia Romana: Zur Rechtsgrundlage des Foderatenstandes der Westogoten im 4 Jahrhundert', *Dacoromania* 1, 52–64, 1973

Clauss, M. *Der Magister Officiorum in der Spatantike 4–6 jahrhundert*, Munich 1980

Connolly, P. *Greece and Rome at War*, London 1988

Cooper, K. Insinuations of Womanly Influence; An Aspect of the Christianisation of the Roman Aristocracy, *JRS*, 1992

Cracco Ruggini, L. 'Uomini senza terra e terra senza uomini nell'Italia Antica', *Quaderni di Sociologia Rurale* 3, 20–42, 1963

Croke, B. 'Arbogast and the Death of Valentinian II', *Historia* 25, 235–44, 1976

Crump, G.A. 'Ammianus and the Late Roman Army', *Historia* 22, 91–103, 1973

Daly, L.J. 'The Mandarin and the Barbarian: The Response of Themistius to the Gothic Challenge', *Historia* 21, 351–79, 1972

Demandt A, *Der Fall Roms*, Munich 1984

'Der Tod des Alteren Theodosius', *Historia* 18, 598–626, 1969

'Magister Militum', *PWRE* 12, 553–790, 1970

Demouget E, *De l'unité à la division de l'empire romain 395–410*, Paris 1951

'Modalités d'établissement des fédéres barbares de Gratien et de Theodose', *Mélanges d'histoire ancienne offerts a W. Seston*, 143–60, Paris 1974

'Note sur la politique orientale de Stilicon de 405–407', *Byzantion* 20, 27–37, 1950

Diesner, H.J. 'Das Buccellariertum von Stilicho und Sarus bis auf Aetius', *Klio* 54, 321–50, 1972

Domaszewski, A. von. *Die Rangordnung des romischen heeres*, Cologne 1967 rev. Dobson, B.

Dudden, F.H. *The Life and Times of St. Ambrose*, Oxford 1935

Ensslin, W. *Die Religionspolitik des Kaiser Theodosius der Grosse*, 1953 *Staat und Kirche von Konstantin bis Theodosius*, 1956

Ferril, A. *The Fall of the Roman Empire: The Military Explanation*, London 1986

Fléchier, V. *Histoire de Théodose le Grand*, Paris 1682

Frere, S.S. *Britannia: A History of Roman Britain*, London 1978

Gasperini, N. La Morte di Teodosio Padre, *Instituto di storia antica*, Milan 1972

Garbsch, J. *Der Spatromische Donau-Iller-Rhein Limes*, Stuttgart 1970

Gibbon, E. *Decline and Fall of the Roman Empire*, 1782

Gluschanin, E.P. 'Die Politik Theodosius I und die Hintergrund des Sogenannten Antigermanismus im Öströmischen Reich', *Historia* 38, 224–49, 1989

Godlowski, K. *The Chronology of the Late Roman and Early Migration Periods in Central Europe*, Cracow 1970

Goffart, W. *Caput and Colonate: Towards a History of Late Roman Taxation*, Toronto 1974

Barbarians and Romans: Techniques of Accommodation, Princeton 1980

Goodburn, R. and Bartholomew, P. (eds) *Aspects of the Notitia Dignitatum*, Oxford 1976

Goodman, M.D. and Sperber, D. 'Roman Palestine 200–400', *JRS* 70, 235–236, 1980

Grant, M. *The Fall of the Roman Empire: A Reappraisal*, London 1976

Greene, K. *The Archaeology of the Roman Economy*, London 1986

Guldenpenning and Ifland, J. *Der Kaiser Theodosius der Grosse*, 1878

Hassall, M.W.C. and Ireland, R. *De Rebus Bellicis*, Oxford 1979

Hawkes, S.C. and Dunning, G.C. 'Soldiers and Settlers in Britain, Fourth to Fifth Centuries', *Medieval Archaeology* 5, 1–70, 1970

Heather, P. 'The Crossing of the Danube and the Gothic Conversion', *Greek, Roman and Byzantine Studies* 27, 289–318, 1986

Goths and Romans 332–489, Oxford 1991

Hoeppffner, A. *La mort du magister militum Théodose*, 1936

Hoffman, D. *Das Spatromische Bewegungsheer und die Notitia Dignitatum*, Dusseldorf 1969

Holder, P.A. *The Roman Army in Britain*, New York 1982

Holum, K.G. *Theodosian Empresses: Women and Dominion in Late Antiquity*, Berkeley 1982

Hyland, A. *Equus: A History of the Horse in the Roman World*, London 1990

Johnson, S. *The Roman Forts of the Saxon Shore*, 1976

Late Roman Fortifications, London 1983

Jones, A.H.M. *The Later Roman Empire 284–602*, Oxford 1964

The Decline of the Ancient World, New York 1966

The Roman Economy, Oxford 1974

Jones, A.H.M., Martindale, J.R. and Morris, J. *PLRE I*, Cambridge 1971

Kaegi, W.E. *Byzantium and the Decline of Rome*, Princeton 1968

Keppie, L. *The Making of the Roman Army*, London 1984

King, C.E. (ed.) *Imperial Revenue, Expenditure and Monetary Policy in the Fourth Century A.D.*, Oxford 1980

King, N. *The Emperor Theodosius and the Establishment of Christianity*, 1961

Kopacek, T.A. 'Curial Displacement and Flight in Later Fourth Century Cappadocia', *Historia* 23, 319–42, 1974

Liebeschuetz, J.H.W. *Barbarians and Bishops*, Oxford 1991

Lippold, A. *Theodosius der Grosse und seine Zeit*, Munich 1980

Luttwak, E.N. *The Grand Strategy of the Roman Empire*, Baltimore 1976

MacCormack, S. *Art and Ceremony in Late Antiquity*, Berkeley, 1981

MacMullen, R. 'How big was the Roman Army?', *Klio* 62, 451–60, 1980; *The Roman Government's Response to Crisis*, Yale, 1976

'The Roman Emperors' Army Costs', *Latomus* 43, 571–80, 1984

'Tax Pressure in the Roman Empire', *Latomus* 46, 733–49, 1987

Corruption and the Decline of Rome, New Haven 1988

Maenchen-Helfen, O.J. *The World of the Huns*, Berkeley 1973

Maloney, J. and Hobley, B. *Roman Urban Defences in the West*, London 1983

Martindale, J.R. *The Prosopography of the Later Roman Empire II*, Cambridge 1980

Matthews, J. *Western Aristocracies and Imperial Court AD 364–425*, Oxford 1975

The Roman Empire of Ammianus, London 1989

Mazzarino, S. *Stilicone: La Crisi Imperiale dopo Teodosio*, Rome 1942

Millar, F. (ed.) *The Roman Empire and its Neighbours*, London 1981 (reprint); *The Emperor in the Roman World*, Duckworth, 1977; Emperors, Frontiers and Foreign Relations, 31 BC to AD 378, *Britannia*, 1982

Mocsy, A. *Pannonia and Upper Moesia: A History of the Middle Danube Provinces of the Roman Empire*, London 1974 (Frere, S.)

Momigliano, A. *The Conflict between Paganism and Christianity in the Fourth Century*, 1933

O'Flynn, J. M. *Generalissimos of the Western Roman Empire*, Edmonton 1983

Oman, C. *A History of the Art of War in the Middle Ages*, London 1991

Oost, S.I., 'Count Gildo and Theodosius the Great', *Classical Philology* 57, 27–30, 1962

Palanque, J.R. *S. Ambroise et l'Empire romain*, Paris 1933

Parker, H.M.D. *The Roman Legions*, Cambridge 1958 (reprint)

Pavan, M. *La Politica Gotica di Teodosio*, Rome 1964

Percival, J. *The Roman Villa*, London 1981

Petrikovits, H. Von 'Fortifications in the North-Western Roman Empire From the Third to the Fifth Centuries AD', *JRS* 61, 178–218, 1971

Reece, R. 'Town and Country: The End of Roman Britain', *World Archaeology* 12, 77–92, 1980

Robinson, H.R. *The Armour of Imperial Rome*, London 1975

Samson, R. 'Rural Slavery, Inscriptions, Archaeology and Marx: A Response to Ramsey MacMullen's "Late Roman Slavery"', *Historia* 38, 99–110, 1989

Schönberger, H. 'The Roman Frontier in Germany: An Archaeological Survey', *JRS* 59, 144–97, 1969.

Seeck, O. 'Die Schlacht am Frigidus', *Klio* 13, 451–67, 1913

Soproni, S. *Der Spätromischen Limes zwischen Esztergom und Szentendre*, Budapest 1978

Speidel, M.P. *Guards of the Roman Armies*, Bonn 1978

Ste Croix, G.E.M. de *The Class Struggle in the Ancient Greek World from the Archaic Age to the Arab Conquests*, Oxford 1981

Stein, E. *Histoire du Bas-empire*, Amsterdam 1968

Stevens, C.E. 'Agriculture and Rural Life in the Later Roman Empire', Cambridge 1966 (*Cambridge Economic History of Europe 92–124*)

Stevens, F.P. *From Constantine to Alaric*, 1984

Straub, J. *Regeneration Imperii*, Darmstadt 1972

Sulmirski, T. *The Sarmatians*, London 1970

Szidat, J. 'Die Usurpation des Eugenius', *Historia* 28, 487–508, 1979

Tainter, J. *The Collapse of Complex Societies*, Cambridge 1988

Thompson, E.A. *A History of Attila and the Huns*, Oxford 1948

Romans and Barbarians, Madison 1982

'Barbarian Invaders and Roman Collaborators', *Florilegium* 2, 71–88, 1980

'The Visigoths from Fritigern to Euric', *Historia* 12, 105–26, 1963

Tsangadas, B.C.P. *The Fortifications and Defence of Constantinople*, New York 1980

Wacher, J. *The Towns of Roman Britain*, London 1976

Wallace-Hadrill, J.M. *The Barbarian West 400–1000*, London 1967

'Gothia and Romania', *Bulletin of the John Rylands Library* 44, 213–347, 1961

Early Germanic Kingship in England and on the Continent, 1971

Ward, J.H. 'The *Notitia Dignitatum*', *Latomus* 33, 397–434, 1974

Watson, G.R. *The Roman Soldier*, London 1969

Webster, G. *The Roman Imperial Army*, London 1979
White, L. (ed.) *The Transformation of the Roman World*, 1966
Wightman, E.M. *Gallia Belgica,* London 1985
Wilkes, J.J. *Dalmatia*, London 1969
Williams, S. *Diocletian and the Roman Recovery*, London 1985
Wolfram, H. *History of the Goths*, Berkeley 1988

INDEX

References appearing in footnotes are indexed according to the position of the note number and not to the text of the note.